THE
MICHELIN
GUIDE

EATING OUT IN PUBS

DEAR READER,

We are delighted to present the 2017 edition of the Michelin guide to Eating Out in Pubs – our guide to the best dining pubs in the UK & Ireland.

The standard of pub cooking continues to reach new heights, and there is now an enormous amount of choice available. Some pubs offer British classics beside the fire in the bar, while others offer creative international cooking in smart dining rooms; some showcase homemade or organic ingredients from small local producers, while others import a diverse range of ingredients from abroad. Whatever the style, the quality and consistency required to be in the guide remain the same.

All of the pubs within these pages have been selected by our team of famous Michelin inspectors, who are the eyes and ears of our readers. They always pay their own bills and their anonymity is key to ensuring that they receive the same treatment as any other guest. Each year, they search for new establishments to add – and only the best make it through! The 'best of the best' are then recognised with awards.

Our famous Stars ❁ are awarded to places serving top class cuisine – taking into account the quality of ingredients, the mastery of techniques and flavours, the levels of creativity and, of course, consistency.

These are not our only awards; look out too for the Bib Gourmands 🍽️, which highlight places offering good quality, good value cooking.

Many of our modern day pubs started life as coaching inns, providing refreshment and a place to stay for weary travellers and their horses. The car may have replaced the horse and carriage but the trend for pubs offering accommodation continues – you'll find that many of our recommended pubs also have bedrooms.

Michelin Travel Partner is committed to remaining at the forefront of the culinary world and to meeting the needs of our readers. Please don't hesitate to contact us – we'd love to hear your opinions on the establishments listed within these pages, as well as those you feel could be of interest for future editions.

We hope you enjoy your dining and accommodation experiences – happy travelling with the 2017 edition of the Michelin Eating Out in Pubs guide!

→ Awards
Stars and Bib Gourmands

✿✿	Excellent cooking, worth a detour!
✿	High quality cooking, worth a stop!
🍽️ Bib Gourmand	'Bibs' are awarded for simple yet skilful cooking for under £28 or €40.

CONTENTS

GREAT BRITAIN & IRELAND

REGIONAL MAPS OF...

IRELAND

Republic
of Ireland

SCOTLAND

Northern
Ireland

North
East

North
West

Isle
of Man

Yorkshire &
the Humber

East
Midlands

ENGLAND

West
Midlands

East of
England

WALES

London

South East

South West

Isle of Wight

THE **PUB**
OF **THE YEAR**

The Marksman
254 Hackney Road
Bethnal Green, London, E2 7SJ

Tel: 020 77397393

www.marksmanpublichouse.com - @marksman_pub
➜ See page 157 for more details

Our team of full-time inspectors have spent the year eating in pubs all over Great Britain and Ireland and choosing the best for our 2017 selection. Every year the inspectors decide which pub will be crowned our Pub of the Year: this is one that stands out from the rest – where the atmosphere, the service, and most importantly, the food, offer something special. This year, the award goes to The Marksman.

THE PUB

With its imposing corner position and its quirky façade, the Marksman has long been a local landmark in what is fast becoming a lively and fashionable part of East London. This is a pub, first and foremost, and a great place to come for a pint of local ale or a bottle of craft beer. Inside, it's a place of two halves: the wood-panelled bar with its jukebox and

mirrors retains the cosy, unaffected character of a traditional local, while the first floor dining room is much more modern, with a colourful floor, filament lights and a trendy, retro feel. You can dine in either space, and the summer roof terrace, the friendly atmosphere and the attentive, personable staff also add to the pub's appeal.

THE OWNERS

Chef-owners Tom Harris and Jon Rotheram are St John alumni and their considerable experience – and the influence of Fergus Henderson – is evident in the food that they cook here. Although The Marksman may seem like quite a simple operation on the surface, this is a pub with hidden depths – and the passion that Tom and Jon have for their first venture together is obvious. They like to keeps things fresh, and regular events with guest chefs, live music and DJs draw in the crowds.

THE FOOD

The appealing menu is all about straightforward British dishes like devilled mussels on toast, skate with shrimps and turnip tops, and pheasant and trotter pie. The beef and barley buns with horseradish cream are a must-try and you can even have

a curry – albeit one made with quail, goat or mutton! The fresh seasonal produce is top-notch and includes some lesser-known ingredients; these are used to create carefully cooked dishes which are perfectly balanced and full of flavour. This is gutsy British comfort food at its best!

HOW TO **FIND** A **PUB**

COUNTRY, REGION AND COUNTY NAMES

Coloured tab:

- ■ **ENGLAND**
  - ■ East Midlands
  - ■ East of England
  - ■ London
  - ▨ North East
  - ■ North West
  - ▨ South East
  - ■ South West
  - ▨ West Midlands
  - ■ Yorkshire & the Humber

- ■ **SCOTLAND**
- ▨ **WALES**
- ■ **IRELAND**
  - ▨ Northern Ireland
  - ▨ Republic of Ireland

CONTACT DETAILS & DIRECTIONS

FACILITIES & SERVICES

🏕	Outside dining available
🍷	Particularly interesting wine list
🐕🐕	No dogs allowed • Dog friendly
🚫	Credit cards not accepted

PRICES & CLOSING TIMES

Approximate range of prices for a three-course meal, plus information on booking and annual closures.

Prices are given in £ sterling, and in €uro for the Republic of Ireland.

ENGLAND • East of England • Essex

BELL INN

Run by the same family for over 70 yea...

If you're wondering about the hot cross buns past landlord Jack Turnell took over the p whereupon he nailed a bun to one of the bea has been added every year – cement versie rationing and a wooden one commemora the pub's oldest regular. The Bell has be family for over 70 years, but dates back as the characterful beams and wood par uses quality produce to create classically modern touch, like pan-fried sea bass with new potatoes and creamed crayfish bisq are traditional in style, while those in Hil modern.

High Rd,
HORNDON ON THE HILL, SS17 8LD
Tel.: 01375 642463
Website: www.bell-inn.co.uk

In the centre of the village. Parking.

🏕 🐕

PRICES
Meals: a la carte £ 22/41

CLOSING TIMES
Closed 25-26 December and bank holidays

86

There are 3 ways to search for a pub in this guide:

→ use the regional maps that precede each section,
→ use the alphabetical list of pubs at the end,
→ use the alphabetical list of place names at the end.

FLITCH OF BACON

Come at the weekend for a tasty brunch

ENGLAND • East of England • Essex

The unusual name originates from the 12C Dunmow Flitch Trials that awarded a flitch of bacon to married couples who could swear not to have regretted their marriage for a year and a day! It's a pretty place, where the serving team are confident and the chef is experienced: warm sourdough arrives in a hessian bag and is followed by an extensive range of modern dishes, allied with the odd pub classic. Good ingredients are used in accomplished ways, flavour combinations are great and presentation is top notch. In summer the terrace comes to life, with an old Citroen van acting as a bar and meats cooked on a 'Big Green Egg' barbeque. Contemporary bedrooms are boldly decorated – one has a four-poster bed and a roll-top bath in the room.

NEW PUB IN THE GUIDE

The Street,
LITTLE DUNMOW, CM6 3HT
Tel.: 01371 821660
Website: www.flitchofbacon.co.uk
3 mi east of Great Dunmow by B 1256, in village centre. Parking.

ONE OF OUR FAVOURITES

NUMBER ON THE REGIONAL MAP

PRICES
Meals: a la carte £ 28/53

3 rooms:
£ 160

MAP: 24 ◄

CLOSING TIMES
Open daily
booking essential

87

PUBS WITH BEDROOMS

Room prices range from the lowest-priced single to the most expensive double or twin.

Breakfast is usually included in the price.

They are marked ▬ in blue on the map.

INSPECTORS' **FAVOURITES**

A ll the pubs in this guide have been selected for the quality of their cooking. However, we feel that several of them deserve additional consideration as they boast at least one extra quality which makes them particularly special.
It may be the delightful setting, the charm and character of the pub, the general atmosphere, the pleasant service, the overall value for money or the exceptional cooking.

To distinguish these pubs, we point them out with our "Inspectors' favourites" Bibendum stamp.

We are sure you will enjoy these pubs as much as we have.

ENGLAND

BEER
IN THE **U.K.** & **IRELAND**

→ It's easy to think of beer as just bitter or lager. But that doesn't tell half the story. Between the two there's a whole range of styles and tastes, including pale ales, beers flavoured with spices, fruits and herbs, and wheat beers. It's all down to the skill of the brewer who'll juggle art, craft and a modicum of science to create the perfect pint.

Grist and wort may sound like medieval hangover cures, but they're actually crucial to the brewing process. Malted barley is crushed into grist, a coarse powder which is mashed with hot water in a large vessel called a mash tun. Depending on what sort of recipe's required, the brewer will add different cereals at this stage, such as darker malt for stout. The malt's natural sugars dissolve and the result is wort: a sweet brown liquid, which is boiled with hops in large coppers. Then comes the most important process of all: fermentation, when the hopped wort is cooled and run into fermentation vessels. The final addition is yeast, which converts the natural sugars into alcohol, carbon dioxide and a host of subtle flavours.

Finally, a beer has to be conditioned before it leaves the brewery, and in the case of cask conditioned real ales, the beer goes directly into the cask, barrel or bottle. The yeast is still active in there, fermenting the beer for a second time, often in a pub cellar.

Beer's as natural a product as you can get. This is what's in your pint:

BARLEY
It's the main ingredient in beer and rich in starch. Malted before brewing to begin the release of sugars.

HOPS
Contain resins and essential oils, and used at varying times to give beer its distinctive flavour. Early on they add bitterness, later on they provide a spicy or citrus zest.

YEAST
Converts the sugars from the barley into alcohol and carbon dioxide during fermentation. It produces compounds that affect the flavour of the beer.

WATER
Burton and Tadcaster have excellent local water, and that's why they became great ale brewing centres. Meanwhile, the water of London and Dublin is just right for the production of stouts and porters.

All the time there's a delicate process going on as the beer is vulnerable to attack from micro-biological organisms. But as long as the publican cares about his beer, you should get a tasty, full-flavoured pint.

REAL QUALITY

The modern taste for real ale took off over thirty years ago when it looked like the lager industry was in the process of killing off traditional "warm ale". There are several styles, but the most popular in England and Wales is bitter, which boasts a seemingly inexhaustible variety of appearance, scent and flavour. You can have your bitter gold or copper of colour, hoppy or malty of aroma, dry or sweet of flavour (sweet flavoured bitter? This is where the term "bitter" is at its loosest). Sometimes it has a creamy head; sometimes no head at all. Typically, go to a Yorkshire pub for the former, a London pub for the latter.

Mild developed its popularity in Wales and the north west of England in Victorian times. Often dark, it's a weaker alternative to bitter, with a sweetish taste based on its hop characteristics.

In Scotland, the near equivalent of bitter is heavy, and the most popular draught ales are known as 80 shilling (export) or 70 shilling (special). And, yes, they have a heavy quality to them, though 60 shilling ale – or Light – is akin to English mild.

Full-bodied and rich, stouts (and their rarer porter relatives) are almost a meal in themselves. They're famously black in colour with hints of chocolate and caramel, but it's the highly roasted yeast flavour that leaves the strong after taste.

MICHELIN IS CONTINUALLY INNOVATING FOR SAFER, CLEANER, MORE ECONOMICAL, MORE CONNECTED... BETTER ALL-ROUND MOBILITY.

Tyres wear more quickly on short urban journeys.

TRUE!

You tend to accelerate and brake more often when driving around town so your tyres work harder!
If you are stuck in traffic, keep calm and drive slowly.

Tyre pressure only affects your car's safety.

FALSE!

Driving with underinflated tyres (0.5 bar below recommended pressure) doesn't just impact handling and fuel consumption, it will shave 8,000 km off tyre lifespan.
Make sure you check tyre pressure about once a month and before you go on holiday or a long journey.

Fitting **2 winter tyres** on my car guarantees maximum safety.

FALSE!

In the winter, especially when temperatures drop below 7°C, to ensure better road holding, all four tyres should be identical and fitted at the same time.

2 WINTER TYRES ONLY = risk of compromised road holding.

4 WINTER TYRES = safer handling when cornering, driving downhill and braking.

If you regularly encounter rain, snow or black ice, choose a **MICHELIN Alpin tyre**. This range offers you sharp handling plus a comfortable ride to safely face the challenge of winter driving.

MICHELIN

MICHELIN IS COMMITTED

► MICHELIN IS **GLOBAL LEADER IN FUEL-EFFICIENT TYRES** FOR LIGHT VEHICLES.

► *EDUCATING OF YOUNGSTERS IN ROAD SAFETY,* NOT FORGETTING TWO-WHEELERS. LOCAL ROAD SAFETY CAMPAIGNS WERE RUN IN **16 COUNTRIES** IN 2015.

QUIZ

1 TYRES ARE BLACK SO WHY IS THE MICHELIN MAN WHITE?

Back in 1898 when the Michelin Man was first created from a stack of tyres, they were made of natural rubber, cotton and sulphur and were therefore light-coloured. The composition of tyres did not change until after the First World War when carbon black was introduced. But the Michelin Man kept his colour!

2 FOR HOW LONG HAS MICHELIN BEEN GUIDING TRAVELLERS?

Since 1900. When the MICHELIN guide was published at the turn of the century, it was claimed that it would last for a hundred years. It's still around today and remains a reference with new editions and online restaurant listings in a number of countries.

3 WHEN WAS THE "BIB GOURMAND" INTRODUCED IN THE MICHELIN GUIDE?

The symbol was created in 1997 but as early as 1954 the MICHELIN guide was recommending "exceptional good food at moderate prices". Today, it features on the MICHELIN Restaurants - Bookatable website and app.

If you want to enjoy a fun day out and find out more about Michelin, why not visit the l'Aventure Michelin museum and shop in Clermont-Ferrand, France:
www.laventuremichelin.com

MICHELIN
A better way forward

A vision of England sweeps across a range of historic buildings, monuments and rolling landscapes. This image, taking in wild natural borders extending from the rugged splendour of Cornwall's cliffs to pounding Northumbrian shores, seeks parity with a newer picture of Albion: redefined cities and towns whose industrial past is being reshaped by a shiny, steel-and glass, interactive reality. The country's geographical bones and bumps are a reassuring constant: the windswept moors of the south west and the craggy peaks of the Pennines, the summery orchards of the Kentish Weald, the "flat earth" constancy of East Anglian skies and the mirrored calm of Cumbria's lakes. The pubs of England have made good use of the land's natural bounty over the past decade; streamlined establishments have stripped out the soggy carpets and soggier menus and replaced them with crisp décor and fresh, inventive cooking. England's multi-ethnic culture has borne fruit in the kitchens of your local...

EAST MIDLANDS

—— **England**

© J. Doornkamp / Design Pics / Photononstop

An area that combines the grace of a bygone age with the speed of the 21C. To the east (Chatsworth House, Haddon Hall and Burghley House) is where Pride and Prejudice came to life, while Silverstone to the south hosts the Grand Prix. Market towns are dotted all around: Spalding's cultivation of tulips rivals that of Holland, Oakham boasts its stunning Castle and Great Hall, and the legendary "Boston Stump" oversees the bustle of a 450 year-old market. The brooding beauty of the Peak District makes it the second most visited National Park in the world. Izaak Walton popularised the river Dove's trout-filled waters in "The Compleat Angler" and its surrounding hills are a rambler's dream, as are the wildlife habitats of the National Forest and the wind-swept acres of the pancake-flat fens.

Above it all looms Lincoln Cathedral's ancient spire, while in the pubs, local ale – typically brewed in Bakewell, Dovedale or Rutland – slips down a treat alongside the ubiquitous Melton Mowbray pie.

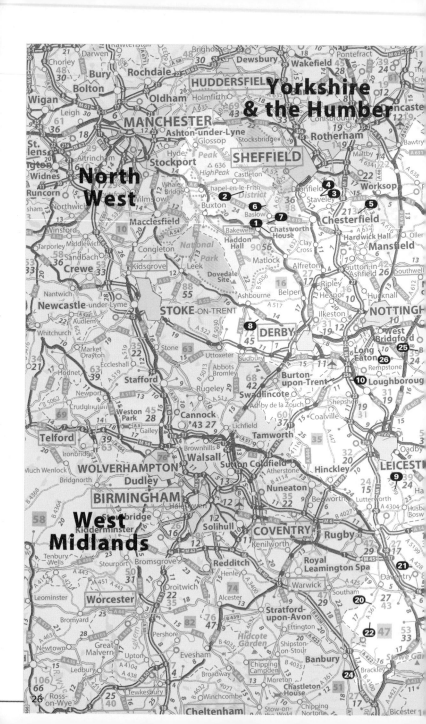

DEVONSHIRE ARMS

Hugely characterful bar and contemporary brasserie

Part of the estate, this inn is just minutes down the road from Chatsworth House, in a small hamlet largely owned by the Duke and Duchess of Devonshire. There are two clear parts to the place: a hugely characterful, homely bar with exposed stone, low oak beams and open fires, and a bright modern brasserie extension with a glass-fronted wine cave and village and stream views. If you're making a flying visit, have afternoon tea; if you've got longer, choose something from the lengthy, classically based main menu. Produce comes from the surrounding villages, as well as from green-fingered locals who swap their wares for beer tokens – the estate game is a speciality. Bedrooms in the main inn and next door are cosy; those opposite are more modern.

Devonshire Sq,
BEELEY, DE4 2NR
Tel.: 01629 733259
Website: www.devonshirebeeley.co.uk

5 mi southeast of Bakewell by A 6 and B 6012. Parking.

PRICES
Meals: a la carte £ 23/35

 14 rooms:
£ 86/209

MAP: 1

CLOSING TIMES
Open daily
booking advisable

SAMUEL FOX COUNTRY INN

Classic cooking with modern and Spanish twists

The dramatic landscape of the Hope Valley will be the first thing to catch your eye, and the curious pub sign depicting a fox beneath an umbrella, the next – it makes sense, however, when you discover that famed local businessman, Samuel Fox, was the inventor of the steel-ribbed umbrella! The attractive light-stone building dates back over 200 years and conceals a cosy room with tables arranged around the semi-circular bar. The cooking is classic with modern touches and makes good use of local produce: choose from dishes such as homemade terrine with chutney and brioche or local slow cooked pork belly with broad beans, celeriac and gooseberries. The 7 course tasting menu is a popular choice; stay over after in one of the smart, cosy bedrooms.

Stretfield Rd,
BRADWELL, S33 9JT
Tel.: 01433 621562
Website: www.samuelfox.co.uk

12 mi northwest of Baslow by A 623 and B 6049. Parking.

PRICES
Meals: £ 20/49 and a la carte £ 25/39

 4 rooms:
£ 75/130

MAP: 2

CLOSING TIMES
Closed 2-25 January, Sunday dinner,
Monday, Tuesday and lunch Wednesday-
Thursday

DEVONSHIRE ARMS

You'll be welcomed by a friendly team

It might be remotely set but that's all part of its charm and the views on the way over are worth the drive alone; look out for the huge horse chestnut tree and you'll find the pub standing proudly beneath. When the sun's shining, the small terrace is a delightful place to be – if it's already full then pick a spot in one of three cosy rooms. Tables are simply laid and the cooking is fittingly understated. Tried-and-tested British dishes are packed with flavour and equal effort is given to the cod wrapped in crispy batter accompanied by light fluffy chips, as to the more adventurous dishes like quail with celeriac, grape and hazelnut. Desserts are a highlight and could include cream cheese mousse with plum sorbet and brown sugar crumble.

Lightwood Ln,
MIDDLE HANDLEY, ECKINGTON, S21 5RN
Tel.: 01246 434800
Website: www.devonshirearmsmiddlehandley.com

8.5 mi southeast of Sheffield by A 61 and B 6056, turning at traffic light in village on to B 6052 then Middle Handley rd. Parking.

PRICES
Meals: £ 28 (weekdays) and a la carte
£ 26/42

MAP: **3**

CLOSING TIMES
Closed Monday except bank holiday lunch
and dinner Sunday

INN AT TROWAY

Hearty portions and regional ales

This early Victorian pub is set in a picturesque location and offers delightful views out over the rolling countryside; make the most of these by grabbing a seat either on the terrace or in the airy rear dining room. This is an area popular with walkers and the food is satisfyingly hearty – perfect for refuelling after a brisk morning hike. Among the options on the extensive menu might be a butchers board, braised lamb shank or beef brisket; be sure to check out the blackboards and keep an eye out for the chipolatas with 3 different mustards. Desserts often include playful elements, so you might find dishes featuring doughnuts or marshmallows. The good value set menu is served from 12-7pm and a fine selection of regional ales are offered 24/7.

Snowdon Ln,
TROWAY, ECKINGTON, S21 5RU
Tel.: 01246 417666
Website: www.relaxeatanddrink.co.uk

7.5 mi southeast of Sheffield by A 61 and B 6056 (Eckington Rd).
Parking.

PRICES   MAP: **4**
Meals: a la carte £ 21/34

CLOSING TIMES
Open daily

ELM TREE

Most ingredients are sourced from within 10 miles

This 18C stone building takes its name from an elm tree which used to stand on the village green. It was once a wheelwright's by day and a pub by night, and the fact that it's now wholly a pub evidently pleases the loyal band of locals sitting at the brightly lit bar. Head left for a seat by the wood-burning stove or through to the rear for a more intimate experience – or, in summer, dine on the terrace. The menu reads like a roll call of pub classics, with the likes of liver and bacon, gammon steak with Ted's egg and chips, homemade Derbyshire steak burger, and specials that could include mushroom and wild garlic ravioli. Dishes are good value and presented in a modern manner, and most ingredients are sourced from within 10 miles.

ELMTON, S80 4LS
Tel.: 01909 721261
Website: www.elmtreeelmton.co.uk

4 mi northeast of Bolsover by A 632 signed off B 6417.
In centre of village. Parking.

PRICES
Meals: £ 15 (weekday lunch) and a la carte
£ 18/40

MAP: 5

CLOSING TIMES
Closed Tuesday

CHEQUERS INN

Built into the stone boulders of Froggatt Edge

This 16C inn is built right into the stone boulders of Froggatt Edge and even has a direct path from its garden up to the peak. As traditional inside as out, it's a comfortingly no-nonsense sort of place, boasting an open fire, gleaming brass, a large bar and a quieter, cosier room across the hall. The majority of diners are walkers, but the jolly team welcome one and all as if they were locals. Cooking is unfussy and wholesome, with classical dishes that always include fish and chips, bangers and mash and a pie, as well as more imaginative specials such as roast partridge or seared scallops and black pudding on the blackboard. No.1, to the rear, is the quietest of the comfy bedrooms; hampers of homemade produce are a popular take-home purchase.

Hope Valley,
FROGGATT, S32 3ZJ
Tel.: 01433 630231
Website: www.chequers-froggatt.com

3 mi north of Baslow on A 625. Situated on the edge of the village. Parking.

PRICES
Meals: a la carte £ 26/39

 7 rooms:
£ 109/119

MAP: 6

CLOSING TIMES
Closed 25 December

DEVONSHIRE ARMS

An ideal base for exploring the area

This is another inn from the Devonshire Group and, as with the others, it comes with bedrooms, making it an ideal choice if you're looking to book a weekend away in the Peak District. Designed by none other than the Duchess herself, the stylish rooms are appealingly contemporary and, with the popular Chatsworth Farm shop in the very same village, you'll want to stock up on supplies to take home. Traditional pub dishes get a makeover on the menu and, as in the shop, much of the produce on your plate will have come directly from farms on the Chatsworth Estate. Servings are generous and dishes like suet pudding or lamb hotpot, satisfyingly filling, so you'll do well to get through three courses. Order at the bar; staff are friendly and efficient.

PILSLEY, DE45 1UL
Tel.: 01246 583258
Website: www.devonshirepilsley.co.uk

3 mi northeast of Bakewell off A 619. In centre of village. Parking

PRICES
Meals: a la carte £ 21/36

 13 rooms:
£ 76/219

MAP: 7

CLOSING TIMES
Open daily
booking advisable

SARACEN'S HEAD

With portions this large, you won't leave hungry

Set opposite a pretty church in a remote, picturesque village, the Saracen's Head may not seem like the kind of place where you need to book, but arrive without a reservation and you could be disappointed. Pass the chefs hard at work in the kitchen and you'll arrive in a bright bar with rustic furnishings, which leads through to a high-ceilinged room with exposed beams and another open-fired room filled with local art. The large, frequently changing menu is chalked up on a blackboard over the fireplace and lists good old pub and restaurant favourites such as prawn cocktail, pressed ham hock or crisp roast duck with orange syrup; consider your options carefully, as with portions this large, it's unlikely you'll make it through three courses!

Church Ln,
SHIRLEY, DE6 3AS
Tel.: 01335 360330
Website: www.saracens-head-shirley.co.uk

Between Ashbourne and Brailsford off A 52. Parking.

PRICES   MAP: **8**
Meals: a la carte £ 21/41

CLOSING TIMES
Open daily

THE JOINERS

The Friday Fish & Chips lunches are a hit

Although they do keep a few tables by the fire for locals to enjoy a pint, this is more of a dining pub than one set up for drinkers. Beams and a tiled floor bring 17C character to the open-plan interior but designer wallpaper and fresh flower displays give it a chic overall feel. Foodwise, there's plenty of choice: as well as the à la carte, there's an extensive list of specials and a good value lunch menu too. You'll find the odd pub classic but in the main expect the likes of pork rillettes, calves' liver and bacon or pot-roast pheasant – and be sure to save room for the soufflé of the day! The experienced staff run the show with a steady hand; on Tuesdays they hold an 'Auberge Night', where they offer a great value 3 course set menu.

Church Walk,
BRUNTINGTHORPE, LE17 5QH
Tel.: 0116 247 8258
Website: www.thejoinersarms.co.uk

Between Leicester and Husbands Bosworth off A 5199. Parking.

PRICES
Meals: £ 16 (weekday lunch) and a la carte
£ 25/35

MAP: 9

CLOSING TIMES
Closed Sunday dinner and Monday
booking essential

ROYAL OAK

In a sleepy village close to East Midlands Airport

This pub may no longer boast the majestic oak tree it was once named after but its grounds still remain a draw; here, from June until September, a large marquee plays host to summer weddings. The pub is set at the heart of a sleepy village, and is owned by two brothers who have totally modernised it. Most people eat in the cosy dining room but there's also a smart bar, its wooden beams decorated with beer pump signs. Menus offer plenty of choice, from sandwiches and soup through to sharing platters, pub favourites and ambitious main courses; some with Indian or Italian influences. Well-equipped, up-to-date bedrooms are in an adjacent block; with East Midlands Airport close by, this is a popular place for a 'night before the holiday' stay.

The Green,
LONG WHATTON, LE12 5BD
Tel.: 01509 843694
Website: www.theroyaloaklongwhatton.co.uk

4 mi northwest of Loughborough by A 6 and B 5324. Parking.

PRICES
Meals: £ 13 (weekday dinner) and a la carte
£ 21/38

 7 rooms:
£ 69/99

MAP: 10

CLOSING TIMES
Open daily

BERKELEY ARMS

Charming service and appealing, good value dishes

This attractive village pub dates back to the 16C and is under the control of an enthusiastic local couple, who have plenty of experience in the hospitality industry. As you enter, a roaring fire greets you; turn left for the wonderfully cosy low-beamed bar with its quarry tiled floor and pine tables or right for a slightly more formal dining room. The relaxed, personable service is overseen by charming owner Louise, while her husband, Neil, is hard at work behind the scenes, preparing a very appealing, constantly evolving menu of locally sourced seasonal produce. Dishes are gutsy and satisfying, and alongside the usual British favourites you'll find the likes of rabbit and prune pâté or local mallard with poached pears and red cabbage.

59 Main St,
WYMONDHAM, LE14 2AG
Tel.: 01572 787587
Website: www.theberkeleyarms.co.uk

7 mi east of Melton Mowbray off B 676. In centre of village. Parking.

PRICES
Meals: £ 16 (weekday lunch)/19
and a la carte £ 25/43

MAP: 11

CLOSING TIMES
Closed first 2 weeks January, 2 weeks summer,
Sunday dinner and Monday
booking essential

BLUE BELL INN

Home-cooked meals for ramblers

Set in a tiny hamlet at the heart of the Lincolnshire Wolds, this welcoming whitewashed pub is a popular stop-off point for ramblers navigating the Viking Way. It was originally named after the bluebell flower but a previous landlord was unhappy with the moniker, so he split the word in two and hung a big blue fibreglass bell outside. You enter into a traditional bar with a copper counter and comfy sofas, which in turn leads through to a bright red dining room – a popular spot come evening time. Menus cover all bases, offering honest, home-cooked dishes which are big on flavour; maybe devilled whitebait or potted shrimps, followed by corned beef hash, twice-baked cheddar soufflé or whole locally smoked trout. Comforting nursery puddings follow.

1 Main Rd,
BELCHFORD, LN9 6LQ
Tel.: 01507 533602
Website: www.bluebellbelchford.co.uk

4 mi north of Horncastle by A 153 and right hand turn east. Parking.

PRICES   MAP: **12**
Meals: a la carte £ 20/34

CLOSING TIMES
Closed 9-23 January

NEW INN

Smart and modern with a stylish terrace

It might have been built in the 18C but the Brocklesby Estate's Grade II listed pub certainly lives up to its name. Having been extensively refurbished, it's now smart and modern, and has a stylishly furnished terrace and bedrooms. With its dartboard and TVs, the bar is a favourite haunt of the locals, while the library-lounge is the perfect spot for a fireside G&T before dinner in the contemporary restaurant with its vibrant modern art and stylish banquettes. Classically based dishes are prepared with care and sophistication and there's a modern touch to both the cooking and presentation. The humble scotch egg is elevated to new heights, scallops might come with squash and yoghurt, and apple crumble could be accompanied by custard espumá.

2 High St,
GREAT LIMBER, DN37 8JL
Tel.: 01469 569998
Website: www.thenewinngreatlimber.co.uk

Between Scunthorpe and Grimsby on A 18. Parking.

PRICES
Meals: a la carte £ 25/38

 10 rooms:
£ 90/135

MAP: 13

CLOSING TIMES
Closed Monday lunch

WIG & MITRE

Come at 9am for a hearty, homemade breakfast

Nestled among period shops on a steep hill, this well-established, part-14C pub is something of a Lincoln institution; standing midway between the castle, used as a court – hence the 'Wig' – and the cathedral – hence the 'Mitre'. There's a cosy bar downstairs, and two period dining rooms and a light, airy beamed restaurant above. The menu changes quarterly, displaying largely classical dishes with the odd Mediterranean or Asian influence. There's a blackboard of daily specials, a good value weekday set selection and, for those who enjoy a hearty homemade breakfast, they open at 9am. With wine books and maps dotted about the place and over 20 wines by the glass, it comes as no surprise to find that they own the next door wine shop too.

30-32 Steep Hill,
LINCOLN, LN2 1LU
Tel.: 01522 535190
Website: www.wigandmitre.com

Close to the Cathedral. Lincoln Castle car parks adjacent.

PRICES

Meals: £ 18 (weekdays) and a la carte
£ 19/52

MAP: 14

CLOSING TIMES
Closed 25 December

ADVOCATE ARMS

Smart modern pub offering afternoon tea

This building started life in the early 19C as the Gordon Arms Hotel and is located just a few steps away from the main market square. Apart from the original revolving door, there's not much of its past to be seen nowadays as, courtesy of a top-to-toe refit, it's now smart and modern, with large etched glass walls dividing the place into a large bar and two dining areas. It's open from early in the morning to late at night, so you can pop in and start your day with a bacon sandwich or break up your shopping with afternoon tea. Lunch sticks to good old pub classics, while at dinner, mature local steaks are a speciality. Puddings are satisfyingly traditional and tasty regional cheeses are a feature. Bedrooms are spacious and well-equipped.

2 Queen St,
MARKET RASEN, LN8 3EH
Tel.: 01673 842364
Website: www.advocatearms.co.uk

In town centre, opposite the main market square. Parking.

PRICES
Meals: £ 19 (weekday lunch) and a la carte
£ 20/43

 10 rooms:
£ 50/130

MAP: 15

CLOSING TIMES
Closed Sunday dinner except in December

HOPE & ANCHOR

Local meats are aged in a glass cabinet

It's known mainly for its cement works, but the experienced chef-owner – who previously worked at Winteringham Fields – is aiming to put South Ferriby on the map for a different reason: his food. This is a pub through and through, with a rustic, nautical theme which takes in wood panelling, slate, ropes, a fish tank and mythical sea paintings on the walls. The bar offers the likes of mini sausage rolls and scotch eggs but most head for the dining room for a meal with a Humber view. Well-priced, tasty British dishes showcase fish from Grimsby, fruit and vegetables from their smallholding and meats from the Lake District – which are aged in a glass-fronted drying cabinet. The homemade burgers and steaks cooked on the Josper grill are a hit.

Sluice Rd,
SOUTH FERRIBY, DN18 6JQ
Tel.: 01652 635334
Website: www.thehopeandanchorpub.co.uk

10 mi northeast of Scunthorpe on A 1077. Parking.

PRICES
Meals: a la carte £ 18/42

MAP: 16

CLOSING TIMES
Closed 1-7 January and Monday except
bank holidays
booking advisable

BUSTARD INN

From the outside it resembles a schoolhouse, but the Bustard Inn is hardly bookish. Its flag-floored bar is simple and uncluttered, while the spacious beamed restaurant, with its cream-tiled floor and exposed brick, has a touch of the Mediterranean about it. There's a great value set lunch menu available Tues-Sat (also offered at dinner Tues-Thurs), while the more ambitious à la carte shows off the chef's talents to the full. Dishes might include fillet of Lincolnshire beef, pan-fried sea trout or homemade venison sausages, as well as satisfying desserts like sticky toffee pudding. Wine isn't overlooked, with reasonable mark-ups and a fine selection of clarets – or you can slay your thirst with a pint of specially brewed 'Cheeky Bustard' beer.

44 Main St,
SOUTH RAUCEBY, NG34 8QG
Tel.: 01529 488250
Website: www.thebustardinn.co.uk

4 mi west of Sleaford by A 17 and minor road south. Parking.

PRICES   MAP: **17**
Meals: £ 15 (weekday lunch) and a la carte
£ 22/45

CLOSING TIMES
Closed 1 January, Sunday dinner
and Monday except bank holidays

BULL & SWAN

The only public house south of the river

This stone-built pub started life as a medieval hall house and was only converted into a travellers' inn during the late 1600s. It changed name several times, eventually settling on the Bull & Swan in 1739, when it was taken over by Walter Robinson, a former coachman to the Earl of Exeter. The menu offers something to suit all tastes, from sharing slates to classics such as Lincoln Red rib-eye steak or haslet with free range fried eggs and bacon – and on Sundays, a roasting pot for four with all the trimmings. Like the characterful beamed bar, the bedrooms have a traditional feel; their names are the pseudonyms of the members of the historic gentlemen's drinking club the 'Order of Little Bedlam' and most have impressive wooden feature beds.

St Martins,
STAMFORD, PE9 2LJ
Tel.: 01780 766412
Website: www.thebullandswan.co.uk

0.5 mi south of the town centre on B 1081. Parking on London Rd.

PRICES
Meals: a la carte £ 25/42

 9 rooms:
£ 90/180

MAP: 18

CLOSING TIMES
Open daily

SIX BELLS

Hand-crafted pizzas from the wood-burning oven

Having admired this early 20C inn for many years, Jim and Sharon Trevor (owners of the Beehive and former owners of Jim's Yard), jumped at the chance to add it to their portfolio when it came on the market. The spacious courtyard is an obvious draw and the bright, stylish interior keeps things cheery whatever the weather. In the bar there's a wood-burning oven where their hand-crafted pizzas are cooked; if these don't take your fancy, then the main menu offers everything from a ploughman's or bangers and mash to more sophisticated offerings such as Lincolnshire Poacher soufflé with smoked haddock or pork belly with sweet and sour apples. Upstairs are three very stylishly appointed bedrooms – Hayloft, with its courtyard view, is the best.

WITHAM ON THE HILL, PE10 0JH
Tel.: 01778 590360
Website: www.sixbellswitham.co.uk

Between Stamford and Bourne off A 6121. Parking.

PRICES
Meals: £ 13 (weekday lunch)/17
and a la carte £ 22/37

 3 rooms:
£ 65/150

MAP: 19

CLOSING TIMES
Closed 1-9 January, Sunday dinner and
Monday in winter

FOX & HOUNDS

A great range of boldly flavoured dishes

The Fox & Hounds has been a fixture in Charwelton since 1871, so when it closed its doors, the despairing villagers decided to take a stand, by buying it themselves and giving it a top to toe refurbishment. They then set about looking for an experienced team to run it and came up trumps when they found Matt to take charge in the kitchen and David and Sarah to keep things running smoothly out front. Menus offer everything from pork faggots with pea purée to stone bass with lobster risotto or a 'duck supper'; Matt is much-travelled, so alongside the odd Spanish influence you'll also find some excellent Indian-spiced dishes. After dinner relax on one of the chesterfields in the bar, beside the locals and their dogs stretched out by the fire.

Banbury Rd,
CHARWELTON, NN11 3YY
Tel.: 01327 260611
Website: www.foxandhoundscharwelton.co.uk

6 miles South of Daventry on A361. Parking.

PRICES
Meals: £ 16 (weekdays) and a la carte
£ 24/42

MAP: 20

CLOSING TIMES
Closed 25 December, 2 weeks January and
Sunday dinner

RED LION

An eclectic mix of dishes; choose the scotch egg!

This large, thatched honey-stone inn is located right in the heart of the attractive village of East Haddon, and boasts a terrace to the front, along with pretty gardens to the rear. It was originally a farmhouse but has been sympathetically extended, resulting in a pleasing mix of wood and slate flooring, wood panelling and exposed bricks and beams. Although there are always plenty of local drinkers, it's the food that's the main focus here. The seasonal menu offers an eclectic mix of dishes: the scotch egg with caper and parsley mayonnaise and the slow-cooked beef in red wine with smoked bacon and cabbage being perennial favourites. Service is enthusiastic and attentive, and bedrooms are chic and cosy – one has a roll-top bath in the room.

Main St,
EAST HADDON, NN6 8BU
Tel.: 01604 770223
Website: www.redlioneasthaddon.co.uk

8.5 mi northwest of Northampton off A 428. Parking.

PRICES
Meals: a la carte £ 21/40

 7 rooms:
£ 80/110

MAP: 21

CLOSING TIMES
Closed 25 December

Veuve Clicquot

■ REIMS FRANCE ■

ROYAL OAK

Creative modern food in 17C surroundings

This large pub sits in a quiet country village and its exposed stone walls and polished flag floors give it plenty of character. There are four different dining areas, plus a courtyard terrace; the locals tend to head for the snug and the regulars all have their favourite room (Annie's is named after one of the original landladies and semi-private table 3 in the Meeting Room is always in demand). If it's traditional pub food you're after, go for the good value set lunch; if you fancy pushing the boat out choose from the à la carte with its ambitious modern dishes such as cured salmon with pickled beetroot to start, followed by duck breast with vanilla mash. It's owned by a local farming family, so you can be sure the produce is top notch.

6 Lime Av,
EYDON, NN11 3PG
Tel.: 01327 263167
Website: www.theroyaloakateydon.co.uk

11 mi south of Daventry by A 45 off A 361, in village centre. Parking.

PRICES
Meals: £ 10 (lunch) and a la carte £ 27/47

MAP: 22

CLOSING TIMES
Closed dinner Monday-Tuesday

FALCON INN

Local game is a feature

In the pretty village of Fotheringhay – the birthplace of Richard III and the deathplace of Mary Queen of Scots – under the shadow of a large church, sits the attractive, stone-built Falcon Inn. It boasts a beamed bar with an unusual display of 15C bell clappers and a conservatory restaurant with formally laid tables, wicker chairs and folding doors which open onto a small paved terrace and garden. You'll find the regulars playing darts and drinking real ales in the small tap bar and, for private parties, there's a lovely annexe called The Cottage. The large menu offers everything from scallops with black pudding to sea bass with salmon mousse and there's always plenty of game in season. Dishes are flavoursome and showcase good ingredients.

FOTHERINGHAY, PE8 5HZ
Tel.: 01832 226254
Website: www.thefalcon-inn.co.uk

3.5 mi north of Oundle by A 427 off A 605. In the centre of the village. Parking.

PRICES
Meals: £ 16 (weekdays) and a la carte
£ 23/39

MAP: 23

CLOSING TIMES
Closed Sunday dinner September-May

WHITE HORSE

Charming pub with low beams and wood fires

This pretty sandstone inn sits on the village green opposite the church; its exact origins are unknown but it dates back to at least the 1750s. It's run by a keen young couple who are putting their hearts and souls into making it a success. Julie keeps things in check out front, while self-taught chef Hendrik always goes the extra mile to exceed guests' expectations. He makes everything from the breads to the ice creams from scratch and his produce is fresh, local and follows a 'when it's gone, it's gone' approach. The main bar is charming and there are two cosy rooms behind. For special occasions, book the chef's table, where you can design a custom tasting menu with the chefs in advance, which they will serve and explain to you on the day.

2 The Square,
KING'S SUTTON, OX17 3RF
Tel.: 01295 812440
Website: www.whitehorseks.co.uk

4.75 mi east of Banbury in centre of village opposite church. Parking.

PRICES
Meals: £ 14 (lunch) and a la carte £ 22/40

MAP: 24

CLOSING TIMES
Closed 27-30 December, Sunday dinner
and Monday

THE MARTINS ARMS

Lots of character and wholesome, gutsy cooking

Blazing log fires cast a welcoming glow in this creeper-clad pub, which is full of feminine touches like fresh flowers, comfy cushions and gleaming copperware. Originally a farmhouse on the Martin family estate, it contains several articles salvaged from the original manor house, including the carved Jacobean fireplace and the old library shelves – now used to hold drinks in the bar. Said bar is the place for an impromptu lunch, while the period furnished dining rooms, adorned with hunting pictures, are more suited to a formal dinner. The menu has a meaty, masculine base with a mix of classical and more modern dishes; portions are hearty and there's plenty of game in season. Unsurprisingly, Colston Bassett stilton is always available too!

School Ln,
COLSTON BASSETT, NG12 3FD
Tel.: 01949 81361
Website: www.themartinsarms.co.uk

East of Cotgrave off A 46. Parking.

PRICES
Meals: a la carte £ 32/53

MAP: 25

CLOSING TIMES
Closed dinner 25 December

RUDDINGTON ARMS

An experienced chef's first solo venture

Chef-owner Mark has certainly done his fair share of relocating – he started his career in Newcastle and then spent time in London, Jersey and Leeds, before settling in this sleepy village just south of Nottingham. A dramatic refurbishment has left the bar of the 'RA' with a faux industrial look and the sofas and open fire make it all feel very relaxed; come summer, however, it's the smartly furnished terrace that's the place to be. Flavoursome dishes cater for all tastes, with everything from light bites and pub classics to scallops with ox tongue and cauliflower purée or confit duck leg with red onion marmalade – and the tasty preserves are available to purchase too. There's no denying that The Ruddy Good Pub Company is, well, ruddy good.

56 Wilford Rd,
RUDDINGTON, NG11 6EQ
Tel.: 0115 984 1628
Website: www.theruddingtonarms.com

5.5 mi south of Nottingham on A 60. Parking.

PRICES
Meals: £ 17 (weekdays) and a la carte
£ 19/34

MAP: 26

CLOSING TIMES
Open daily

OLIVE BRANCH & BEECH HOUSE

The sourcing keeps things fiercely local

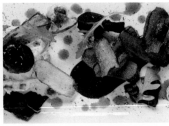

This characterful stone building started life as three farm labourers' cottages, which were knocked together in 1890 to make this 'heart-of-the-village' pub. It's an appealing place with a series of small rooms featuring open fires and exposed beams – most guests make for the cosy bar, where they serve real ales, homemade lemonade and flavoured vodka made from hedgerow berries. The selection of rustic British dishes changes daily, reflecting the seasons and keeping things fiercely local. You can have everything from smoked haddock rarebit to cod with Madeira sauce, ham hock croquettes to whole roast partridge – and at certain times they serve tapas and gourmet menus too. Bedrooms, across the road in Beech House, are cosy and thoughtfully finished.

Main St,
CLIPSHAM, LE15 7SH
Tel.: 01780 410355
Website: www.theolivebranchpub.com

9.5 mi northwest of Stamford by B 1081 off A 1. Parking.

PRICES
Meals: £ 19/33 and a la carte £ 27/46

 6 rooms:
£ 98/195

MAP: 27

CLOSING TIMES
Open daily
booking essential

WHEATSHEAF INN

The aroma of freshly baked bread fills the air

If you're on your way to Rutland Water, it's well worth diverting via this little village for a visit to the Wheatsheaf – but be careful not to overshoot the parking space or you'll end up in the stream. The first thing you notice as you walk through the door is the aroma of freshly baked bread, which sits tantalisingly on the bar. The owners may have spent time in London but they've wisely kept this as a family-friendly country pub, complete with a pool table and a dartboard. Their experience in the kitchen is clear to see: robust British cooking keeps things pleasingly straightforward and cleverly uses cheaper cuts to keep the prices down. Sunday lunch is a steal, desserts are a must, and a jar of homemade chutney makes a great souvenir.

1 Stretton Rd,
GREETHAM, LE15 7NP
Tel.: 01572 812325
Website: www.wheatsheaf-greetham.co.uk

Just off the A1 on the B 668 to Cottesmore and Oakham. Parking.

PRICES
Meals: £ 17 (weekday lunch) and a la carte
£ 23/32

MAP: 28

CLOSING TIMES
Closed first 2 weeks January, Sunday
dinner and Monday except bank holidays

FINCH'S ARMS

Delightful terrace with views over Rutland Water

Cross the threshold of this pretty stone inn and you're transported to a different world, where'll you find a quaint bar, a small anteroom with huge flowers stencilled on the walls, two very stylish dining rooms with vast windows overlooking Rutland Water, and a delightful terrace which shares the view. Assured, seasonal dishes use local lamb, beef and game, and range from appealing sharing boards through to honey-glazed duck breast with stilton salad or grilled cod fillet with gambas and salsa verde. The set menus are good value; desserts are satisfyingly old school and feature the likes of rice pudding with homemade plum jam; and afternoon tea is also an option. Modern bedrooms complete the picture – Room 3 has a balcony with water views.

Oakham Rd,
HAMBLETON, LE15 8TL
Tel.: 01572 756575
Website: www.finchsarms.co.uk

3 mi east of Oakham by A 606. Parking.

PRICES
Meals: £ 14 (weekday lunch) and a la carte
£ 22/43

 10 rooms:
£ 75/130

MAP: 29

CLOSING TIMES
Open daily

MARQUESS OF EXETER

They keep chickens and pigs and grow their own veg

This attractive 16C thatched pub is located in a pleasant village in the heart of the Rutland countryside. Locals gather in the cosy, flag-floored bar, beside inglenook fireplaces and under characterful exposed beams; while further on through, there's a relaxed, rustic dining room with chunky scrubbed tables, old leather chairs and a range. The daily menu offers tasty, classical combinations that let good quality ingredients stand out; they even grow their own vegetables and keep chickens and pigs at the bottom of the garden. There's an appealing 'Lunch for Less' menu and specials written up on gilt mirrors, while the sharing plates – maybe rib of beef or shoulder of lamb – are firm favourites too. Comfy bedrooms are found across the car park.

52 Main St,
LYDDINGTON, LE15 9LT
Tel.: 01572 822477
Website: www.marquessexeter.co.uk

Just south of Uppingham, signposted off A 6003; in the middle of the village. Parking.

PRICES
Meals: £ 14 (weekday lunch) and a la carte
£ 25/39

 17 rooms:
£ 80/135

MAP: 30

CLOSING TIMES
Closed 25 December

OLD WHITE HART

Sit in the garden and watch the petanque team

This pub offers all you'd expect from a traditional 17C coaching inn – and a lot more besides. It's got the chocolate box village setting, the open fires, the comfy corners and the seasonally changing menu of hearty, classic dishes like shoulder of lamb, beef Wellington and bread and butter pudding; but it also has a cosy, relaxing ambience, charming service led by the lovely owner, a 10-piste petanque pitch (plus a petanque team), and stylish, individually decorated bedrooms with excellent bathrooms and homely extras. It will come as no surprise to hear they're usually busy, but there's plenty of space for everyone, whether that be in the beamed bar, out at a picnic table in the neat garden or on the smart, canopy-covered front terrace.

51 Main St,
LYDDINGTON, LE15 9LR
Tel.: 01572 821703
Website: www.oldwhitehart.co.uk

Just south of Uppingham signposted off A 6003; opposite the village green. Parking.

PRICES
Meals: a la carte £ 12/37

 10 rooms:
£ 75/110

MAP: 31

CLOSING TIMES
Closed 25 December and Sunday dinner
in winter

JACKSON STOPS INN

Lovely thatched pub run by a family team

This lovely stone and thatch pub started life as the White Horse but was later jokingly renamed by the locals when the 'Jackson-Stops' estate agent sign stood outside for so long. When the previous owner left, the chef and manager (also husband and wife), stepped up and bought the place and, having been joined by their son, it's a real family affair. Inside it's divided into several areas, each with its own unique feel – sit in the open-fired bar, the cosy barn or one of several beamed rooms. There's plenty of choice when it comes to the food too: there are lunch, dinner and 'Pub Specials' menus, alongside some good value set selections. You can have anything from a steak baguette to a salmon and prawn timbale, and the sharing boards are a hit.

Rookery La,
STRETTON, LE15 7RA
Tel.: 01780 410237
Website: www.thejacksonstops.com

8 mi northwest of Stamford by B 1081 off A 1. Parking.

PRICES
Meals: £ 15 (weekday lunch) and a la carte
£ 25/37

MAP: 32

CLOSING TIMES
Closed Monday except bank holidays and
Sunday dinner

EAST OF ENGLAND

England

© D. Potter / Design Pics / Photononstop

Wide lowland landscapes and huge skies, timber-framed houses, a frowning North Sea canvas: these are the abiding images of England's east. This region has its roots embedded in the earth and its taste buds whetted by local seafood. Some of the most renowned ales are brewed in Norfolk and Suffolk. East Anglia sees crumbling cliffs, superb mudflats and saltmarshes or enchanting medieval wool towns such as Lavenham. Areas of Outstanding Natural Beauty abound, in the Chilterns of Bedfordshire and Hertfordshire, and in Dedham Vale, life-long inspiration of Constable. Religious buildings are everywhere, from Ely Cathedral, "the Ship of the Fens", to the fine structure of Long Melford church. The ghosts of great men haunt Cambridge: Newton, Darwin, Pepys and Byron studied here, doubtless deep in thought as they tramped the wide-open spaces of Midsummer Common or Parker's Piece.

Look out for Cromer crab, samphire, grilled herring, Suffolk pork casserole and the hearty Bedfordshire Clanger.

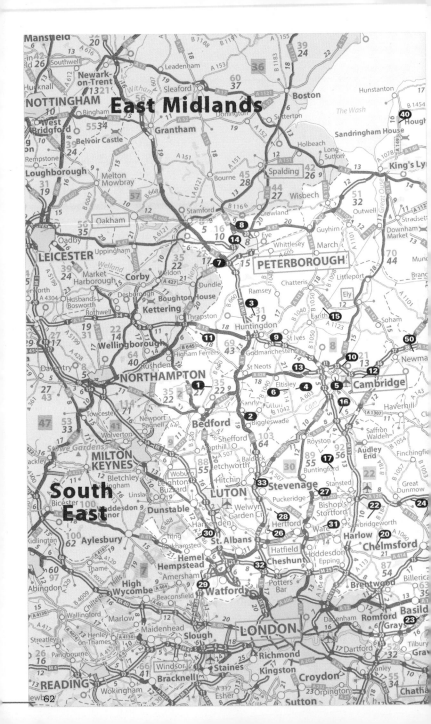

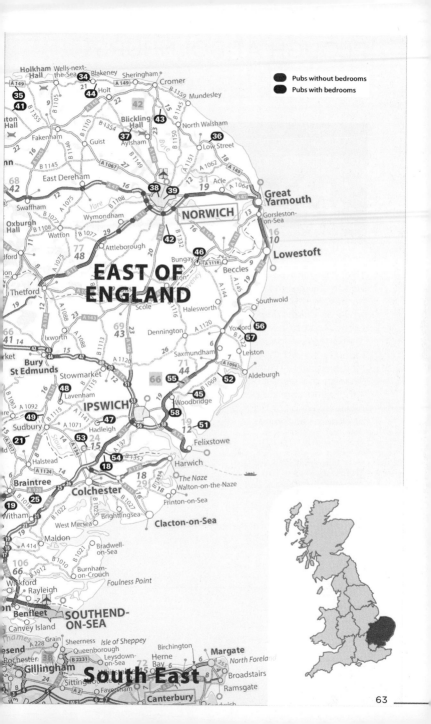

Pubs without bedrooms
Pubs with bedrooms

PLOUGH AT BOLNHURST

Go for dishes with a Mediterranean slant

This charming pub has 15C origins and is a hit with locals and visitors alike, who frequent the place come rain or shine. The garden, with its trickling stream, is the place to be in summer, while on colder days there's the choice of the bar or restaurant; both with cosy low beams and fires – the latter a little smarter, with its modern wallpaper and upholstered chairs. The same seasonal menu is served throughout, with many dishes displaying strong Mediterranean influences; you might find roast chorizo or sweet Spanish pickles, followed by 28-day aged Aberdeenshire steaks – including côte de boeuf for two – and other dishes containing Sicilian olive oil or black olive purée. There's also a great selection of cheeses and wines by the glass.

Kimbolton Rd,
BOLNHURST, MK44 2EX
Tel.: 01234 376274
Website: www.bolnhurst.com

On B 660, 7 mi north of Bedford. Parking.

PRICES

Meals: £ 22 (weekdays) and a la carte
£ 31/52

MAP: 1

CLOSING TIMES

Closed 2 weeks January, Sunday dinner
and Monday

JOHN O'GAUNT INN

Beautiful gardens overlooking the wheat fields

This cosy, honest village inn is located on the edge of a pretty village and its delightful gardens overlook the wheat fields behind. It started life as three 18C cottages; was first licenced in 1835; and is named after the 1st Duke of Lancaster, who held the manor of Sutton in the 14C. The current owners have plenty of experience when it comes to running pubs and it now has a welcoming open-fired bar – complete with a skittle game owned by the villagers themselves – and a smart dining room with a plush feel. Everything on the menu is homemade, from the fresh crisps with zingy pesto dip to the chicken liver parfait with onion marmalade or the cheddar tart with roasted local asparagus – and they also serve some tasty 'Crumps Butchers' steaks.

30 High St,
SUTTON, SG19 2NE
Tel.: 01767 260377
Website: www.johnogauntsutton.co.uk

5 mi northeast of Biggleswade by B 1040. Parking.

PRICES
Meals: a la carte £ 24/40

MAP: **2**

CLOSING TIMES
Closed Monday except bank holidays and
Sunday dinner

ABBOT'S ELM

A passionately compiled wine list

It's hard to believe that this attractive thatched inn is actually a reconstruction of its 17C predecessor; part destroyed by fire in 2010, now only the elegant brick fireplace remains from its former days. The interior is surprisingly modern and spacious, with an open-plan layout, homely touches and a vaulted, oak-beamed roof. Cooking is hearty and flavoursome, with a wide choice that includes good value set price lunch and dinner menus and an evening tasting menu – and the passionately compiled wine list offers most choices by the glass or carafe. Cosy, comfortable bedrooms come with complimentary water and wi-fi as well as fluffy bathrobes – and there's even a cookery school here should you wish to brush up on your culinary skills.

Moat Ln,
ABBOTS RIPTON, PE28 2PA
Tel.: 01487 773773
Website: www.theabbotselm.co.uk

6 mi north of Huntingdon by B 1514, A 141 and B 1090. Parking.

PRICES
Meals: a la carte £ 20/43

 3 rooms:
£ 65/90

MAP: 3

CLOSING TIMES
Closed Sunday dinner

WILLOW TREE

A quirky look and adventurous cooking

It may be named after a majestic British tree – the likes of which you'll find blowing elegantly in the wind as you enter the car park – but this pub is far from your usual affair. The life-sized cow model in the garden is the first clue as to the quirky nature of the place, followed inside by the feeling of being in a 'House and Home' magazine, courtesy of chandeliers, gilt mirrors and Louis XV style furniture dotted about the place. Menus offer everything from old pub classics to more ambitious dishes such as scotch duck egg, rabbit terrine or venison haunch Rossini, and they offer a 'Summer Deckchair' menu and afternoon tea from May-September. These are accompanied by an appealing wine list, with most selections available by the glass.

29 High St,
BOURN, CB23 2SQ
Tel.: 01954 719775
Website: www.thewillowtreebourn.com

3 mi south of Cambourne by A 1198 off B 1046, in the centre of the village. Parking.

PRICES
Meals: a la carte £ 16/42

MAP: 4

CLOSING TIMES
Open daily

PINT SHOP

Gutsy British cooking in simple surroundings

'MEAT. BEER. BREAD.' is written on the window – and that pretty much sums this place up. Set in the city centre, it's styled on an old Beer House, the likes of which gave birth to the modern day pub. Turn left and you'll find yourself in a retro bar where warm sausage rolls sit on the counter and a large blackboard on the wall details their 10 keg and 6 cask beers (there are also over 70 different gins on offer). If you're after a meal, there's an intimate ground floor area and an airy first floor room, both clad in pale grey wood and simply furnished. Cooking is fittingly gutsy and satisfying and the charcoal grill takes centre stage; choose from the likes of beer-brined chicken, beef and ale suet pudding or pork belly with cabbage and bacon.

10 Peas Hill,
CAMBRIDGE, CB2 3NP
Tel.: 01223 352293
Website: www.pintshop.co.uk

In city centre just east of King's Par. Nearest public car park on Corn Exchange St.

PRICES
Meals: £ 13 (lunch and early dinner)
and a la carte £ 20/35

MAP: **5**

CLOSING TIMES
Closed 25-26 December and 1 January

NO 77

Extensive Thai menu and a Sunday cinema club

This isn't your usual kind of pub – but then neither is Craig and Shania's other pub, the Willow Tree. The cream and blue exterior of No 77 leads through to a rustic interior with a copper bar and a room with blue velvet cushioned chairs from an old cinema. It comes as something of a surprise to discover a selection of Thai cocktails on the blackboard – and a menu to match. The extensive list of dishes includes the likes of prawn tempura and spicy fishcakes; stir fries and noodles; and red, green, yellow and jungle curries served with a choice of seafood, meats and vegetables. The Kantok sharing platters are a hit, dishes are available to take away, and during the screenings for their Sunday cinema club they serve Thai popcorn and satay skewers.

77 Ermine St,
CAXTON, CB23 3PQ
Tel.: 01954 269577
Website: www.77cambridge.com

7.5 mi east of St Neots, village signposted off A 428. Parking.

PRICES
Meals: a la carte £ 16/37

MAP: 6

CLOSING TIMES
Closed Tuesday lunch and Monday

CROWN INN

Pub favourites in a quintessential English inn

With its 17C honey-stone walls, its charming thatched roof, and its lovely location in a delightful country parish, the Crown Inn most definitely comes under the heading of 'quintessential English pub'. Sup a cask ale or two beside the characterful inglenook fireplace in the bar, then head through to the cosy dining room or out onto the terrace. The same seasonally changing menu is served throughout, featuring old British favourites such as steak and ale pie, homemade cider and apple sausages or lamb with bubble and squeak. Bedrooms are smart, modern and individually designed – some have four-posters, sleigh beds or roll-top baths – and if you fancy treating yourself in the morning, you can order a hamper and enjoy breakfast in your PJs.

8 Duck St,
ELTON, PE8 6RQ
Tel.: 01832 280232
Website: www.thecrowninn.org

Midway between Oundle and Peterborough signposted off A 605.
Parking.

PRICES
Meals: a la carte £ 24/35

 8 rooms:
£ 68/145

MAP: 7

CLOSING TIMES
Open daily

BLUE BELL

Don't leave before trying their tasty desserts

The pretty village of Glinton is home to the Blue Bell and also to its experienced owners who, after some time away, have returned to their roots. A pretty flower display greets you at the front and there's a pleasant terrace round the back, while inside there are plenty of nooks and crannies in which to hide yourself away. In true pub style, there's plenty of space beneath the old 18C beams for the local drinkers, and the atmosphere is suitably warm and welcoming. Lunch offers pub favourites, generously filled sandwiches and tempting salads in a choice of sizes, while dinner steps things up a gear with dishes like maple-glazed duck breast with confit leg croquette – and be sure to save room for one of their tasty desserts.

10 High St,
GLINTON, PE6 7LS
Tel.: 01733 252285
Website: www.thebluebellglinton.co.uk

5 mi north of Peterborough off A 15 in centre of village. Parking.

PRICES
Meals: a la carte £ 23/39

MAP: 8

CLOSING TIMES
Closed Sunday dinner

THE COCK

They make 110 varieties of sausage!

As you approach this 17C country pub you'll come across two doors: one marked 'Pub', leading to a split-level bar, and the other marked 'Restaurant', leading to a spacious dining room. It's run by an experienced team and has a homely feel, with warm fabrics, comfy seating and attractively papered walls. In winter, the best spot is beside the fire, while in summer, it's by the French windows. Tried-and-tested dishes might include lamb shank or belly pork, the set lunches are good value, and there's an extensive list of daily changing fish specials. There are plenty of gluten-free choices too, including homemade sausages from their repertoire of 110 different varieties, which come with a choice of sauce and various types of mashed potato.

47 High St,
HEMINGFORD GREY, PE28 9BJ
Tel.: 01480 463609
Website: www.cambscuisine.com

The village is 5 mi east of Huntingdon signposted off A 14. Parking.

PRICES
Meals: £ 14 (weekday lunch) and a la carte
£ 23/37

MAP: **9**

CLOSING TIMES
Open daily
booking essential

CROWN & PUNCHBOWL

Choose one of the fish specials

A top-to-toe refurbishment has transformed this into a smart, laid-back pub. Watch your head on the beams as you enter the bar – where you'll find frequently changing cask ales behind the counter – then take your pick from several different seating areas including the intimate Oak Room and the smart conservatory, which is a great spot on a sunny day. Start with rustic bread and zingy olive oil then move on to modern seasonal dishes such as chicken breast stuffed with truffle mousse or wild mushroom and herb cakes. There's a good value set menu to consider and a wide range of specials chalked on the fish board too, with the likes of cod cheek and chorizo risotto or whole baked lemon sole. Cosy, welcoming bedrooms are named after local writers.

High St,
HORNINGSEA, CB25 9JG
Tel.: 01223 860643
Website: www.cambscuisine.com

4 mi northeast of Cambridge by A 1303, in village centre. Parking.

PRICES
Meals: £ 19 (weekdays) and a la carte
£ 24/38

 5 rooms:
£ 120/130

MAP: 10

CLOSING TIMES
Open daily

PHEASANT

A lovely country feel and a great value set menu

This thatched, picture postcard pub is, quite simply, delightful. Hidden away in a sleepy hamlet, it has a lovely relaxed, countryside feel, with exposed beams and hunting scenes galore; John Bull wallpaper features and, in the dining room, bread is carved under the watchful eye of a stuffed albino pheasant. The wide-ranging seasonal menu has something for everyone, from nibbles like salted almonds or crispy squid through to tasty dishes like venison terrine or sea trout with shrimp butter. There's a classic section for the more traditional diner and an incredible value set menu too. Drinks are top notch, with an excellent selection of wines chosen by a Master of Wine; the atmosphere is buzzing and staff are warm, gracious and attentive.

Village Loop Rd,
KEYSTON, PE28 0RE
Tel.: 01832 710241
Website: www.thepheasant-keyston.co.uk

Signposted off junction 15 of A 14. Parking.

PRICES
Meals: £ 15 (lunch and early dinner)
and a la carte £ 24/40

MAP: 11

CLOSING TIMES
Closed 2-15 January, Sunday dinner and Monday
booking essential

HOLE IN THE WALL

Run with passion by a young team

Local workers used to leave their empty tankards in a hole in this charming 16C pub's wall; these would then be filled, ready for them to pick up on their way home. The hole may have long since been closed up, but you can still sup a pint in the pub's cosy beamed bar. Better still, enjoy a meal prepared with zeal by the young chef-owner, a past MasterChef finalist. The regularly changing seasonal menu offers starters like sardines on toast, main courses such as Blythburgh pork chop or Barbury duck breast, and heartwarming, classical desserts like rice pudding. Lunch is a steal, homemade bread is baked twice a day and they are partial to a bit of meat curing and smoking too. For the full experience, try one of the evening tasting menus.

2 High St,
LITTLE WILBRAHAM, CB21 5JY
Tel.: 01223 812282
Website: www.holeinthewallcambridge.com

Just off the A 14 east of Cambridge, the Wilbrahams are signposted off A 1303. Parking.

PRICES

MAP: 12

Meals: £ 20/35

CLOSING TIMES
Closed 2 weeks January, Sunday dinner,
Monday and Tuesday lunch
booking advisable

THREE HORSESHOES

Adventurous cooking and a lively bar

Set in a pretty village, famous for its stunning hall, this appealing pub with its whitewashed walls and attractive thatched roof fits right in. To the front, scrubbed wooden tables are set beside a small bar and a welcoming fireplace; to the rear, a more formal conservatory with Lloyd Loom chairs looks out over the garden. Ambitious, modern dishes have international influences: expect choices like sugar-cured sea trout with black quinoa, broad beans and olive oil jam or roast duck breast with orange, turnips and hazelnuts. Desserts are well presented with a playful edge and the wine list, well-chosen, with plenty available by the glass. The bar is a lively place, so if you're looking for a romantic table for two, head for the conservatory.

High St,
MADINGLEY, CB23 8AB
Tel.: 01954 210221
Website: www.threehorseshoesmadingley.com

West of Cambridge signposted off A 1303. Parking.

PRICES

MAP: **13**

Meals: a la carte £ 25/45

CLOSING TIMES

Closed Sunday dinner November-February
booking advisable

BEEHIVE

A great spot for weary shoppers

Just off the city centre ring road might not be your first choice of location for a pub but it's close at hand for shoppers and has stood here long enough to have built up a steady group of regulars. Owners James and Sharon have lived in the area all their lives and, remembering the pub in its heyday, jumped at the chance to get the place up and running again when it was closed and put on the market. It now has a smart modern interior with stripped floorboards, a zinc-topped bar and a mix of high stools, armchairs and banquettes. When it comes to the food, it's well-presented, flavoursome and satisfying; the house pâté with chutney is a must, followed by a classic like slow-cooked shoulder of lamb or a pub favourite such as toad in the hole.

62 Albert Pl,
PETERBOROUGH, PE1 1DD
Tel.: 01733 310600
Website: www.beehivepub.co.uk

In the centre of the city just off Bourges Boulevard. Pay and display parking across the road.

PRICES **MAP: 14**
Meals: a la carte £ 20/39

CLOSING TIMES
Closed 1 January and Sunday dinner

ANCHOR INN

Tempting dishes and river views

It may seem like a strange name for a pub that's nowhere near the coast – but it does have some watery connections. Built in 1650, this building was originally used to house the workers who created the Hundred Foot Wash in order to alleviate flooding in the fens. If you fancy a river view, head for the wood-panelled rooms to the front of the bar, where you'll discover a pleasant outlook and a tempting menu, which might include smoked eel, pork loin in Parma ham, tea-infused duck or the house speciality of grilled dates wrapped in bacon. There are always some fish specials chalked on the board, while other dishes occasionally use produce from the nearby Denham Estate. Neat, pine-furnished bedrooms include two suites; one has a river outlook.

SUTTON GAULT, CB6 2BD
Tel.: 01353 778537
Website: www.anchor-inn-restaurant.co.uk

Off B 1381; from Sutton village follow signs to Sutton Gault; pub is beside the New Bedford River. Parking.

PRICES
Meals: £ 15 (weekday lunch)/35
and a la carte £ 25/44

 4 rooms:
£ 60/145

MAP: 15

CLOSING TIMES
Open daily

TICKELL ARMS

Sit in the orangery, overlooking the pond

This 17C pub is named after a local squire and former landlord, who had a reputation for being rather irascible – his regulars used to wind him up, just to see if he would throw them out! His coat of arms still hangs on the walls, as a distant relative owns the place, but thankfully the staff are now much more welcoming. Constantly evolving menus offer everything from bar snacks to more adventurous dishes such as rabbit and bacon ballotine. Fish is delivered 6 days a week; on Tuesdays diners can select their own cuts for 'Steak and Chop' night; and on Sundays, freshly roasted potatoes are put out on the bar. Make for the orangery-style extension overlooking the pond and be sure to pay a visit to the WC to listen to the Blackadder tracks!

1 North Rd,
WHITTLESFORD, CB22 4NZ
Tel.: 01223 833025
Website: www.cambscuisine.com

7 mi south of Cambridge, signposted from junction 10 of M 11. Parking

PRICES
Meals: £ 14 (weekdays)/19 and a la carte
£ 23/39

MAP: 16

CLOSING TIMES
Open daily

CRICKETERS

Traditional pub with a lively, buzzy vibe

This deceptively spacious pub sits close to the cricket pitch in a sleepy village and is popular with locals and visitors alike – it also has plenty of welcoming bedrooms for those wishing to stay. The blackboard menu above the fire in the bar lists the dishes of the day; head to the dining room with its exposed beams, horse harnesses and polished brass if you're after a more 'restauranty' feel. The menu offers a mix of hearty British classics and some Italian-influenced dishes, so expect to find tasty homemade pastas alongside a pie of the day, local beef, and fruit crumble. Bread is baked daily and produce is sourced as locally as possible; the owners' son, Jamie Oliver, supplies fruit, vegetables and herbs from his organic garden.

CLAVERING, CB11 4QT
Tel.: 01799 550442
Website: www.thecricketers.co.uk

On the main road through the village close to the cricket pitch. Parking.

PRICES
Meals: a la carte £ 22/42

 20 rooms:
£ 70/135

MAP: 17

CLOSING TIMES
Closed 25-26 December
booking essential

SUN INN

Interesting wine list chosen by the owner

This characterful yellow inn is located in a picturesque spot in the heart of Constable Country; in fact, it dates back to the 15C, so it would have been around in Constable's day. Inside it has an appealing shabby-chic style: there's a cosy panelled lounge, a characterful beamed dining area and a bar with an attractive elm counter. In winter, follow the smell of warm sausage rolls; in summer, head out to the bar in the garden. The monthly menu offers generous Italian-inspired dishes: you'll always find pastas and risottos, alongside maybe sea bass with saffron and bagna cauda sauce. The well-chosen wine list offers plenty by the glass; look out for the 'Desert Island Cellared Wines'. Bedrooms are cosy – two have a modern New England style.

High St,
DEDHAM, CO7 6DF
Tel.: 01206 323351
Website: www.thesuninndedham.com

8 mi northeast of Colchester signposted off A 12, in village centre. Parking.

PRICES
Meals: a la carte £ 19/40

 7 rooms:
£ 90/145

MAP: 18

CLOSING TIMES
Closed 25-26 December

SQUARE & COMPASSES

A hugely characterful pub located on the Essex Way

It's hidden down rural Essex lanes but this mustard yellow pub with its neat and tidy garden is well worth seeking out. Inside it's hugely characterful, with lots of little rooms, plenty of beams and a wood-burning stove or two – and it's run with passion by its welcoming owners and their friendly team. Real ale is served from gravity fed casks, which goes down well with the locals, while the framed menus displayed on the walls are witness to the owners' love of good food. Two menus are offered: one rarely changes and lists classics like homemade steak and ale pie or locally made sausages and mash, while the other, chalked up on blackboards, features more adventurous choices, including fish caught off the Essex coast and local game in season.

FULLER STREET, CM3 2BB
Tel.: 01245 361477
Website: www.thesquareandcompasses.co.uk

Between Braintree and Chelmsford off the A 131. Parking.

PRICES
Meals: a la carte £ 19/33

MAP: 19

CLOSING TIMES
Open daily
booking essential

QUEENS HEAD

Sit outside, looking down to the river

Don't make the mistake of trying to go in the front door – you have to enter either to the side or the rear of this characterful 16C pub. It's located in the heart of the village and has a pretty garden which leads down to the banks of the river. The interior is just as inviting though, with its original beams, inglenook fireplaces and galleried upper level. The extensive menu changes regularly and is supplemented by blackboard specials and a particularly good value set selection; classic dishes showcase produce from small local suppliers and feedback from the regulars helps the menus to evolve. The place is run by a mother and son team and they host regular Garrett sessions, where respected artists play folk, roots and acoustic sets.

Queen St,
FYFIELD, CM5 0RY
Tel.: 01277 899231
Website: www.thequeensheadfyfield.co.uk

3 mi northeast of Chipping Ongar on B 184 in centre of village.
Parking.

PRICES   **MAP: 20**
Meals: £ 22 (weekdays) and a la carte
£ 28/47

CLOSING TIMES
Closed 26 December and Mondays

PHEASANT

They grow their own veg and keep chickens and bees

Set on the edge of a pretty little village, this appealing 16C pub is every bit a true country inn. Run by a former landscape gardener and his wife, it centres around sustainability, with a one acre garden over the road where they grow vegetables and keep chickens and bees. The hub of the pub is a very inviting low-beamed bar and the locals come in their droves for biweekly 'Thirsty Thursday'. The cooking keeps things simple, offering heartwarming dishes in traditional combinations; maybe a prawn cocktail, followed by belly pork or local venison, finished off with an apple crumble. They also serve takeaway fish and chips, which keeps the regulars happy. Bedrooms are modern and stylish; those at the rear offer views over rolling fields.

GESTINGTHORPE, CO9 3AU
Tel.: 01787 465010
Website: www.thepheasant.net

Between Sudbury and Castle Hedingham off B 1058. Parking.

PRICES
Meals: a la carte £ 25/41

 5 rooms:
£ 125/185

MAP: 21

CLOSING TIMES
Closed January and Monday in winter

DUKE'S HEAD

Hosts many of the village's community events

Run by an enthusiastic couple who help support nearby sports clubs and host plenty of community events, this spacious 17C pub is the very definition of a proper village local. It features a large terrace and a pleasant garden with a children's tree house, and behind its smart modern façade, has a bright, relaxed feel. When it comes to the food, dishes are tasty, well-crafted and of a good size; you might find omelette Arnold Bennett or bubble and squeak, followed by chicken Kiev, king prawn spaghetti or pumpkin and chestnut gnocchi. These can be eaten in a laid-back, pine-furnished room or in the more formal, pre-laid dining room. If you're just after some nibbles, the bar, with its open fire and low level seating, is always a good bet.

High St,
HATFIELD BROAD OAK, CM22 7HH
Tel.: 01279 718598
Website: www.thedukeshead.co.uk

In the centre of the village. Parking.

PRICES
Meals: a la carte £ 22/30

MAP: 22

CLOSING TIMES
Closed 25-26 December

BELL INN

Run by the same family for over 70 years

If you're wondering about the hot cross buns, the story goes that past landlord Jack Turnell took over the pub on Good Friday, whereupon he nailed a bun to one of the beams; since then, a bun has been added every year – cement versions marking wartime rationing and a wooden one commemorating the passing of the pub's oldest regular. The Bell has been run by the same family for over 70 years, but dates back nearly 12 times that, as the characterful beams and wood panelling attest. Cooking uses quality produce to create classically based dishes with a modern touch, like pan-fried sea bass with spring onion crushed new potatoes and creamed crayfish bisque. The pub bedrooms are traditional in style, while those in Hill House are thoroughly modern.

High Rd,
HORNDON ON THE HILL, SS17 8LD
Tel.: 01375 642463
Website: www.bell-inn.co.uk

In the centre of the village. Parking.

PRICES
Meals: a la carte £ 22/41

 27 rooms:
£ 65/145

MAP: 23

CLOSING TIMES
Closed 25-26 December and bank holidays

FLITCH OF BACON

Come at the weekend for a tasty brunch

The unusual name originates from the 12C Dunmow Flitch Trials that awarded a flitch of bacon to married couples who could swear not to have regretted their marriage for a year and a day! It's a pretty place, where the serving team are confident and the chef is experienced: warm sourdough arrives in a hessian bag and is followed by an extensive range of modern dishes, allied with the odd pub classic. Good ingredients are used in accomplished ways, flavour combinations are great and presentation is top notch. In summer the terrace comes to life, with an old Citroen van acting as a bar and meats cooked on a 'Big Green Egg' barbeque. Contemporary bedrooms are boldly decorated – one has a four-poster bed and a roll-top bath in the room.

The Street,
LITTLE DUNMOW, CM6 3HT
Tel.: 01371 821660
Website: www.flitchofbacon.co.uk

3 mi east of Great Dunmow by B 1256, in village centre. Parking.

PRICES
Meals: a la carte £ 28/53

 3 rooms:
£ 160

MAP: 24

CLOSING TIMES
Open daily
booking essential

COMPASSES AT PATTISWICK

Great views and local game

This remotely set pub started life as two estate workers' cottages, and its name comes from its far-reaching, 360 degree countryside views. Large gardens with plenty of seating make the most of this panorama, while the mini playground ensures any kids in your party will be kept happy. Inside, it's smart and spacious, with open fires, chatty local staff and a warm, relaxing feel. Lunch sees the likes of sandwiches, a ploughman's or a Melton Mowbray pork pie with piccalilli, while the wide-ranging à la carte keeps things traditional with potted shrimps, ox cheek or a hearty roast mutton shepherd's pie. Food is laudably local, with game from the surrounding estate. Nursery puddings might include warm treacle tart or a fruit crumble with custard.

Compasses Rd,
PATTISWICK, CM77 8BG
Tel.: 01376 561322
Website: www.thecompassespattiswick.co.uk

Between Braintree and Coggeshall signposted off A 120. Parking.

PRICES
Meals: a la carte £ 23/39

MAP: 25

CLOSING TIMES
Open daily

WAGGONERS

Set on the edge of the Brocket Hall Estate, this 17C pub was once a popular stop-off point for stagecoaches and a favourite haunt of the estate workers. With a welcoming owner, a charming young team and a buzzy atmosphere, it's no surprise to find that it's as popular now as it was then; its delightful open-fired bar providing a pleasant spot for weary walkers, locals and their dogs, while another, larger room is set up more formally for diners. The bar menu lists typically pubby dishes like burgers and chips while the à la carte presents more ambitious French dishes like sautéed frogs legs, foie gras ballotine or duck leg confit. Some of the dishes – like the chateaubriand and crêpes Suzettes – are presented on gueridon trolleys.

Brickwall Cl,
AYOT GREEN, AL6 9AA
Tel.: 01707 324241
Website: www.thewaggoners.co.uk

2.5 mi south of Welwyn off B 197. Parking.

PRICES   MAP: **26**
Meals: £ 15 (weekday lunch)/26
and a la carte £ 25/53

CLOSING TIMES
Closed Sunday dinner
booking advisable

GOLDEN FLEECE

The Golden Fleece Smokey is a speciality

This part-16C property was left to go to rack and ruin for ten long years, so when it finally found a buyer, it was in need of some real TLC. Who better to take on the challenge than a couple who grew up in the village: one of whom had their first job – aged 13 – at this very pub? It's not hard to see why they – and their many regulars – are so fond of it, with its spacious garden, pretty terrace overlooking the village and period features like a vast inglenook fireplace. Food is tasty and comforting, with popular dishes including the Millionaire's bun (fillet steak in a bread roll), suet pudding and the Golden Fleece Smokey. Old-school puddings might include a warming blackberry sponge with custard. Gluten and dairy free options are available.

20 Green End,
BRAUGHING, SG11 2PG
Tel.: 01920 823555
Website: www.goldenfleecebraughing.co.uk

In the middle of the village, on B 1368. Parking.

PRICES   MAP: **27**
Meals: a la carte £ 22/38

CLOSING TIMES
Closed 25-26 December and Sunday
dinner

TILBURY

Charming 18C inn offering something for everyone

This charming 18C inn is found just off the green of an equally delightful village. It's had many names over the years but has now reverted back to its original; the logo providing a clue as to its meaning – a two-wheeled horse-drawn carriage. There's a lovely heated terrace and a mature garden where they grow herbs and, inside, three rustic rooms with exposed beams and brick floors. It's owned by two brothers and heavily supported by the villagers, and there's something on offer here for one and all. Pub classics please traditionalists, while more creative dishes such as potted rabbit with carrot cake or maple-roasted guinea fowl really showcase the kitchen's skills. Add to this a selection of Brakspear's ales and everyone is happy.

1 Watton Rd,
DATCHWORTH, SG3 6TB
Tel.: 01483 815550
Website: www.thetilbury.co.uk

4 mi southeast of Stevenage signposted off A 602. Parking.

PRICES   MAP: **28**
Meals: a la carte £ 24/39

CLOSING TIMES
Closed Monday and Sunday dinner

BRICKLAYERS ARMS

Good old-fashioned French-inspired dishes

This pub is tucked away by itself on the outer reaches of a small hamlet, so you'll need a good navigator when trying to find it. Part-built in 1722, it was originally two cottages before becoming a butcher's, a blacksmith's and later, an alehouse. Inside it's rather smart, with polished tables and fresh flowers everywhere; the areas to the side of the bar being more formally laid than those in front. This isn't the place for a quick snack (a glance at the menu will show there are none), but somewhere serving good old-fashioned, French-inspired dishes. Sunday lunch is a real family affair and if you've only time for a fleeting visit, have a hearty pudding on the terrace. The wine list is a labour of love, featuring boutique Australian wines.

Hogpits Bottom,
FLAUNDEN, HP3 0PH
Tel.: 01442 833322
Website: www.bricklayersarms.com

5 mi northeast of Amersham signposted off the A 404. Parking.

PRICES   MAP: **29**
Meals: £ 17 (weekdays) and a la carte
£ 25/44

CLOSING TIMES
Closed 25 December

ALFORD ARMS

Set among the network of paths that run across the Chilterns, this attractive Victorian pub is a popular destination for hikers – and when you're trying to squeeze your car into a tight space on the narrow country lane, arriving by foot may suddenly seem the better option. The pleasant garden flanks the peaceful village green – where you might spot the odd Morris dancer or two – and the warm bar welcomes four-legged friends as equally as their owners. The traditional menu has a strong British stamp and follows the seasons closely, so you're likely to find salads and fish in summer and comforting meat or game dishes in winter; these might include belly pork with sticky parsnips, a lamb and rabbit shepherd's pie or a tempting special.

FRITHSDEN, HP1 3DD
Tel.: 01442 864480
Website: www.alfordarmsfrithsden.co.uk

4.5 mi northwest of Hemel Hempstead signposted off A 4146. Parking.

PRICES

MAP: 30

Meals: a la carte £ 22/40

CLOSING TIMES
Closed 25-26 December

FOX AND HOUNDS

Try one of their tasty hand-rolled pastas

London to Hertfordshire isn't the biggest of moves but swapping the hustle and bustle of the crowded streets for the peace and quiet of the countryside is a move that childhood sweethearts James and Bianca (now husband and wife) believe was well worth making. If the weather's good, sit in the garden or on the terrace; if not, find a spot in the pleasant bar or dining room. Menus are British at heart, with distinct Mediterranean influences, and offer tasty, unfussy dishes that display a clear understanding of flavours. The delicious pastas are homemade, they smoke their own fish, and desserts are not to be missed. Push the boat out with an English Shorthorn chateaubriand steak for two or half a Cornish lobster cooked on the Josper grill.

2 High St,
HUNSDON, SG12 8NH
Tel.: 01279 843999
Website: www.foxandhounds-hunsdon.co.uk

Between Hertford and Harlow signposted off A 414, in the village centre. Parking.

PRICES   MAP: **31**
Meals: £ 15 (weekdays) and a la carte
£ 24/43

CLOSING TIMES
Closed 25-26 December, Sunday dinner
and Monday

SUN AT NORTHAW

Ingredients are sourced from the East of England

This restored, part-16C pub sits by the village green and is deceptively spacious, with a contemporary style and a traditional edge. Cooking is original, so expect a wide range of dishes like crispy pigs' ears, spiced lamb pie, red gurnard or maybe even sea urchin. There's a strong regional slant here too: ingredients are sourced from the East of England, there are local ales and ciders behind the bar – as well as some English bottles on the wine list – and the toilet walls are even papered with Ordnance Survey maps of the area. Look out for wooden crates of veg scattered about the place and expect to see a chef coming to grab an onion or two. Service is friendly and the pub's affectionate dog, Smudge, may well wander over to welcome you too.

1 Judges Hill,
NORTHAW, EN6 4NL
Tel.: 01707 655507
Website: www.thesunatnorthaw.co.uk

Beside village green on main road through the village. Parking.

PRICES
Meals: a la carte £ 24/33

MAP: 32

CLOSING TIMES
Closed Sunday dinner and Monday except
bank holidays when closed Tuesday

FOX

Can't decide? Try the 'Fox Slate' for two

Set right in the heart of the village, next to the beautiful church and opposite the pond, is this smart, bright pub, which is proving extremely popular. Drinkers and diners vie for tables in the modern bar but there's also a contemporary, slightly Scandic-style dining room and a sheltered terrace at the back. Light wood floors and matching furniture feature throughout and the keener eye will notice a host of subtle references to Norfolk – home to the owner's other pubs. Dishes are modern and there's a good choice of game in season; they also take their seafood seriously here, with the likes of herb-crusted Cromer crab and pan-fried golden ray on the menu. For those who can't decide, the 'Fox Slate' for two provides the perfect solution.

WILLIAN, SG6 2AE
Tel.: 01462 480233
Website: www.foxatwillian.co.uk

3 mi northeast of Hitchin by A 505 and side road. Parking.

PRICES
Meals: a la carte £ 23/35

MAP: 33

CLOSING TIMES
Open daily

PRACTISE THE ART
of FINE FOOD.

Live in Italian

WHITE HORSE

Smart bedrooms and unfussy cooking

Whether you've been out on a boat to see the seals, bird watching along the beautiful coastline or wandering the quaint High Street, the sea air will no doubt have stoked your appetite. Head for this brick and flint pub, just behind the harbour, and if the sun's shining, find a spot on the suntrap terrace. Inside it's bright and airy with pastel colours, modern artwork and a pleasant conservatory. The menu champions local produce in tried-and-tested combinations, with seafood a feature in summer. Expect ingredients from the nearby Cley Smokehouse, along with chutney and beer-batter made from Adnams ales – the pub is owned by Adnams Brewery after all! Smart bedrooms are named after nautical knots – spacious 'Bowline' looks out to sea.

4 High St,
BLAKENEY, NR25 7AL
Tel.: 01263 740574
Website: www.blakeneywhitehorse.co.uk

Just off the quay. Parking.

PRICES
Meals: a la carte £ 16/34

 9 rooms:
£ 89/159

MAP: 34

CLOSING TIMES
Closed 25 December
booking advisable

WHITE HORSE

Great views over the marshes

There's no denying that when sitting on the rear terrace or in the spacious conservatory, the views over the Brancaster Marshes and Scolt Head Island really make this pub. If you can't get a seat in either, panic not, as there's still the bar or the landscaped front terrace complete with its pleasant southerly aspect and patio heaters. On the all-day bar menu you'll find old favourites, a selection of tapas-style dishes and a few more ambitious offerings; while on the seasonally changing à la carte and daily specials, there'll be dishes such as dressed Cromer crab, confit Norfolk pork belly or marinated slow-cooked veal breast. Bedrooms have a crisp New England stylo; go for one of the Garden Rooms, as each comes with a private terrace.

BRANCASTER STAITHE, PE31 8BY
Tel.: 01485 210262
Website: www.whitehorsebrancaster.co.uk

On A 149 Hunstanton to Wells Rd. Parking.

PRICES		**MAP: 35**
Meals: a la carte £ 26/38	15 rooms: £ 85/180	

CLOSING TIMES
Open daily
booking essential

INGHAM SWAN

More of a dining than a drinking pub

If you're visiting the Norfolk Broads, be sure to pay a visit to this attractive thatched pub, which stands in the shadow of a fine 11C church. Sit surrounded by flint walls under exposed wooden beams or in one of two cosy banquette-lined snugs – one designed for drinking and the other for dining. There's an array of menus – including a good value 'menu du jour' – all of which feature produce from their farm. Eye-catching dishes are made up of many different elements and could include the likes of pan-roast sea trout with crispy Cromer crab cakes or fillet, breast and loin of lamb with caramelised red onion. Service is formal but has personality. Bedrooms come with muted colour schemes and designer furnishings; breakfast is a highlight.

Sea Palling Rd,
INGHAM, NR12 9AB
Tel.: 01692 581099
Website: www.theinghamswan.co.uk

In the centre of the village. Parking.

PRICES
Meals: £ 17 (weekday lunch)/28
and a la carte £ 27/45

 4 rooms:
£ 85/195

MAP: 36

CLOSING TIMES
Closed 25-26 December
booking essential at dinner

WALPOLE ARMS

The owners are farmers and use their own produce

This pretty 18C inn with carefully manicured gardens is set in a sleepy little village not far from Oulton, where the owners' family have been farming since the 1930s. The interior is surprisingly modern but has been sympathetically designed in keeping with the building's age: the beamed bar provides a warm welcome and leads through to a more formal room with mock-bookshelf wallpaper. The menu champions local ingredients and features produce from their own farm, with rare breed beef a speciality. Dishes have a refined modern style and are attractively presented – choose from the likes of chicken breast Caesar salad with a crispy hen's egg and bacon jam or cod with wild garlic risotto, cockles and acidulated butter. Service is bright and bubbly.

The Common,
ITTERINGHAM, NR11 7AR
Tel.: 01263 587258
Website: www.thewalpolearms.co.uk

In the centre of the village. Parking.

PRICES   MAP: **37**
Meals: a la carte £ 18/39

CLOSING TIMES
Closed 25 December and Sunday dinner
in winter

GEORGIAN TOWNHOUSE

Laid-back pub with a pleasingly flexible menu

'TGT', as the locals like to call it, spent time as a schoolhouse, a wartime hospital and a hotel before finding its calling as a pub. It's an appealing place with a pleasingly laid-back atmosphere and the menu takes on a similar approach: you can have small plates either to start or to share; dishes 'for the table' for 2 or 4; or something to keep to yourself 'from the store'. They use home-grown fruit and veg and heritage preparation methods, including home-smoking cheeses and spit-roasting and flame-grilling meats. In the cosy bar and bustling restaurant, Georgian charm blends seamlessly with modern styling and to the rear there's an attractive terrace. Boldly coloured bedrooms come with retro furniture, Smeg fridges and coffee machines.

30-34 Unthank Rd,
NORWICH, NR2 2RB
Tel.: 01603 615655
Website: www.thegeorgiantownhousenorwich.com

Just off the ring road at the top of Unthank Rd. Parking.

PRICES
Meals: a la carte £ 20/41

 22 rooms:
£ 85/170

MAP: 38

CLOSING TIMES
Open daily

REINDEER

Proudly British cooking uses lesser-known cuts

Despite being located on a busy main street just west of the ring road, the Reindeer's young owners seem to have found a niche for themselves and they have been steadily building up a keen local following. Inside, the pub has a good old rustic feel and, satisfyingly, plenty of space is kept aside for drinkers, who have 10 real ales and 12 keg beers, lagers and ciders to choose from. Cooking is straightforward and proudly British, employing lesser-used cuts in many of the dishes; bar snacks might include potted rabbit and duck hearts or beef dripping on toast, while the main menu features plenty of dishes for sharing. The old brewing room is now a venue for private groups and makes the perfect place for a celebration. Service is friendly.

10 Dereham Rd,
NORWICH, NR2 4AY
Tel.: 01603 612995
Website: www.thereindeerpub.co.uk

On A 1074 west of the city centre. Parking.

PRICES
Meals: a la carte £ 20/32

MAP: **39**

CLOSING TIMES
Closed 25-26 December and Monday

ROSE AND CROWN

14C inn with honest, hearty cooking

Its warren of rooms and passageways, uneven floors and low beamed ceilings place the Rose and Crown squarely into the quintessentially English bracket of inns; and the bright dining rooms, the paved terrace and the impressive pirate ship for children in the garden add some 21C zing to the pub's 14C roots. Cooking is gutsy by nature and makes good use of local produce, with neatly presented dishes such as pan-fried hake fillet alongside trusty classics like steak and chips, and local mussels in season. Service is efficient, they are well used to being busy and a crowd of locals from the village can often be found enjoying a tipple at the bar. Bedrooms are quite a contrast to the rustic pub, being light and modern in style.

Old Church Rd,
SNETTISHAM, PE31 7LX
Tel.: 01485 541382
Website: www.roseandcrownsnettisham.co.uk

In the middle of the village. Parking.

PRICES
Meals: a la carte £ 21/38

16 rooms:
£ 100/140

MAP: 40

CLOSING TIMES
Closed 25 December

DUCK INN

Thick, juicy local steaks are a highlight

Fairy lights decorate the picket fence which fringes the garden and a flock of ducks waddle over from their pond around the corner: this is the Duck Inn, in the pretty village of Stanhoe. In the buzzy slate-floored bar you'll find locals enjoying Elgood's ales – check out the blackboard for bar bites like scotch quail's egg. Lunch sees open sandwiches like 'Fruit Pig Co.' bangers, mustard and onions and dishes such as confit smoked salmon with roasted beetroot. At dinner there's plenty of fresh fish but the mature meats are what you should go for, with thick, juicy local steaks a highlight. The three dining rooms have a rustic, relaxed feel; their walls adorned with local art and vintage kitchen utensils. Bedrooms are cosy and well-kept.

Burnham Rd,
STANHOE, PE31 8QD
Tel.: 01485 518330
Website: www.duckinn.co.uk

3 mi southwest of Burnham Market on B 1155. Parking.

PRICES
Meals: a la carte £ 23/46

 2 rooms:
£ 80/150

MAP: 41

CLOSING TIMES
Closed 25 December

WILDEBEEST

Refined cooking in a modern setting

Local boy Dan Smith worked here for 10 years before opening his own pub, the Ingham Swan. Five years later and looking for his next adventure, he found himself at the Wildebeest once more, only this time as its owner. It's a smart place, where comfy leather chairs are set at chunky tree trunk tables. Don't expect to find a burger and chips here – this is a pub where the cooking is modern and refined, with colourful dishes blending many different ingredients to create pleasing contrasts of flavour. The 'Menu du Jour' offers the best value; if you're looking to push the boat out, go for the 6 course evening tasting menu. This being a pub, you are always welcome to come just for a drink and you'll find the local book club here every Wednesday.

82-86 Norwich Rd,
STOKE HOLY CROSS, NR14 8QJ
Tel: 01508 492497
Website: www.thewildebeest.co.uk

Just off the A 140, 5.5 mi south of Norwich. Parking.

PRICES
Meals: £ 17/28 and a la carte £ 32/47

MAP: 42

CLOSING TIMES
Closed 25-26 December
booking essential

GUNTON ARMS

Lovely views over the 18C deer park

Much of the 1,000 acre Gunton Estate has been lovingly restored over the last few decades, including the early 18C deer park, several ruined buildings and this charming pub. It has a super terrace for summer BBQs and an appealing mix of period furnishings and provocative modern art. Nibble on a venison sausage roll or Blythburgh pork crackling in the bar – over a game of pool or darts – or head for a gnarled wood table beside the fireplace in the flag-floored Elk Room. Here you can choose something cooked on the fire – such as an Aberdeen Angus steak – or from a selection of unfussy, fiercely seasonal British dishes like Barnsley lamb chop or mixed grill of Gunton fallow deer. Well-equipped bedrooms have a stylish, country house feel.

Gunton Park,
THORPE MARKET, NR11 8TZ
Tel.: 01263 832010
Website: www.theguntonarms.co.uk

5.5 mi south of Cromer on A 149. Parking on edge of the estate.

PRICES
Meals: a la carte £ 23/40

12 rooms:
£ 85/240

MAP: 43

CLOSING TIMES
Closed 25 December
booking advisable

WIVETON BELL

Proper pub food in a modern setting

With its lightly painted façade bearing a stylised scribble of its name, this place has all the hallmarks of a 'modernised' pub. Thankfully, this modernisation has been undertaken with style and care, so you'll find an attractive interior with beams, stripped floors, wood-burning stoves and a corner just for drinkers; as well as an airy restaurant and conservatory, a beautiful landscaped rear terrace and picnic benches out the front. The seasonal menu offers all the usual pub classics, carefully crafted from quality ingredients – many of which are locally sourced. You'll find bedrooms stylish and cosy; breakfast is continental and this could come as something of a relief considering the size of the portions served in the pub!

Blakeney Rd,
WIVETON, NR25 7TL
Tel.: 01263 740101
Website: www.wivetonbell.com

Signposted off the A 149 just south of Blakeney. Parking.

PRICES
Meals: a la carte £ 25/37

 6 rooms:
£ 90/160

MAP: 44

CLOSING TIMES
Open daily
booking essential

UNRULY PIG

Choose something from the charcoal grill

This pig is far from unruly, its owner – a former lawyer – sees to that, and he makes sure it stays that way by taking an active role in its day-to-day running. It's a cosy kind of a place, with wooden panelling, open fires and an interesting collection of artwork and photographs on display. The Mediterranean-inspired menu offers plenty of choice: for starters try smoked potato and pig croquettes or brisket and bone marrow on toast; for main course, whole grilled sea bream with black olive hollandaise, roasted rump of lamb with baked polenta or rib-eye steak from the charcoal-fired Inka grill. The set menus are good value and there's usually a daily main course for £10 – keep an eye out for the manager's red and white wine of the month too.

Orford Rd,
BROMESWELL, IP12 2PU
Tel.: 01394 460310
Website: www.theunrulypig.co.uk

2.5 mi northeast of Woodbridge on the A 1152. Parking.

PRICES
Meals: £ 15 (weekday lunch)/25
and a la carte £ 27/38

MAP: **45**

CLOSING TIMES
Closed Sunday dinner and Monday
booking advisable

CASTLE INN

Great local sausages and game in season

This sky-blue pub's open-plan interior includes dining areas and an intimate rear bar – the perfect spot for a coffee or a flick through a magazine. Cooking is fresh, simple and seasonal, and while lunch might see a burger and chips or creamy risotto verde alongside doorstop sandwiches, the evening menu might include slow-cooked salt marsh lamb shoulder or pheasant breast wrapped in Parma ham. The Innkeeper's Platter is a perennial favourite and showcases local produce, including a great pickle made by the "Rockin' Grannies" – keep an eye out for the cake stands too, with their homemade cakes and cookies. Themed evenings include 'pie and wine' night and 'film and food' night, complete with popcorn. Bedrooms are homely, warm and comfortable.

35 Earsham St,
BUNGAY, NR35 1AF
Tel.: 01986 892283
Website: www.thecastleinn.net

In the centre of town. Parking.

PRICES
Meals: £ 20 (lunch) and a la carte £ 20/32

 4 rooms:
£ 70

MAP: 46

CLOSING TIMES
Closed 25 December, Sunday dinner and Monday in winter

HADLEIGH RAM

Elaborate modern cooking in a stylish dining pub

The smart cream façade emblazoned with its name suggests that this isn't your typical town pub and, once inside, modern colours and tables neatly laid up for dining confirm suspicions. If you've come just for a drink you will be welcomed but with most others around you dining, you'll start to wonder why you're not eating too. The large menu features just one pub classic – fish and chips – while the rest of the dishes are much more modern and elaborate in style, with lots of different ingredients appearing in some unusual combinations. Your rabbit terrine might come with anchovy mousse and apricot gel; your chicken breast with a smoked sausage and chicken bon bons; and your rump steak with a pork faggot and black truffle jus.

5 Market Pl,
HADLEIGH, IP7 5DL
Tel.: 01473 822880
Website: www.thehadleighram.co.uk

In the centre of the town off the High St. Pay and display parking adjacent.

PRICES
Meals: £ 22 (weekdays) and a la carte
£ 28/43

MAP: **47**

CLOSING TIMES
Closed 26-27 December and Sunday dinner

SIX BELLS

Characterful pub with a hunting theme

Tom and Ed Martin's first pub outside of London is this attractive brick and timber build in the hamlet of Preston St Mary. Ignore the '1416' sign above the door – it was rebuilt during the 18C; but at over 270 years old it still has plenty of character. Open fires punctuate brick walls, rustic tables stand on parquet floors and heavy timbers are hung with tankards and antlers. A hunting theme runs throughout, so you'll also discover an array of stuffed animals and a wire cage filled with old shotguns. Cooking is careful and shows respect for ingredients; alongside pub snacks like crackling with apple sauce, you'll find confidently prepared restaurant-style dishes such as clam, tomato and basil tagliatelli or roebuck tartare with sourdough.

The Street,
PRESTON SAINT MARY, CO10 9NG
Tel.: 01787 247440
Website: www.thesixbellspreston.com

2.75 mi northeast of Lavenham signposted off A 1141. Parking.

PRICES
Meals: £ 12 (weekday lunch) and a la carte
£ 22/31

MAP: 48

CLOSING TIMES
Closed Monday and Tuesday

SWAN

Stay in one of the stylish bedrooms

This smart double-fronted pub is just the sort of place you'd hope to find in this characterful old wool town. The Swan was the first in a small family-run group and every member plays their role – dad oversees the finances, his daughter is in charge of interior design and his son is the chef. To the front there's the bar, in the middle, a beamed dining room and behind it, The Pantry – so-called because it looks into the kitchen. The appealing menu provides plenty of choice, from refined French classics to dishes with an Asian bent; start with Dorset snails or frogs' legs, followed by wild halibut supreme or loin of Lavenham lamb. From the flavoursome cooking to the eye-catching décor, this is a place where you can really see that they care.

Hall St,
LONG MELFORD, CO10 9JQ
Tel.: 01787 464545
Website: www.longmelfordswan.co.uk

14 mi south of Bury St Edmunds by A 134. On-street parking.

PRICES
Meals: a la carte £ 26/53

 8 rooms:
£ 95/175

MAP: 49

CLOSING TIMES
Open daily

PACKHORSE INN

Interesting dishes and plush bedrooms

This smart modern pub is set near the green in the pretty village of Moulton and is named after its famous flint bridge which has spanned the River Kennett since the 15C. Cooking keeps things classical, with the focus firmly on the ingredients' natural flavours: to start you might find truffled goat's cheese, pear, hazelnut and beetroot salad, which could be followed by a burger with Suffolk Gold cheese and red onion marmalade or loin of venison with boulangère potatoes, parsnips, broccoli and blackberries for two to share; for dessert, the assiettes are a good way to go. Bedrooms are ultra-stylish with plush furnishings, roll-top baths and good quality toiletries. For that extra special occasion, they sell a £1,500 magnum of champagne!

Bridge St,
MOULTON, CB8 8SP
Tel.: 01638 751818
Website: www.thepackhorseinn.com

5 mi east of Newmarket by A 1304, B 1506 and B 1085. Parking.

PRICES
Meals: £ 19 (weekday lunch) and a la carte
£ 28/41

 8 rooms:
£ 85/250

MAP: 50

CLOSING TIMES
Open daily

RAMSHOLT ARMS

Honest pub food and river views

The Ramsholt Arms: it may well be at the end of a long and winding road but, boy, is it worth it when you get there, as this striking inn sits against the spectacular backdrop of the River Deben. Sister to the Ufford Crown, it specialises in honest, well-priced pub food and Suffolk ales. Summer days bring hordes to the terrace but, with seating for over a hundred, there's no lack of outside space. When the weather is inclement, a window seat's the ticket: watch the pleasure boats bobbing as you eat. The menu's printed daily and might include such dishes as black pudding scotch egg, local crayfish cocktail or baked camembert to share. After come 'proper' puddings like spotted dick or plum and almond tart. Locals walk here and bring their dogs.

Dock Rd,
RAMSHOLT, IP12 3AB
Tel.: 01394 411209
Website: www.theramsholtarms.com

8 mi south of Woodbridge by A 1152 and B 1083. Parking.

PRICES
Meals: a la carte £ 20/31

MAP: 51

CLOSING TIMES
Closed weekdays January-mid
February and Monday-Wednesday dinner
114 October-April

CROWN INN

Home-reared meats and home-grown fruit and veg

These days any pub worth its salt is serving produce sourced from the local area, but there aren't many who can claim to provide most of the meat for their menus themselves, as well as the majority of the fruit and veg. The affable young owners of this characterful 15C smugglers' inn raise pigs, goats, lambs, calves, ducks, turkeys and chickens in the fields at the back. They'll show you around if you ask – although it's probably best to eat first – and you can check out the rosettes in the bar, won by their Gloucester Old Spot pigs. It's easy to find dishes which appeal on the regularly changing menu; perhaps home-reared pork terrine, braised faggots or a cured meat platter. Staying over? Rustic bedrooms have beamed ceilings and sloping floors.

Bridge Rd,
SNAPE, IP17 1SL
Tel.: 01728 688324
Website: www.snape-crown.co.uk

On B 1069, just north of Snape Maltings. Parking.

PRICES
Meals: a la carte £ 20/36

 2 rooms:
£ 70/90

MAP: 52

CLOSING TIMES
Open daily

CROWN

Large, luxurious bedrooms in a great spot

If you find the newspapers on the bar too depressing, the wine list here is a great read: a well-priced, top quality selection with over 25 available by the glass – bottles are displayed in a glass-fronted room and can also be bought to take home. Globally influenced, generously proportioned dishes feature the latest produce from local farms and estates, and might include game terrine, king prawn linguine or a locally reared rump steak, while a separate menu lists fresh seafood sourced from the east coast. Set in a great spot overlooking the Box and Stour river valleys, this smart pub also offers luxurious, ultra-spacious, superbly equipped bedrooms; all have king or super king sized beds, while some feature French windows and terraces.

STOKE-BY-NAYLAND, CO6 4SE
Tel.: 01206 262001
Website: www.crowninn.net

8 mi north of Colchester by A 134. In the centre of the village. Parking.

PRICES
Meals: a la carte £ 20/43

 11 rooms:
£ 95/260

MAP: 53

CLOSING TIMES
Closed 25-26 December

SWAN

Try one of their natural ciders

This 16C coaching inn has been nursed back to health by experienced pub owners Mark and Sophie, who also run The Anchor in Walberswick. At the back is an extensive garden which they have planted with hops and over the road to the front is a second garden beside the river. The interior is suitably homely, with a bar, a snug and a dining room featuring whitewashed walls, low beams and open fires. The short menu changes daily and uses local ingredients in time-honoured ways that Elizabeth David would advocate. They are gaining quite a reputation for their natural ciders and offer a good range of wines by the glass courtesy of their Enomatic machine, but beer lovers aren't forgotten – each dish is matched not only with a wine but also an ale.

Lower St,
STRATFORD ST MARY, CO7 6JR
Tel.: 01206 321244
Website: www.stratfordswan.com

8 mi north of Colchester signposted off A 12, in centre of village.
Parking.

PRICES   MAP: **54**
Meals: a la carte £ 23/40

CLOSING TIMES
Closed Monday and Tuesday

UFFORD CROWN

Hearty daily menus from a family team

Close to a nursery of the same name, you'll find this former coaching inn, which offers a warm welcome to one and all. A few steps lead down to a small walled terrace and the choice of two doors – one opening into a bright bar comprising a series of narrow rooms and the other into a chic, intimate restaurant. It's run by enthusiastic husband and wife team, Max and Polly, and the head chef is Polly's brother, Will. Menus change daily, with hearty dishes ranging from a crispy pork belly sandwich, chargrilled duck hearts or rib of Ketley beef for 3 to Mediterranean dishes like linguine with pistachio pesto and sun-blushed tomatoes. Portions are generous and service is keen; finish with a maple and pecan tart or a tasty Valrhona brownie.

High St,
UFFORD, IP13 6EL
Tel.: 01394 461030
Website: www.theuffordcrown.com

3 mi northwest of Woodbridge on B 1348. Parking.

PRICES   MAP: **55**
Meals: a la carte £ 22/41

CLOSING TIMES
Closed Tuesday

ANCHOR

Global flavours punctuate the menu

The Anchor is a welcoming and relaxing place, run by an enthusiastic, friendly team. Unusually for a pub, it's housed in an Arts and Crafts building, with a pleasant terrace and a path leading directly from the garden – with its wood-fired oven – to the beach. Owners Sophie and Mark are passionate about sourcing local, seasonal produce; they grow various herbs and vegetables themselves and also bake their own bread, which is available to buy. Dishes are prepared with real care and global flavours punctuate the menu; Mrs Kirkham's White Gold cheese gives a clue as to Mark's roots. Some of the bedrooms are in the house, but ask for one of the wood-clad chalet rooms in the garden – and breakfast like a king on smoked haddock and jugged kippers.

Main St,
WALBERSWICK, IP18 6UA
Tel.: 01502 722112
Website: www.anchoratwalberswick.com

In the centre of the village. Parking.

PRICES
Meals: £ 12 (weekday lunch) and a la carte
£ 23/35

 10 rooms:
£ 95/160

MAP: 56

CLOSING TIMES
Closed 25 December

WESTLETON CROWN

They cater well for gluten-free and special diets

The rustic 17C bar of this former coaching inn welcomes you with its beams and open fires; venture a little further in, and you'll find an attractive, surprisingly modern conservatory, as well as an appealing terrace and garden. The same seasonally pertinent menu is offered throughout, so you can eat your trio of Blythburgh pork or saddle of venison wherever you choose. If you're counting the pennies, come at lunchtime, when you'll find a second menu offering the likes of sausage and mash or Suffolk lamb stew, and if you are vegetarian or have special dietary requirements, you'll find that you're also well catered for. Bedrooms have a crisp, uncluttered style and are named after birds found on the adjacent RSPB nature reserve.

The Street,
WESTLETON, IP17 3AD
Tel.: 01728 648777
Website: www.westletoncrown.co.uk

3 mi east of Yoxford signed off A 12. In the centre of the village. Parking.

PRICES
Meals: a la carte £ 26/39

 34 rooms:
£ 90/215

MAP: 57

CLOSING TIMES
Open daily

CROWN

Modern town centre pub with minimalist bedrooms

With its farmers' markets, restaurants and cafés, the delightful riverside town of Woodbridge is up there with the best of them when it comes to foodie credentials; and all the more so since the arrival of the Crown. After a top-to-toe 21C makeover, this pub retains little evidence of its 17C roots – a glass-roofed, granite-floored bar sits at its centre, with four smart dining areas arranged around it. Bedrooms are modern, minimalistic and very cosy, with good facilities, and service is polite, friendly and copes well when busy. Seasonal menus are made up of modern classics – perhaps roast local partridge or Suffolk honey ham, with plenty of shellfish, including Deben oysters and mussels from the new beds – and the set menu offers terrific value.

Thoroughfare,
WOODBRIDGE, IP12 1AD
Tel.: 01394 384242
Website: www.thecrownatwoodbridge.co.uk

At town centre crossroads. Parking.

PRICES
Meals: £ 15 (weekdays) and a la carte
£ 26/46

10 rooms:
£ 100/200

MAP: 58

CLOSING TIMES
Open daily

LONDON

© J. Arnold Images/ hemis.fr

Twenty-first century London may truly be called the definitive world city. Time zones radiate from Greenwich, and global finances zap round the Square Mile, while a vast smorgasbord of restaurants is the equal of anywhere on the planet. A stunning diversity of population now calls the capital its home, mixing and matching its time between the urban sprawl and enviable acres of green open space. From Roman settlement to banking centre to capital of a 19C empire, London's pulse has rarely missed a beat. Along the way, expansion has gobbled up surrounding villages, a piecemeal cocktail with its ingredients stirred to create the likes of Kensington and Chelsea, Highgate and Hampstead, Twickenham and Richmond.

Apart from the great range of restaurants, London boasts over three and a half thousand pubs, many of which now see accomplished, creative cooking as an integral part of their existence and appeal. And you can find them sprinkled right the way across from zones one to five...

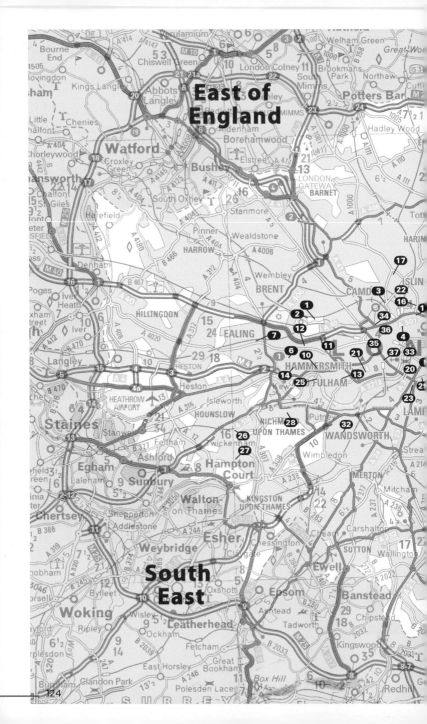

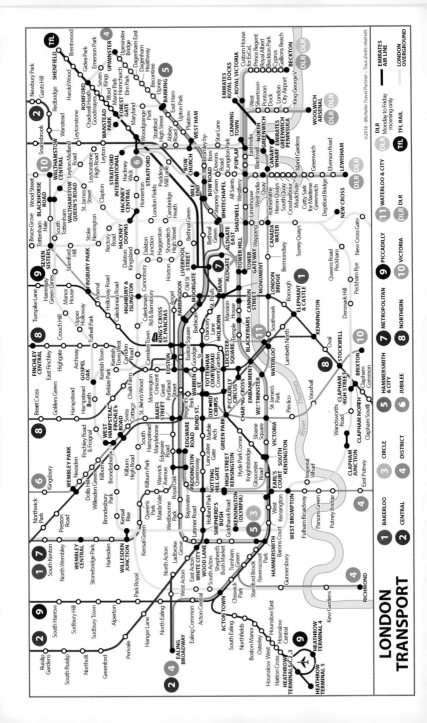

LONDON TRANSPORT

PARADISE BY WAY OF KENSAL GREEN

A quirky fun palace with something for everyone

Calling 'Paradise' a pub hardly does it justice – this is a veritable fun palace. Named after a line from a GK Chesterton poem, this gloriously bohemian place is spread over three floors and means different things to different people: some come along for comedy nights and cocktails or party nights and DJs; others pop in for drinks in the Reading room or snacks in the bar; many come to eat in the restaurant; and you can even get married here. The food is a reassuring mix of British favourites and European themed dishes, all made using good ingredients from trusted suppliers and prepared with obvious care. The surroundings are wonderfully quirky and idiosyncratic, the staff are contagiously enthusiastic and the vibe, effortlessly cool.

BRENT
19 Kilburn Ln,
KENSAL GREEN, W10 4AE
Tel.: 020 8969 0098
Website: www.theparadise.co.uk

⊖ Kensal Green. - On-street parking.

PRICES   MAP: **1**
Meals: a la carte £ 26/45

CLOSING TIMES
Open daily
dinner only and lunch Saturday and
Sunday

PARLOUR

A fun neighbourhood hang-out

It may not quite be a pub but nor is it a restaurant, so let's focus more on what Parlour actually is – a fun, warmly run and slightly quirky neighbourhood hangout. Open from breakfast until late, it has one room dominated by a large bar and the other, with an appealingly higgledy-piggledy look, set up for eating. They do a decent cocktail and a great range of beers and the menu is a wonderfully unabashed mix of tradition, originality and reinvention. Approaching legendary status is their cow pie which even Dan, however Desperate, would struggle to finish. The vegetable 'ravioli' is a cleverly thought-out construction and the marshmallow Wagon Wheel something for the children. On warm nights ask for one of the cabanas in the garden.

BRENT
5 Regent St,
KENSAL GREEN, NW10 5LG
Tel.: 020 8969 2184
Website: www.parlourkensal.com

⊖ Kensal Green - On-street parking.

PRICES   MAP: **2**
Meals: £ 15 (weekday lunch) and a la carte
£ 20/40

CLOSING TIMES
Closed 1 week August, 10 days Christmas-
New Year and Monday

BULL & LAST

Great for Sunday lunch – they know their meats

This Victorian corner pub is well loved by the locals and it's easy to see why. It's full of character and life – and the food is gloriously robust and wholesome. Stay on the ground floor as it has more character than upstairs; if you haven't booked, it's worth trying your luck anyway as they keep the odd table back – mind you, with enticing bar snacks like ham and corn croquettes and buttermilk chicken wings, you may simply find happiness at the bar ordering these with a pint. The daily menu can sometimes change between services, depending on what ingredients come in. The kitchen knows its way around an animal – the charcuterie boards and terrines are very good, and game in season is not to be missed. They do a pretty good breakfast too.

CAMDEN
168 Highgate Rd,
DARTMOUTH PARK, NW5 1QS
Tel.: 020 7267 3641
Website: www.thebullandlast.co.uk

⊖ Tufnell Park. - On-street parking.

PRICES
Meals: a la carte £ 25/44

MAP: 3

CLOSING TIMES
Closed 23-25 December
booking essential

LADY OTTOLINE

A charmingly traditional feel and a keen sense of history have always defined this classic Victorian pub – and a change in ownership appears to have had little effect, which is good news for all its many regulars. It was named after a member of the Bloomsbury Set, although you can still see its original name, the King's Arms, etched on the windows. The ground floor is where the drinkers gather so head up the steep wooden stairs to their neatly laid out dining room if you want a bit more comfort with your food. The regularly changing menu delivers some robustly flavoured dishes, with choices like chicken liver parfait or Cornish plaice with capers hitting the spot. What the service team lack in acuity, they make up for in politeness.

CAMDEN
11a Northington St,
BLOOMSBURY, WC1N 2JF
Tel.: 020 7831 0008
Website: www.theladyottoline.com

⊖ Chancery Lane. - On-street parking.

PRICES   MAP: **4**
Meals: a la carte £ 26/43

CLOSING TIMES
Closed bank holidays

JUGGED HARE

Stout British dishes for meat lovers

The famous 18C recipe created by Hannah Glasse, the UK's first domestic goddess, provided the inspiration for the renaming of this Grade II listed pub, previously known as The King's Head. It's an apt name because committed vegetarians may feel ill at ease – and not just because of the collection of glass cabinets in the bar which showcase the art of taxidermy. The atmospheric and appealingly noisy dining room, which has a large open kitchen running down one side, specialises in stout British dishes, with Denham Estate venison, Yorkshire guinea fowl and Cumbrian Longhorn steaks from the rotisserie and grill being the highlights. If the main course doesn't fill you, puddings like treacle tart or bread and butter pudding will.

CITY OF LONDON
42 Chiswell St,
CITY OF LONDON, EC1Y 4SA
Tel.: 020 7614 0134
Website: www.thejuggedhare.com

⊖ Barbican. - Limited on-street parking.

PRICES
Meals: a la carte £ 30/60

MAP: 5

CLOSING TIMES
Closed 25-26 December
booking essential

DUKE OF SUSSEX

Moorish cooking in a classic old gin palace

The Duke of Sussex may seem like a typical London pub, even from the front bar, but step through into the dining room and you'll find yourself in what was once a variety theatre from the time when this was a classic gin palace, complete with proscenium arch, glass ceiling and chandeliers. If that wasn't unusual enough, you could then find yourself eating cured meats or fabada, as the menu has a strong Spanish influence. Traditionalists can still get their steak pies and treacle tart but it's worth being more adventurous and trying the sardines, the paella and the crema Catalana. This is a fun, enthusiastically run and hustling pub and the kitchen's enthusiasm is palpable. On Mondays it's BYO; Sunday is quiz night.

EALING
75 South Par,
ACTON GREEN, W4 5LF
Tel.: 020 8742 8801
Website: www.realpubs.co.uk

⊖ Chiswick Park. - Parking on adjacent street.

PRICES
Meals: a la carte £ 23/35

MAP: **6**

CLOSING TIMES
Open daily

EALING PARK TAVERN

Bespoke ales come from the brewery at the back

This west London landmark, an impressive Arts and Crafts property dating from 1886, has been reborn and brought right up-to-date thanks to a splendid refurbishment from the Martin Brothers. With a panelled bar complete with stuffed animals, a bright, cavernous dining room, a suntrap terrace and the 'Long Arm Brewing Co.' at the back of the pub providing three bespoke ales (try the American IPA-OK), this is the sort of place we'd all like to live near. Service is charming and friendly and the cooking is robust yet comes with a refined edge, whether that's the freshest fish from Billingsgate, Yorkshire game in season, the chop or pie of the day, or the delightful old school puds. For larger groups, 'Feasting' menus can be arranged.

EALING
222 South Ealing Rd,
SOUTH EALING, W5 4RL
Tel.: 020 8758 1879
Website: www.ealingparktavern.com

⊖ South Ealing - On B455, on-street parking.

PRICES

MAP: 7

Meals: £ 19 (lunch and early dinner)
and a la carte £ 33/57

CLOSING TIMES
Open daily

EMPRESS

This 1850s pub used to be known as the Empress of India but was changed after people came expecting chicken tikka – information which will dishearten history teachers everywhere. Queen Victoria was then demoted to Empress E9, and eventually ended up as plain old Empress. Food is at the centre of what they do here, although don't be surprised to see locals sprawled on the sofas enjoying a drink, as this is a neighbourhood pub at heart. The menu is short, simple and pleasingly seasonal, with dishes like smoked eel, blood orange and mustard leaf salad or crispy polenta, burrata, chilli and wild garlic pesto demonstrating that this is a kitchen with confidence and intelligence. Prices are kept in check and Sunday lunch is a very languid affair.

HACKNEY
130 Lauriston Rd,
VICTORIA PARK, SOUTH HACKNEY, E9 7LH
Tel.: 020 8533 5123
Website: www.empresse9.co.uk

⊖ Homerton. - On-street parking meters.

PRICES
Meals: a la carte £ 25/33

MAP: 8

CLOSING TIMES
Closed 25-26 December and Monday lunch
except bank holidays

PRINCESS OF SHOREDITCH

An appealingly priced, daily changing menu

Apparently there has been a pub on this corner site since 1742 but it is doubtful many of the previous incarnations were as busy or as pleasant as the Princess is today. The owners have always been very hands-on and their welcoming attitude has rubbed off on their friendly staff; the pub comes with an appealing buzz and, to cap it all off, the prices are more than fair. It's set over two floors and the same menu is served throughout – although you can book upstairs. The menu changes daily, and sometimes between services; the food appears quite simple but the best dishes are those that come with a satisfyingly rustic edge, whether that's the buttery goose rillettes, the chicken pie with terrific mash or the tender pulled pork.

HACKNEY
76-78 Paul St,
SHOREDITCH, EC2A 4NE
Tel.: 020 7729 9270
Website: www.theprincessofshoreditch.com

⊖ Old Street - On-street parking meters.

PRICES   MAP: **9**
Meals: a la carte £ 27/38

CLOSING TIMES
Closed 24-26 December
booking essential

ANGLESEA ARMS

One of London's original gastropubs

The Anglesea Arms was one of the daddies of the gastropub movement, and for several decades has given those who live nearby an excuse never to venture too far for dinner; with its warm, laid-back atmosphere, friendly young staff – and food that's a cut above your usual pub fodder. The nicely seasonal menu gives the impression that it's written by a Brit who occasionally holidays on the Med – there are some suitably robust dishes but the kitchen is also capable of displaying a pleasing lightness of touch. Plates are never overly crowded with ingredients and modern versions of old-school desserts like rice pudding and apple crumble certainly hit the spot. The pub also offers a regularly changing selection of regional real ales.

HAMMERSMITH AND FULHAM
35 Wingate Rd,
HAMMERSMITH, W6 0UR
Tel.: 020 8749 1291
Website: www.angleseaarmspub.co.uk

⊖ Ravenscourt Park

PRICES
Meals: a la carte £ 22/34

MAP: 10

CLOSING TIMES
Closed 24-26 December

HARWOOD ARMS

Wonderful food, with game a speciality

It may be a very handsome pub in a smart postcode and have all its tables laid up for dining but there's nothing stuck-up or snooty about this place – in fact, the only thing that's superior is the cooking. It's British to its core, with its reassuringly concise, daily changing menu resolutely governed by our country's own seasonal produce. Cornish fish, Herdwick lamb, Cumbrian chicken and Wiltshire pork can all feature and game is a real strength of the kitchen whether it's rabbit, grouse or Hampshire muntjac. Dishes have real depth and flavours are bold and satisfying. Service is smooth and assured and comes courtesy of a young yet experienced team and the well-chosen wine list offers a particularly good choice of mature claret.

HAMMERSMITH AND FULHAM
Walham Grove,
FULHAM, SW6 1QP
Tel.: 020 7386 1847
Website: www.harwoodarms.com

⊖ Fulham Broadway. - On-street parking with restrictions until 8pm.

PRICES
Meals: £ 36 (weekday lunch)/43

MAP: 11

CLOSING TIMES
Closed 24-27 December, 1 January and
Monday lunch except bank holidays
booking essential

PRINCESS VICTORIA

A fine-looking Victorian grande dame

London has a wealth of fine Victorian gin palaces but few are as grand as the Princess Victoria. From the friezes to the etched glass, the portraits to the parquet floor, the last restoration created a terrific pub. Mind you, that's not all that impresses: there's a superb, wide-ranging wine list, with carafes and glasses providing flexibility; enticing bar snacks ranging from quail eggs to salt cod croquettes; a great menu that could include roasted skate wing or homemade pork and herb sausages; and, most importantly, cooking that's executed with no little skill. Those with proclivities for all things porcine will find much to savour – charcuterie is a passion here and the board may well include pig's cheeks and rillettes.

HAMMERSMITH AND FULHAM
217 Uxbridge Rd,
SHEPHERD'S BUSH, W12 9DH
Tel.: 020 8749 5886
Website: www.princessvictoria.co.uk

⊖ Shepherd's Bush. - On-street parking.

PRICES   **MAP: 12**
Meals: £ 13 (weekday lunch) and a la carte
£ 23/47

CLOSING TIMES
Closed 24-27 December

TOMMY TUCKER

Brighter inside than its dark façade suggests

Locals will remember this as The Pelican, a relatively quiet pub that would get overwhelmed whenever Chelsea were playing at home. The people behind Claude's Kitchen in nearby Parsons Green then gave it a head-to-toe revamp and the TT, as they call it, is now the sort of place everyone would want on their street. The black façade doesn't really give the right impression because inside it's bright and open-plan – the nicest part is the 'Music Room' with its sheet music wallpaper. The menu is unstructured and divided under headings of 'meat', 'fish' and 'fruit and veg', with asterisks marking the dishes available as starters. The food is rustic, earthy and satisfying and the service is thoughtful and sincere.

HAMMERSMITH AND FULHAM
22 Waterford Rd,
FULHAM, SW6 2DR
Tel.: 020 7736 1023
Website: www.thetommytucker.com

⊖ Fulham Broadway. - Limited on-street parking.

PRICES   MAP: **13**
Meals: a la carte £ 19/35

CLOSING TIMES
Closed 25 December

SMOKEHOUSE

Head for the delightful garden

The success of the first Smokehouse in Canonbury meant a second was inevitable, although the owners were sensible enough to avoid making a carbon copy. The menu at this sizeable pub, which has a lovely rear garden, still centres around barbeque but it's not quite as 'in your face' as Islington – residents of Chiswick are perhaps a little more demure. The Belted Galloway burgers with pulled pork fly out of the kitchen but the winning dish is the short rib Bourguignon with creamy mash. The kitchen frequently cook a whole beast, like a Gloucester Old Spot and then make terrines and potted meats, hams and charcuterie. There are lighter dishes on offer and, if you make it to dessert, they do a mean rum and raisin rice pudding.

HOUNSLOW
12 Sutton Ln North,
CHISWICK, W4 4LD
Tel.: 020 3819 6066
Website: www.smokehousechiswick.co.uk

⊖ Chiswick Park. - On-street parking.

PRICES   MAP: **14**
Meals: a la carte £ 28/34

CLOSING TIMES
dinner only and lunch Friday to Sunday

DRAPERS ARMS

Gutsy, satisfying and good value British food

Good food, decent prices and an easy-going atmosphere are all on offer at this busy Islington pub, whose shabby chic interior contrasts with its handsome Georgian façade. It understands that celebrating British cuisine means more than just putting a few old favourites on the menu – it's about making intelligent use of indigenous ingredients and introducing them to a wider audience. Dishes are gutsy and affordable and offal is a highlight, yet the kitchen can also demonstrate a light touch when needed. The wine list is well thought out and dominated by the Old World, with a well-priced selection by the glass and carafe. The bar snacks are the size of a generous starter and are well worth exploring.

ISLINGTON
44 Barnsbury St,
ISLINGTON, N1 1ER
Tel.: 020 7619 0348
Website: www.thedrapersarms.com

⊖ Highbury & Islington. - On-street parking.

PRICES
Meals: a la carte £ 23/32

MAP: 15

CLOSING TIMES
Closed 25-26 December
bookings advisable at dinner

PIG AND BUTCHER

This corner pub dates from the mid-19C, when cattle drovers taking their livestock to Smithfield Market would stop for a swift one. Now sympathetically restored, it enjoys the same ownership as the Princess of Shoreditch as well as Islington and Chiswick's 'Smokehouse's. The busy bar offers an impressive number of bottled beers, while the dining room is secreted behind shelves of bric-a-brac. There's a strong British element to the menu and not just because they use words like 'Beeton' and 'Mrs'. Meat comes straight from the farm and is butchered and smoked in-house; fish comes from day boats off the south coast. Roasts take centre stage on Sundays; "just like your mother's" they claim, which presumably means something different to us all.

ISLINGTON
80 Liverpool Rd,
ISLINGTON, N1 0QD
Tel.: 020 7226 8304
Website: www.thepigandbutcher.co.uk

⊖ Angel. - Free on-street parking after 6.30pm.

PRICES   MAP: **16**
Meals: a la carte £ 28/44

CLOSING TIMES
Closed 25-27 December
dinner only and lunch Friday-Sunday
booking advisable

ST JOHN'S TAVERN

A shining beacon of hope on this busy thoroughfare

A Junction Road landmark, St John's Tavern has been providing sustenance to the good people of Islington since the 1860s – generally in the form of beer. Tapas is a rather more modern addition – these days served in the front bar – so choose from such delights as plaice goujons, globe artichoke, patatas bravas and jamon croquetas. For a more structured meal, head to the vast and hugely appealing rear dining room with its art and lithographs. The well-crafted dishes are mainly British with a nod to the Med, and could include pig's head terrine with piccalilli, octopus risotto or pork belly with quince aioli. Add in friendly service and a great selection of artisan beers and you'll see why this is still very much a favourite with the locals.

ISLINGTON
91 Junction Rd,
ARCHWAY, N19 5QU
Tel.: 020 7272 1587
Website: www.stjohnstavern.com

⊖ Archway. - Pay & display parking; free after 6.30pm.

PRICES
Meals: a la carte £ 18/36

MAP: 17

CLOSING TIMES
Closed 25-26 December, 1 January and
Monday lunch
booking advisable

SMOKEHOUSE

Enticing aromas rise from the wood-chip smokers

If, to you, barbecuing means a burnt chicken leg, warm wine and a wet garden then a visit to Smokehouse will set you straight. You can smell the oak chips in the smoker as you approach this warm, modern pub, which was previously called The House. Meat is the mainstay of the very appealing menu – the peppered ox cheeks have understandably become a firm favourite – but whilst the flavours are undeniably gutsy, the smoking and barbecuing manages to add a little something to the ingredients without ever overpowering them. With portion sizes to appease Desperate Dan, only the committed may make it to dessert but chocolate lovers should try the Friday pie. The pub is enthusiastically run and staff are eager to recommend dishes.

ISLINGTON
63-69 Canonbury Rd,
CANONBURY, N1 2DG
Tel.: 020 7354 1144
Website: www.smokehouseislington.co.uk

⊖ Highbury & Islington. - Free on-street parking after 6.30pm.

PRICES   MAP: **18**
Meals: a la carte £ 28/34

CLOSING TIMES
Closed 24-26 December
dinner only and lunch Saturday-Sunday
booking advisable

WELL

Well-supported local; dishes cooked with care

This well-supported neighbourhood pub may be one of the smallest in the Martin brothers' portfolio but it's also one of the easiest to find thanks to its wide expanse of blue canopy. There's an intimate basement with sofas and bright artwork, but most of the dining takes place on the ground floor, where the windows open wide and the rather wonky tables are shoehorned in. The seasonal menu is a joy to read and whether you choose potted rainbow trout with pickled nectarines or Devonshire kid sausages with creamed polenta, dishes are carefully cooked and not short on flavour. Ingredients are sourced from all over the British Isles: mussels from the Shetland Isles, squid from Cornwall and steak from the artisan butcher round the corner.

ISLINGTON
180 St John St,
FINSBURY, EC1V 4JY
Tel.: 020 7251 9363
Website: www.downthewell.com

⊖ Farringdon. - On-street parking meters.

PRICES   MAP: **19**
Meals: a la carte £ 26/41

CLOSING TIMES
Closed 25-26 December

BUILDERS ARMS

Mediterranean food to match the colourful interior

The Builders Arms is very much like a packed village local – the only difference being that, in this instance, the village is Chelsea and the villagers are all young and prosperous. The inside delivers on the promise of the smart exterior but don't expect it to be quiet as drinkers are welcomed just as much as diners. In fact, bookings are only taken for larger parties but just tell the staff that you're here to eat and they'll sort you out. The cooking reveals the effort that has gone into the sourcing of some decent ingredients; the rib of beef for two is a perennial favourite. Dishes are robust and satisfying and are not without some flair in presentation. Wine is also taken seriously and their list has been thoughtfully put together.

KENSINGTON AND CHELSEA
13 Britten St,
CHELSEA, SW3 3TY
Tel.: 020 7349 9040
Website: www.geronimo-inns.co.uk

⊖ South Kensington. - On-street parking.

PRICES   MAP: **20**
Meals: a la carte £ 23/42

CLOSING TIMES
Open daily
bookings not accepted

CROSS KEYS

A much-loved local saved from the developers

Chelsea's oldest pub, dating from 1708, was in danger of being converted into a house but a well-organised campaign persuaded the council to see sense and refuse permission – and in 2015 this delightful neighbourhood pub triumphantly reopened, much to the joy of those fortunate enough to live in this neck of the woods. It's now operated by the team who run the Brown Cow and they've made a great job of updating the place while respecting its past. The style of cooking is largely contemporary, with Asian influences being especially prevalent, although there is a section marked 'traditional dishes' for those who prefer classic pub fare. Service comes from well-meaning chaps who appear to be known to most of the customers.

KENSINGTON AND CHELSEA
1 Lawrence St,
CHELSEA, SW3 5NB
Tel.: 020 7351 0686
Website: www.thecrosskeyschelsea.co.uk

⊖ Sloane Square. - Limited on-street parking meters.

PRICES   MAP: **21**
Meals: a la carte £ 29/44

CLOSING TIMES
Closed 24 December dinner and
25 December

FELLOW

Atmospheric and fun; cooking done with care

This clever Fellow established itself well before the regeneration of King's Cross finished so was all ready for the influx of new customers. Don't be fooled by its rather anonymous façade – this is a pub 'de nos jours', complete with a slick cocktail bar and a kitchen with worthy ingredient-sourcing credentials. Most of the action takes place on the ground floor which looks a little dark and moody but the atmosphere is brightened considerably by the staff who make a genuine effort to look after their customers. A relatively small kitchen means they keep the menu lean and clean and influences remain largely within Europe. Fish from the Cornish day boats is often a highlight; cheeses are British and puds are well worth a flutter.

KING'S CROSS ST PANCRAS
24 York Way,
ST PANCRAS, N1 9AA
Tel.: 020 7833 4395
Website: www.thefellow.co.uk

⊖ King's Cross St Pancras. - Limited on-street parking.

PRICES   MAP: **22**
Meals: a la carte £ 24/37

CLOSING TIMES
Closed 25-27 December

CANTON ARMS

Wholesome, satisfying and well-priced food

Its appreciative audience proves that the demand for fresh, honest, seasonal food is not just limited to smart squares in Chelsea or Islington. The oval-shaped bar dominates the room; the front half busy with drinkers and the back laid up for diners, although it's all very relaxed and you can eat where you want. The kitchen's experience in places like the Anchor & Hope and Great Queen Street is obvious on their menu which features rustic, earthy British food, of the sort that suits this environment so well. Lunch could be a kipper or tripe and chips; even a reinvented toasted sandwich. Dinner sees a short, no-nonsense menu offering perhaps braised venison or grilled haddock, with daily specials like steak and kidney pie for two.

LAMBETH
177 South Lambeth Rd,
STOCKWELL, SW8 1XP
Tel.: 020 7582 8710
Website: www.cantonarms.com

⊖ Stockwell. - Free on-street parking in the evening.

PRICES
Meals: a la carte £ 19/35

MAP: 23

CLOSING TIMES
Closed Christmas-New Year, Monday lunch,
Sunday dinner and bank holidays
bookings not accepted

PALMERSTON

Gutsy cooking suits the lived-in look

The Palmerston has long realised that success for any pub lies in being at the heart of the local community. Since its last makeover, this Victorian pub has been popular with families – just look at all those highchairs – and local artists' work decorates the walls. It has a comfortable, lived-in feel, along with a snug, wood-panelled rear dining room with an original and quite beautiful mosaic floor. The menu is as reassuring as the service and the cooking has a satisfying, gutsy edge. There's plenty of choice, from chowders and soups to well-judged fish dishes but it's the meat dishes that stand out, like the mature steaks or lamb chops – and if they have grouse on the menu, then forsake all others and get in quick.

LAMBETH
91 Lordship Ln,
EAST DULWICH, SE22 8EP
Tel.: 020 8693 1629
Website: www.thepalmerston.co.uk

⊖ East Dulwich (Rail). - Free on-street parking in the evening.

PRICES   MAP: **24**
Meals: £ 15 (weekday lunch) and a la carte
£ 28/55

CLOSING TIMES
Closed 25-26 December and 1 January

BROWN DOG

Homely, comforting and tucked away

To the untrained eye, this dog can look a little forlorn, but then, if you live on one of the many residential streets adjoining it, what your local looks like from the outside is not going to be your primary concern. Mind you, this is a pub which needn't bother looking too attractive because it's concealed within a maze of terraced houses and passing trade is rare. Inside, the lived-in look gives the place a relaxed and homely feel, especially as it's accompanied by easy-going service executed with a smile. The balanced menu offers a decent range of traditional fare like venison pie or haddock fishcake, all done 'properly'; the dishes are flavoursome and the kitchen uses some lesser cuts like bavette to keep the prices down.

RICHMOND UPON THAMES
28 Cross St,
BARNES, SW13 0AP
Tel.: 020 8392 2200
Website: www.thebrowndog.co.uk

⊖ Barnes Bridge (Rail). - On-street parking.

PRICES   MAP: **25**
Meals: a la carte £ 23/42

CLOSING TIMES
Closed 25 December

CROWN

Ample portions of globally influenced dishes

Much to the delight of St Margarets residents, this fine-looking Georgian pub has been revived and revitalised. Setting the scene are an old lantern hanging above the entrance and a mosaic floor inlaid with the pub's name, while inside it feels relaxed and stylish, with parquet floors, feature fireplaces and bright colours; sit in the airy, elegant rear restaurant, with its high vaulted ceiling and garden view. There's something for everyone on the global menus, from sharing boards and classic pub dishes to Mediterranean-influenced fish stew or Asian-inspired Tom Yum Thai prawns and squid. Portions are ample and cooking fresh, tasty and reliable. Service is enthusiastic and the pretty beer garden is popular with drinkers and diners alike.

RICHMOND UPON THAMES
174 Richmond Rd,
ST MARGARETS, TWICKENHAM, TW1 2NH
Tel.: 020 8892 5896
Website: www.crowntwickenham.co.uk

⊖ St Margarets (Rail). - Parking.

PRICES   MAP: **26**
Meals: a la carte £ 21/40

CLOSING TIMES
Closed 26 December

KING'S HEAD

Familiar brasserie-style classics

Britain has its pubs and France its brasseries; The King's Head does its bit for the entente cordiale by combining both. Raymond Blanc's team has given this Victorian pub a tidy makeover and, although there might not be much character left, they have created a suitably warm environment. The brasserie at the back is run by a pleasant, enthusiastic team and the menus offer all comers plenty of choice. Classic brasserie dishes such as Toulouse sausages and beef stroganoff come with a satisfyingly rustic edge, while the dual-nationality element is maintained through the inclusion of a ploughman's board alongside the charcuterie. Steaks from the charcoal grill are popular and families are lured in by the decent kiddies menu.

RICHMOND UPON THAMES
123 High St,
TEDDINGTON, TW11 8HG
Tel.: 020 3166 2900
Website: www.whitebrasserie.com

⊖ Teddington (Rail). - On-street parking.

PRICES   MAP: **27**
Meals: £ 10 (weekday lunch) and a la carte
£ 23/40

CLOSING TIMES
Open daily

VICTORIA

Lies at the heart of the local community

Chef-owner Paul Merrett is something of a food hero in these parts: he gives cookery classes at the school next door and the ethos of his pub is, first and foremost, to serve the local community. It has a pleasant lived-in feel, with the nooks and crannies of the bars usually busy with loungers and drinkers; if you're here to eat you're better off heading for the conservatory, which overlooks their terrace. The appealing menu offers a good range of dishes and comes with a distinct Mediterranean slant, with Middle Eastern influences never far away. You can start with chickpea and basil hummus, then move on to chargrilled lemon chicken or falafel or, if you prefer something simpler, there's a well-priced selection of burgers available.

RICHMOND UPON THAMES
10 West Temple Sheen,
EAST SHEEN, SW14 7RT
Tel.: 020 8876 4238
Website: www.thevictoria.net

⊖ Mortlake (Rail). - Parking.

PRICES
Meals: a la carte £ 26/44

 7 rooms:
£ 95/135

MAP: 28

CLOSING TIMES
Open daily

ANCHOR & HOPE

Hearty, no-nonsense and confident cooking

The Anchor & Hope is still running at full steam and its popularity shows no sign of abating. It's not hard to see why: combine a menu that changes with each service and is a paragon of seasonality, with cooking that is gutsy, bold and wholesome, and you end up with immeasurably rewarding dishes like suckling kid chops with wild garlic, succulent roast pigeon with lentils or buttermilk pudding with poached rhubarb. The place has a contagiously congenial feel and the friendly staff all pull in the same direction; you may spot a waiter trimming vegetables or a chef delivering dishes to the tables. The no-reservation policy remains, so either get here early or be prepared to wait a while; you can, however, book for Sunday lunch.

SOUTHWARK
36 The Cut,
SOUTHWARK, SE1 8LP
Tel.: 020 7928 9898
Website: www.anchorandhopepub.co.uk

⊖ Southwark. - On-street parking meters.

PRICES
Meals: £ 15 (weekday lunch) and a la carte
£ 18/34

MAP: **29**

CLOSING TIMES
Closed Christmas-New Year, Sunday dinner,
Monday lunch and bank holidays
bookings not accepted

GARRISON

You'll leave feeling good about life in general

You'd be hard pressed to find a more charming pub than The Garrison. With its appealing vintage look, warm atmosphere and delightful staff, it's the perfect antidote to those hard-edged boozers that we've all accidentally found ourselves in at some point. Open from 8am for smoothies and breakfast, it gets busier as the day goes on – and don't bother coming for dinner if you haven't booked. Booth numbers 4 and 5, opposite the open kitchen, are the most popular while number 2 at the back is the cosiest. Daily specials on the blackboard supplement the nicely balanced menu and the cooking is perky and bright, with a subtle Mediterranean slant. Salads are done well and there's a daily steak, while puds are of a more traditional bent.

SOUTHWARK
99-101 Bermondsey St,
BERMONDSEY, SE1 3XB
Tel.: 020 7089 9355
Website: www.thegarrison.co.uk

⊖ London Bridge. - On-street parking.

PRICES
Meals: £ 24/29 and a la carte £ 26/38

MAP: 30

CLOSING TIMES
Closed 25-26 December
booking essential at dinner

MARKSMAN

Our Pub of the Year 2017!

With its quirky, brown-tiled façade, the Marksman has long been a local landmark. Inside, it's a place of two halves: the wood-panelled bar retains the cosy, unaffected feel of a traditional boozer, while the first floor dining room is far more modern. There's a roof terrace for alfresco dining and the friendly atmosphere really adds to the pub's appeal. Owners Tom Harris and Jon Rotheram are St John alumni and their considerable experience is evident in the food. The simply cooked, seasonal dishes are wonderfully fresh, perfectly balanced and full of flavour – we're talking proper British cooking with the likes of devilled mussels on toast, skate with shrimps and turnip tops, or pheasant and trotter pie for two.

TOWER HAMLETS
254 Hackney Rd,
BETHNAL GREEN, E2 7SJ
Tel.: 020 7739 7393
Website: www.marksmanpublichouse.com

⊖ Hoxton. - On-street parking.

PRICES
Meals: a la carte £ 19/35

MAP: 31

CLOSING TIMES
Closed 25 December, 1 January, Sunday
dinner and Monday

EARL SPENCER

Traditional food prepared with genuine care

The owner worked at this Edwardian pub over a decade ago and so jumped at the chance of actually buying it himself – he felt he had "unfinished business" here. It's a handsome pub, standing a baseline lob away from the All England Tennis Club and its small terrace overlooks a showroom of the finest 4-wheel thoroughbreds. Inside is bright and welcoming, with many of the original features and fittings restored, but it's the cooking that really sets it apart. The experienced brigade are strict apostles of seasonality – the menu can sometimes change twice a day – and everything is homemade. The one entry in the debit column is that you have to keep going up to the bar to order everything.

WANDSWORTH
260-262 Merton Rd,
SOUTHFIELDS, SW18 5JL
Tel.: 020 8870 9244
Website: www.theearlspencer.com

⊖ Southfields. - On-street parking.

PRICES
Meals: a la carte £ 24/35

MAP: **32**

CLOSING TIMES
dinner only and lunch Friday-Sunday

THE ALFRED TENNYSON

Handsome Georgian pub with upstairs dining room

What used to be The Pantechnicon is now The Alfred Tennyson; the esteemed Victorian poet who wrote 'The Charge of the Light Brigade' used to live nearby and you feel he would have approved of the parquet floor and leather armchairs that give this cosy pub its clubby feel – although it's a moot point whether he'd enjoy seeing quotations from his work on the backs of the toilet doors! The ground floor is crammed with tables and works on a first-come-first-served basis; upstairs you'll find a more formal, Georgian-style dining room and, above that, there's even a cocktail bar – this is Belgravia after all. Classic dishes have light, modern touches, so expect potted smoked mackerel to come with rhubarb purée or Scottish scallops with chorizo dressing.

WESTMINSTER
10 Motcomb St,
BELGRAVIA, SW1X 8LA
Tel.: 020 7730 6074
Website: www.thealfredtennyson.co.uk

⊖ Knightsbridge. - On-street parking.

PRICES
Meals: a la carte £ 29/50

MAP: **33**

CLOSING TIMES
Closed 25 December
booking advisable

NEWMAN ARMS

Cornish produce, modern cooking, Georgian charm

Matt Chatfield, a farmer's son from Launceston, is fiercely proud of all the wonderful produce his home county has to offer and has spent several years creating a network to supply some of the best restaurants in London; in turn, creating jobs for Cornish folk. This charming Georgian pub – a one-time haunt of Dylan Thomas – is the latest to benefit, and this time it's Matt himself who's the owner. Downstairs is a real boozer, great for a pie and a pint, but the quaint wood-panelled upstairs room is where most of the eating happens; ask for one of the window tables. The menu may be short but every ingredient is super-fresh, often arriving from the sea or field within 24 hours. Beef and lamb are the stars – along with fish from the day boats.

WESTMINSTER
23 Rathbone St,
REGENT'S PARK AND MARYLEBONE, W1T 1NG
Tel.: 020 3643 6285
Website: www.newmanarmspub.com

⊖ Goodge St - On street parking nearby.

PRICES
Meals: £ 15 (weekday lunch) and a la carte
£ 26/39

MAP: **34**

CLOSING TIMES
Closed 24-26 December and bank holidays

THE ORANGE

As delightful as its façade suggests

The former home of the Orange Brewery is a handsome pub that's as charming as its stucco-fronted façade suggests. The locals will no doubt have filled the bar, where the wood-burning oven is quite a feature, but it's still worth trying your luck to get one of the tables here or in the adjacent room; if you book ahead you'll be upstairs which is just as pleasantly decorated but a little more sedate. There's a clear Mediterranean bias to the menu which also includes plenty of salads along with spelt or wheat-based pizzas which come with some original toppings; there are also roasts on a Sunday and pies for the traditionalists. Unusually for a London pub, there are bedrooms upstairs: these are stylish and comfortable.

WESTMINSTER
37 Pimlico Rd,
VICTORIA, SW1W 8NE
Tel.: 020 7881 9844
Website: www.theorange.co.uk

⊖ Sloane Square. - On-street parking.

PRICES
Meals: a la carte £ 28/40

 4 rooms:
£ 210

MAP: 35

CLOSING TIMES
Open daily

PORTMAN

Head upstairs and order a sharing plate

When it went by the name of The Masons Arms this pub was widely known for its gruesome history. It was here that the condemned, on their way to Tyburn Tree gallows, would take their last drink, which purportedly led to the phrase "one for the road". Reincarnated as the Portman, the pub these days boasts a less disreputable clientele who are more attracted by the quality of the cooking. Food is served all day and you can choose to eat in the busy ground floor bar or in the unexpectedly formal upstairs dining room, all thick-pile carpet and starched tablecloths. Fortunately, the style of food remains thoroughly down-to-earth and satisfying and is accompanied by a well-organised wine list and an interesting selection of cocktails.

WESTMINSTER
51 Upper Berkeley St,
REGENT'S PARK AND MARYLEBONE, W1H 7QW
Tel.: 020 7723 8996
Website: www.theportmanmarylebone.com

⊖ Marble Arch. - On-street parking.

PRICES   MAP: **36**
Meals: a la carte £ 25/48

CLOSING TIMES
Open daily

THOMAS CUBITT

There's certainly no spit 'n' sawdust here

Thomas Cubitt was the master builder behind Eaton and Belgrave Squares so it's appropriate that the pub bearing his name is an unquestionably handsome establishment. Regency and Georgian styles have been combined to good effect, especially in the discreet and surprisingly genteel upstairs dining room, where you'll find an impeccably behaved clientele enjoying a sophisticated menu of quite elaborate constructions that are British at their core. The ground floor, where bookings aren't taken, is more relaxed, more fun and distinctly louder, although on sunny days when the French windows are thrown open, it's hard to get a table. The menu here is more accessible, both in content and price, although some dishes are served on both floors.

WESTMINSTER
44 Elizabeth St,
VICTORIA, SW1W 9PA
Tel.: 020 7730 6060
Website: www.thethomascubitt.co.uk

⊖ Sloane Square. - Parking meters in Elizabeth Street.

PRICES
Meals: a la carte £ 29/44

MAP: 37

CLOSING TIMES
Open daily
booking essential

NORTH EAST

England

© J. Arnold Images / hemis.fr

This his region cradles some of England's wildest and most dramatic scenery typified by Northumberland National Park, a landscape of rolling purple moorlands and roaring rivers bursting with salmon and trout. Kielder Forest's mighty wilderness has been called "the country's most tranquil spot" while Bill Bryson has waxed lyrical upon the glories of Durham Cathedral. Those who love the wind in their hair are equally effusive about the eleven-mile footpath that accompanies the pounding waves of Durham's Heritage Coast; further north are the long, dune-backed beaches of Northumberland. Rambling across the region is Hadrian's Wall, 73 miles of iconic Roman history, while a modern slant on architectural celebrity is proffered by the Millennium Bridge, BALTIC Centre and Angel of the North.

The famously bracing air whets hearty appetites for local Cheviot lamb, Coquetdale cheese or Holy Island oysters. And what could be more redolent of the North East than a breakfast of Craster kippers?

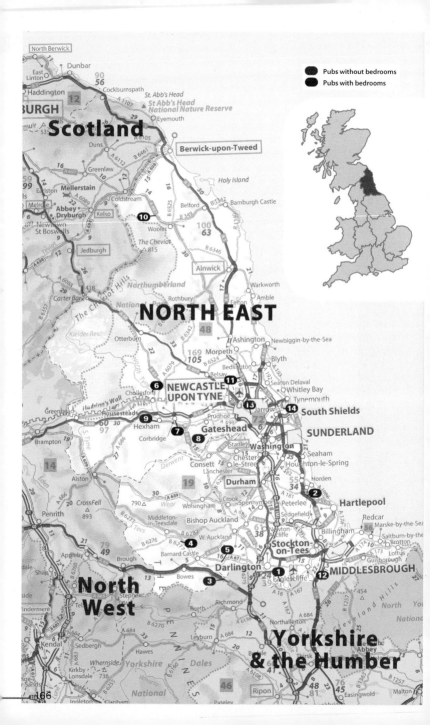

BAY HORSE

Everything from bread to ice cream is homemade

Sitting pretty in a delightful village, this dining pub provides a pleasing mixture of the old and the new. A former coaching inn, its beams, open fires and antique furnishings give it the air of a traditional pub, but there's nothing old-fashioned about this place – on the contrary, it's smart and cosy, with a warm, welcoming feel. Each of the three rooms has a slightly different ambiance: it's buzzy in the bar; quieter in the restaurant and if you're a party of six or more, try the private dining room on the first floor. The fourth option – and the best on a hot day – is the pleasant garden with its multitude of picnic benches. Wide-ranging menus offer ambitious dishes with distinctive flavours, and friendly locals provide charming service.

45 The Green,
HURWORTH ON TEES, DL2 2AA
Tel.: 01325 720663
Website: www.thebayhorsehurworth.com

5.5 mi south of Darlington; signed off A 167; in the middle of the village. Parking.

PRICES   **MAP: 1**
Meals: £ 15 (weekday lunch) and a la carte
£ 32/52

CLOSING TIMES
Closed 25-26 December

CASTLE EDEN INN

Experienced owners know their customers well

A former coaching inn of indeterminate age, on what was formerly the main road to London: local gossip says that Dick Turpin was once tied up outside while his captors enjoyed some refreshment – torture indeed! The experienced owners know their customers well and offer a wide choice of dishes, from classics like steak and ale pie to smoked cheese soufflé or pork belly with black pudding, and the 'monthly specials' menu offers great value. The central bar splits the place in two: on one side is the lounge where you can drink, eat or watch TV from the comfort of a sofa. On the other, is a rather smart restaurant with dressed tables; head to the far end – which used to be the stables – as it offers more character, especially in the evening.

Stockton Rd,
CASTLE EDEN, TS27 4SD
Tel.: 01429 835137
Website: www.castleedeninn.com

Just off A 19, 1 mi south of Peterlee. Parking.

PRICES   MAP: **2**
Meals: £ 15 (weekdays) and a la carte
£ 23/42

CLOSING TIMES
Closed Sunday dinner

OAK TREE INN

Charming little place run by a husband & wife team

They say good things come in small packages and that's definitely the case with this charming whitewashed pub. Found on the main street of a small hamlet, it consists of a single room with a proper old-fashioned counter, six wooden tables flanked by green settles and a bench table for the locals. Claire – who both serves the drinks and delivers the food – provides a warm welcome at the bar, while behind the scenes in the kitchen, Alastair single-handedly holds the fort. The short menu takes on a fairly formal format, offering generous portions of hearty, flavoursome cooking with a rustic British style and some subtle modern twists: you might find confit belly pork, onion and thyme tart, turbot with orange or Best End of lamb with artichokes.

HUTTON MAGNA, DL11 7HH
Tel.: 01833 627371
Website: www.theoaktreehutton.co.uk

7 mi southeast of Barnard Castle off A 66. Parking.

PRICES
Meals: a la carte £ 32/44

MAP: 3

CLOSING TIMES
Closed 24-27 and 31 December, 1-2 January
and Monday dinner only
booking essential

ROSE AND CROWN

Delightful inn overlooking three village greens

This delightful Georgian inn occupies a very pleasant spot overlooking three village greens. It's run by the Robinsons – the owners of nearby Headlam Hall – and a charming, chatty team who are always willing to help. The wonderfully characterful open-fired bar is filled with gleaming horse brasses and there's a smart wood-panelled dining room for those after a slightly more formal feel; eat in either, from a menu of British pub classics which showcase local, seasonal produce. Well-equipped bedrooms are spread between the main building, the courtyard and the "Monk's House" (the latter come complete with cosy lounges). In the morning you'll find the Rose and Crown Post on your breakfast table, which recommends walks and activities for your stay.

ROMALDKIRK, DL12 9EB
Tel.: 01833 650213
Website: www.rose-and-crown.co.uk

3.5 mi south of Middleton-on-Teesdale, on B 6177, next to church on village green. Parking.

PRICES
Meals: a la carte £ 23/40

 14 rooms:
£ 90/160

MAP: 4

CLOSING TIMES
Closed Christmas

BRIDGEWATER ARMS

Choose one of their fish dishes

A copperplate alphabet edging the ceiling and the cast list from a 1957 production of Jack and the Beanstalk are reminders that this traditional pub spent the first hundred years of its life as the village school. When chef Paul Grundy's lease on the brewery-owned pub ran out after several successful years, he was faced with a move. Spotting an opportunity, one of the pub's regulars decided to buy it himself, and to the locals' delight, reinstated Paul as chef. There's local beef and game on the menu along with the legendary cheddar cheese and spinach soufflé, but it's fish and seafood that the chef is known for, so let that lead your choice. Dishes are unashamedly classic, accurately executed and extremely satisfying.

WINSTON, DL2 3RN
Tel.: 01325 730302
Website: www.thebridgewaterarms.com

Between Barnard Castle and Darlington just off A 67. Parking.

PRICES   **MAP: 5**
Meals: a la carte £ 22/59

CLOSING TIMES
Closed 25-26 December, 1 January, Sunday
and Monday

BARRASFORD ARMS

At the heart of the local community

In the heart of the Northumbrian countryside, close to Kielder Water and Hadrian's Wall, sits this family-run stone inn, which provides an ideal base for exploring the North Tyne Valley. Retaining plenty of traditional character, it creates the perfect home from home. Bedrooms are comfortable and sensibly priced, and the cosy fire is a huge draw – as are the regular vegetable, darts and quoits competitions – but the star attraction is the food. Menus differ between lunch and dinner; the former being a touch less formal. Local rib-eye is a permanent feature, as is the twice-baked cheese soufflé, and many come for the local game, which is handled deftly. The owner works closely with his suppliers to ensure that the ingredients are tip-top.

BARRASFORD, NE48 4AA
Tel.: 01434 681237
Website: www.barrasfordarms.co.uk

7 mi north of Hexham signed off A 6079. Parking.

PRICES
Meals: £ 15 (weekday lunch) and a la carte
£ 25/33

 7 rooms:
£ 67/87

MAP: 6

CLOSING TIMES
Closed 24-26 December, Sunday dinner,
Monday and bank holidays

DUKE OF WELLINGTON

Head to the terrace for Tyne Valley views

Dating from the 1823 – and named after the Duke, who was busy winning battles in France at this time – this pub is reputedly the oldest licensed premises in the county. Despite being tucked away in a tiny hamlet, it's clear that a good few people know about it, and when you're out on the terrace taking in the valley view, it'll soon become one of your favourite spots too. Within its stone walls is a smart, modern country style bar and a more formal dining room. Breakfast features brioche French toast and local eggs Benedict, and is followed by a good value set lunch and evening à la carte, where pub classics sit alongside more adventurous dishes such as saddle of roe deer. Bedrooms are stylish and luxurious and have characterful exposed beams.

Newton,
CORBRIDGE, NE43 7UL
Tel.: 01661 844446
Website: www.thedukeofwellingtoninn.co.uk

3.5 mi from Corbridge signposted off A 69. Parking.

PRICES
Meals: £ 15 (weekdays) and a la carte
£ 26/43

 7 rooms:
£ 85/140

MAP: 7

CLOSING TIMES
Open daily

FEATHERS INN

The bookshelves are crammed with cookbooks

All three rooms in this characterful village centre pub have their bookshelves crammed with cookbooks and their walls filled with photos of those who supply their produce, both of which suggest that this is a place which takes its food seriously. The kitchen certainly does things properly, whether that's making its own black pudding or preparing the popular game dishes. The food is generous in both flavour and size and seasonality plays a large part – the menu changes on a daily basis and it's worth exploring the selection of local cheeses. The pub has a warm and welcoming feel thanks to its large central fireplace and stove, and feels genuinely part of the local community. It also offers really nice views of the surrounding countryside.

HEDLEY ON THE HILL, NE43 7SW
Tel.: 01661 843607
Website: www.thefeathers.net

6 mi north of Consett by A 694, B 6309 and minor road. Parking.

PRICES
Meals: a la carte £ 18/33

MAP: 8

CLOSING TIMES
Closed first 2 weeks January, Sunday dinner, Monday except bank holidays and lunch Tuesday-Wednesday

RAT INN

Relax among the arbours in the multi-level garden

There are several suggestions as to how this 18C drovers' inn got its name – theories include rat catchers using it as a meeting place, a large rat once residing here and it being home to the local snitch during the Jacobite rebellion. Nobody knows the answer, so just sit back and enjoy the pleasant Tyne Valley views. Situated in a small hillside hamlet, it's the perfect place to escape the rat race of the city, with its multi-level garden boasting arbours and picnic benches, and a traditional interior displaying wooden beams and an open range. The daily blackboard menu covers a good range of dishes from ground rib burger in a homemade bun to chop, belly and heart of lamb with goat's cheese mash. Produce is good quality and locally sourced.

Anick,
HEXHAM, NE46 4LN
Tel.: 01434 602814
Website: www.theratinn.com

1.75 mi northeast of Hexham signposted off A 6079. Parking.

PRICES
Meals: a la carte £ 22/42

MAP: **9**

CLOSING TIMES
Closed 25 December, Monday except bank
holidays and Sunday dinner

RED LION INN

Catch up with the locals and the latest sports

The Red Lion started life as a mid-18C drovers' inn, before becoming a stop-off point for the mail stagecoach between 1785 and 1835. It really is the heart of the village, so if you'd rather not catch up with the locals and the latest sporting events, head for the open-fired dining room instead of the bar. The traditional menu offers plenty of choice, showcasing produce from both England and across the border. Dishes range from a prawn cocktail to scallops with black pudding, the Shetland mussels are not to be missed and the hearty homemade burger has become a cult dish. Specials are chalked up the board and if you make it to pudding, you'll be rewarded with a tasty nursery selection. Bedrooms are homely – most are set in wooden lodges.

Main Rd,
MILFIELD, NE71 6JD
Tel.: 01668 216224
Website: www.redlionmilfield.co.uk

7 mi southeast of Coldstream by A 697. In the village centre. Parking.

PRICES
Meals: a la carte £ 19/30

5 rooms:
£ 45/80

MAP: 10

CLOSING TIMES
Closed 1 January and 25 December
booking advisable

ST MARY'S INN

Set in a striking old hospital building

The old St Mary's Hospital sits deep in the heart of the Northumbrian countryside. The striking red-brick offices at its centre have been turned into a pub and the rest of the buildings are being transformed into houses. The pub is a spacious place consisting of several individually styled rooms and it has a smart, homely feel – keep an eye out for the much sought-after works by Norman Cornish in their eclectic art collection. The experienced owners have created a repertoire of dishes that people will know and love; meat and fish are cooked on the lump wood charcoal grill, portions are hearty to say the least and afternoon tea is a hit. Bright, airy bedrooms are named after nearby reservoirs and feature ultra-modern bathrooms and local art.

St Mary's Ln,
ST MARY'S PARK, STANNINGTON, NE61 6BL
Tel.: 01670 293293
Website: www.stmarysinn.co.uk

2.5 mi west of Stannington by Saltwick rd. Parking

PRICES
Meals: a la carte £ 19/31

 11 rooms:
£ 80/150

MAP: 11

CLOSING TIMES
Open daily

CHADWICKS INN

The live acoustic sessions are a hit

Formerly named The Pathfinder, this pub dates back over 200 years and was where the Spitfire pilots used to stop for a noggin before flying out on their missions. It's the only pub in the village, so you'll find regulars nursing their pints alongside those out for an evening meal. In warmer weather find a spot in the garden or on the sheltered patio area; in winter, head for the large open-fired bar or either of the two dining rooms with their smartly laid polished tables. The main à la carte features ambitious, intricate dishes, and is supplemented by a simpler early evening bistro menu and a good value set selection. The live acoustic sessions are popular, as are the wine and tapas evenings. Service is friendly and fittingly formal.

High Ln,
MALTBY, TS8 0BG
Tel.: 01642 590300
Website: www.chadwicksinnmaltby.co.uk

7 mi south of Middlesborough by A 19 and A 1045. Parking at rear.

PRICES

Meals: £ 14 (weekday lunch)/28
and a la carte £ 31/50

MAP: **12**

CLOSING TIMES

Closed 26 December, 1 January and
Monday except bank holidays
booking advisable

BROAD CHARE

A choice of over 40 ales – some custom-made

Owned by Terry Laybourne and set next to its sister operation Caffé Vivo, Broad Chare really hit the ground running. It's located on the quayside, close to the Millennium Bridge and, with its 'Proper Beer, Proper Food' motto, is a hit with the locals. The snug ground floor with its low level stool seating offers a choice of over 40 ales – some custom-made for the pub – and a bar snack menu featuring the likes of scotch eggs, cauliflower with curried mayonnaise and deep-fried pig's ears. Dining also takes place upstairs, where, along with this affectionately named 'Geordie Tapas', you'll find everything from an appealing 'on toast' selection to hearty daily specials such as steak and kidney pudding – all followed by tasty nursery puddings.

25 Broad Chare,
NEWCASTLE UPON TYNE, NE1 3DQ
Tel.: 0191 211 2144
Website: www.thebroadchare.co.uk

Close to Millennium Bridge in Quayside area of city centre.
On-street parking.

PRICES
Meals: a la carte £ 21/37

MAP: 13

CLOSING TIMES
Closed 25-26 December and Sunday
dinner
booking advisable

STAITH HOUSE

Cosy, quayside pub serving good value food

When you're dining on a fishing quay (or staith) with the smell of sea in the air, it makes sense to bypass typical pub fare like a burger and chips – nice though it is – and plump for something brought in by the fishing fleets... perhaps some halibut, sea bass, cod or shellfish. Dishes change almost daily depending on the catch and cooking is robust, tasty and well-priced. The pub is cosy and simply furnished, with an open kitchen and décor that makes many a reference to the pub's location, with portholes, ship's lights and nautical charts. The music is loud and the service, although friendly, can be disorganised – but it just seems to add to the appeal. Check out the enormous whale's jaw bone outside the back door before you leave.

57 Low Lights,
NORTH SHIELDS, NE30 1JA
Tel.: 0191 270 8441
Website: www.thestaithhouse.co.uk

On the fish quay. Pay and display parking adjacent.

PRICES
Meals: a la carte £ 21/43

MAP: 14

CLOSING TIMES
Closed 25-26 December and 1-2 January
booking essential at dinner

NORTH WEST

—— England

© R. Harding / hemis.fr

Liverpool's UNESCO World Heritage Site status, dovetailed by the confident sophistication of a reinvigorated Manchester means that the country's oldest industrial heartland boasts an impressive cultural profile. And yet arty urban centres are a million miles away from the rural grandeur of the region: trails and paths criss-cross the area all the way from the Solway Firth to Cheshire. Cumbria is a walker's paradise: from Hadrian's Wall to the glories of the Lake District, and along the vast shoreline of Morecambe Bay with its rich gathering of waders and wildfowl, there's a vivid contrast in scenery. The architectural landscape of the region covers the ages, too. Lancaster Castle reverberates to the footsteps of ancient soldiers, while Chester's walled city of medieval buildings is a true gem.

Blackpool is now Europe's biggest seaside resort while the flavour of the north west is hotpot, black pudding and Morecambe Bay shrimps.

183

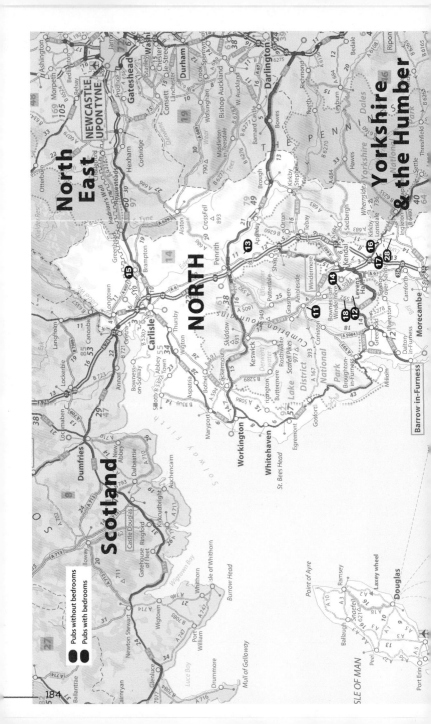

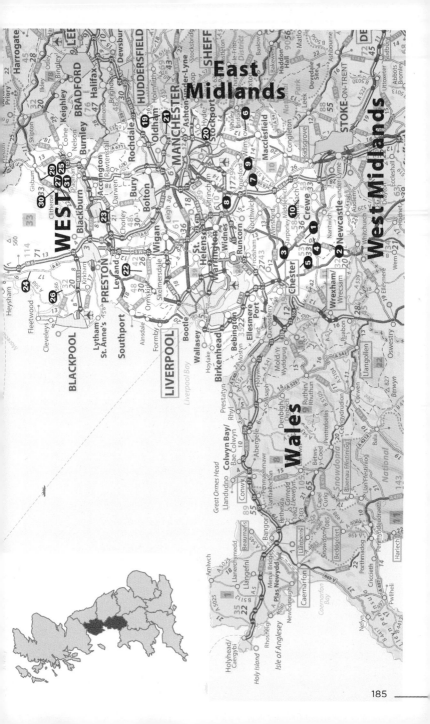

YEW TREE INN

Come for their quarterly farmers' market

Satisfyingly, this handsome part red-brick, part black and white timbered pub does come complete with a large yew tree. It also comes with a lovely terrace, a pleasingly relaxed feel and numerous snug rooms featuring brightly coloured fabrics, quirky wallpapers and photographs from yesteryear – not forgetting toilet doors made from old drawer fronts! They host events throughout the year, including two beer festivals and a quarterly farmers' market and, unsurprisingly, the freshest local and seasonal ingredients appear in their cooking. Dishes include all of the favourites, from tasty homemade pies to sticky baby back ribs – and the bar is chock-full of different ales, some of which the dedicated owner drives all the way to London to collect.

Long Ln,
SPURSTOW, BUNBURY, CW6 9RD
Tel.: 01829 260274
Website: www.theyewtreebunbury.com

7.5 mi northwest of Nantwich by A 51, A 534 and A 49. Parking.

PRICES
Meals: a la carte £ 21/37

MAP: **1**

CLOSING TIMES
Open daily

CHOLMONDELEY ARMS

Choose from over 200 types of gin!

The Cholmondeley Arms started life in 1862 as the eponymous estate's schoolhouse and details like school blackboards, an 'old school favourites' section on the menu and an ale called 'teacher's tipple' are a reminder that it spent more than a century as a place of learning. High vaulted ceilings and large windows let in lots of light, while roaring fires give the place a cosy, welcoming feel. The menu offers tasty, modern pub favourites like devilled lamb's kidneys on toast, stalker's venison pie or homemade lamb faggots. Cask beers come from within a 30 mile radius and gin-lovers will be in clover with over 200 to choose from, plus five types of tonic. Head to the Old Headmaster's House to sleep it all off in one of the 6 comfy bedrooms.

Wrenbury Rd,
CHOLMONDELEY, SY14 8HN
Tel.: 01829 720300
Website: www.cholmondeleyarms.co.uk

11 mi west of Nantwich by A51 and A 534 on A 49. Parking.

PRICES
Meals: a la carte £ 22/34

 6 rooms:
£ 65/100

MAP: 2

CLOSING TIMES
Open daily

FOX AND BARREL

With wood-panelled walls filled with framed pictures and shelves lined with books, you could be mistaken for thinking you're in a Brunning and Price pub, but then that's probably because the owners have both worked for the group in the past. The front bar with its open log fire is very much the drinkers' domain, while the smart terrace and large garden, complete with vintage tractor, attract one and all. Menus change virtually daily and offer plenty of originality and interest; you might find twice-baked cheese soufflé followed by loin of venison with spiced red cabbage, alongside old favourites like fish and chips. Dishes are generously proportioned, neatly presented and sensibly priced – and there's a good list of wines by the glass too.

Foxbank,
COTEBROOK, CW6 9DZ
Tel.: 01829 760529
Website: www.foxandbarrel.co.uk

On A 49 northeast of Tarporley. Parking.

PRICES
Meals: a la carte £ 21/35

MAP: **3**

CLOSING TIMES
Closed dinner 25-26 December
and 1 January

NAG'S HEAD

The delightful garden even has a bowling green

Arguably the prettiest of the Ribble Valley Inns, this attractive timbered property sits within a peaceful hamlet. The garden is a delightful spot and comes complete with a bowling green for those who fancy a game, while inside exposed beams, tiled floors and open fires provide plenty of character, helped along by saddle-shaped stools and tables made from shotguns. Photos of local Cheshire producers line the walls – giving a clue as to the importance regional ingredients play – and a charcoal grill takes pride of place in the kitchen, so it's no surprise to find plenty of steaks among the classic dishes. The nearby Weetwood Brewery provides most of the real ales but you'll also find Thwaites 1629 – named after the year that the pub was built.

Long Ln,
HAUGHTON MOSS, CW6 9RN
Tel.: 01829 260265
Website: www.nagsheadhaughton.co.uk

5.5 mi northwest of Nantwich signposted off A 534. Parking.

PRICES
Meals: £ 14 (weekdays) and a la carte
£ 22/46

MAP: 4

CLOSING TIMES
Open daily

PHEASANT INN

Look out across the Cheshire Plains

This well-run, modern pub is set atop a sandstone escarpment, with views across the Cheshire Plains to Wrexham and Liverpool. Outside space is plentiful, with various terraces and a garden, while the interior feels fresh and clean with its reclaimed beams and open fires. The snug is quite cosy, the dining room more formal – and the window tables are the first to be nabbed in either. The seasonal menu focuses on simple pub classics like ale, steak and mushroom pie, with some interesting specials, nibbles and deli boards to complement. The no-nonsense cooking has clear, gutsy flavours and the smartly dressed staff are keen to please. Spacious, beamed bedrooms are set in the main building; more modern rooms with views are located in the barn.

HIGHER BURWARDSLEY, CH3 9PF
Tel.: 01829 770434
Website: www.thepheasantinn.co.uk

2.5 mi southeast of Tattenhall. Parking.

PRICES		MAP: 5
Meals: a la carte £ 20/38	12 rooms: £ 95/145	

CLOSING TIMES
Open daily

LORD CLYDE

Complex modern cooking in a rustic pub

This keenly run village pub started life in 1843 as two weavers' cottages. It's a small place, with a simple, rustic feel courtesy of quarry tiled floors, polished wood tables and black and white photos of local scenes. The cooking, however, is a complete contrast. Chef Ernst has experience in some top Scandinavian restaurants and his creative, extremely eye-catching dishes exhibit a wide range of complex modern techniques. Hay-baked beetroot with goat's curd could tempt you to start, followed by monkfish at 46 degrees with asparagus and razor clams, then iced lemon mousse and pickled blueberries. The 7 and 10 course tasting menus are a hit, the terrace is a popular spot on warmer days and a loyal band of drinkers add to the atmosphere.

36 Clarke Ln,
KERRIDGE, SK10 5AH
Tel.: 01625 562123
Website: www.thelordclyde.co.uk

3 mi north of Macclesfield by A 523, with village signposted off B 5090 to Bollington. Parking.

PRICES   MAP: **6**
Meals: a la carte £ 28/46

CLOSING TIMES
Closed Sunday dinner and Monday lunch

BELLS OF PEOVER

Cooking has a Mediterranean feel

So, why does this 16C coaching inn have the Stars and Stripes flying over it? Because, apparently, Generals Eisenhower and Patton were stationed nearby and were regulars. And the Bells? No, not from the delightful church behind, but the name of a family who once owned it. You'll have to be quick to nab one of the handful of tables in the cosy fire-lit bar but there's always plenty of space in the three contemporary dining rooms; and on a sunny day, a spot on the terrace beneath the wisteria is hard to beat. Service is friendly and the cooking will get you thinking of warmer climes, with influences coming from the Med – in particular, Italy, Greece and Turkey; start with jalapeno hummus and move onto a feta and spinach pie with sun-blushed tomatoes.

The Cobbles,
LOWER PEOVER, WA16 9PZ
Tel.: 01565 722269
Website: www.thebellsofpeover.com

Off the B 5081, which runs through the village. Parking.

PRICES   MAP: **7**
Meals: a la carte £ 24/40

CLOSING TIMES
Open daily

CHURCH GREEN

They take pride in their kitchen garden

This double-fronted Victorian pub stands on the green next to St Mary's Church. Its experienced chef-owner, Aiden Byrne, is supported by a well-structured team, who take pride in the pub's kitchen garden, which supplies everything from beetroot to soft fruits. The open-plan bar and restaurant are decorated in modern hues and there's a pleasant conservatory and an attractive decked terrace to the rear. There's plenty to choose from, with an appealing set menu; a grill menu where you choose a cut, then add sauce, garnish and extras; and an extensive small plates menu, where you can try a selection of the most popular dishes since their opening in 2008. They also serve tasty breakfasts at the weekend, which includes a full English for children.

Higher Ln,
LYMM, WA13 0AP
Tel.: 01925 752068
Website: www.thechurchgreen.co.uk

7 mi west of Altrincham by A 56. Parking.

PRICES   MAP: **8**
Meals: £ 30 (weekdays) and a la carte
£ 28/58

CLOSING TIMES
Closed 25 December
booking essential

CHURCH INN

Sit on the terrace and admire the 12C church

Beside the village bowling green you'll find this 18C brick pub, where candles flicker against exposed brick walls and a curious mix of antiques and curios are on display, from stuffed animals to a grandfather clock. Regularly changing menus reflect the seasons, featuring light dishes in summer and hearty stews in winter. On a sunny afternoon, grab a hand-pumped beer (two of which are produced within 15 miles of the pub), and make for the terrace, where you can sit and admire the 12C architecture of the neighbouring church. Those after a private dinner will be shown upstairs to the George Mallory room (his father was once the church rector), via a corridor chock full of old photos of the party who took part in the first Everest expedition.

Church Ln,
MOBBERLEY, WA16 7RD
Tel.: 01565 873178
Website: www.churchinnmobberley.co.uk

2.5 mi northeast of Knutsford by A 537 and B 5085. Parking.

PRICES
Meals: a la carte £ 21/44

MAP: 9

CLOSING TIMES
Open daily

BEAR'S PAW

Sizeable pub with an equally large menu

Sister to the Pheasant at Tattenhall is this handsome 19C inn; probably best described as very big and very, very busy. There's a spacious, semi wood panelled bar with two vast fireplaces and a huge array of local ales. The menu is also sizeable, with enough choice to please all appetites; from nibbles like flavoured chipolatas or olives to deli boards including charcuterie and cheese selections – all served with rustic bread and house chutney. Main dishes look to Europe for their inspiration, but it's the good old British favourites like fish and chips or steak and ale pie that win the day. You can cook your own steak on a hot stone – and make sure you try the Bear's Paw Sundae for dessert. Bedrooms are stylish and well worth the money.

School Ln,
WARMINGHAM, CW11 3QN
Tel.: 01270 526317
Website: www.thebearspaw.co.uk

3.5 mi west of Sandbach by A 533. Parking.

PRICES
Meals: a la carte £ 20/41

 17 rooms:
£ 105/145

MAP: 10

CLOSING TIMES
Open daily

DRUNKEN DUCK INN

Easy to see why it's always so busy

Situated in the heart of the beautiful Lakeland countryside, this attractive inn takes its name from an old legend about a landlady, some ducks and a leaky beer barrel. The popular fire-lit bar is the cosiest place to sit, among hop bines, pictures of the hunt and old brewery advertisements; but there are also two more formal dining rooms. The same menu is served throughout, offering simple lunches and much more elaborate dinners, with prices to match; cooking is generous and service, attentive. Ales come from the on-site micro-brewery and are made with water from their own tarn. Boutique, country house bedrooms – some with patios – boast extremely comfy beds and country views. Afternoon tea can be taken in the lounge or residents' garden.

Barngates,
AMBLESIDE, LA22 0NG
Tel.: 015394 36347
Website: www.drunkenduckinn.co.uk

3 mi southwest of Ambleside by A 593 and B 5286 on Tarn Hows road. By the crossroads at the top of Duck Hill. Parking.

PRICES
Meals: a la carte £ 29/50

 17 rooms:
£ 79/325

MAP: 11

CLOSING TIMES
Closed 25 December
booking essential at dinner

HARE AND HOUNDS

Cosy, characterful and charming

This charming 17C Lakeland pub is situated in the delightful village of Bowland Bridge, where Arthur Ransome wrote the book 'Swallows and Amazons'. There's a large terrace with chunky wooden tables to the front, leading through into a rustic, open-fired inner with stone walls, black and white village photos and exposed beams draped with hop bines. Menus offer typical, hearty, pub-style dishes – such as homemade pies or Lakeland hotpot with black pudding and home-pickled cabbage – and much of the produce is locally sourced. There's also a fine selection of ales to choose from, including 'Hare of the Dog', which is specially brewed for them by a Lakeland brewery. Bedrooms are well-equipped and elegant with smart bathrooms; some have roll-top baths.

BOWLAND BRIDGE, LA11 6NN
Tel.: 015395 68333
Website: www.hareandhoundsbowlandbridge.co.uk

7 mi south of Windermere signed off A 5074. In the village centre. Parking.

PRICES
Meals: a la carte £ 21/33

5 rooms:
£ 72/145

MAP: 12

CLOSING TIMES
Closed 25 December

GEORGE AND DRAGON

Game from the moors and meat from estate farms

Consisting of 75,000 acres and covering much of Cumbria, the Lowther family estate includes properties ranging from a castellated mansion to this whitewashed coaching inn. Its characterful 18C bar features a flag floor, panelling and a wood burning stove, while the spacious restaurant takes on a more modern style, with its open kitchen and smart wood furnishings. When it comes to the food, it doesn't get more local than this, with vegetables from the kitchen garden, game from the surrounding moors and organic meats from the estate's farms. Appealing dishes might include twice-baked Cumbrian cheese soufflé, followed by Askham pork sausages or pan-fried wild sea bass. Modern bedrooms showcase furniture and paintings from the family's collection.

CLIFTON, CA10 2ER
Tel.: 01768 865381
Website: www.georgeanddragonclifton.co.uk

3 mi south of Penrith on A 6. In centre of village. Parking.

PRICES
Meals: £ 15 (weekdays) and a la carte £ 25/36

 11 rooms:
£ 85/155

MAP: 13

CLOSING TIMES
Closed 26 December

PUNCH BOWL INN

Charming pub in a picturesque valley setting

Nestled among the hills in the heart of the picturesque Lyth Valley, this attractive 17C inn enjoys a truly delightful setting – and it's not just the views that are glorious: the pub itself is truly charming, with its antiques, cosy open fires and exposed wooden beams. Cooking has a classical base but displays some modern touches, and dishes display a degree of complexity that you wouldn't usually find in a pub. Dine in the rustic bar or, for more of an occasion, in the more formal restaurant. Smart, individually styled bedrooms boast good quality linen, roll-top baths and fluffy towels; 'Noble' features twin bath tubs and 'Danson' offers the best views. If you fancy sending a postcard, the reception also doubles as the village post office!

CROSTHWAITE, LA8 8HR
Tel.: 015395 68237
Website: www.the-punchbowl.co.uk

5.25 mi west of Kendal by All Hallows Lane; next to the church.
Parking.

PRICES
Meals: a la carte £ 26/39

 9 rooms:
£ 85/305

MAP: 14

CLOSING TIMES
Open daily

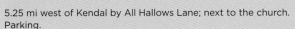

GOLDEN FLEECE

A cosy place to stay near Hadrian's Wall

Yan, Tahn, Tethera, Methera, Pimp: words traditionally used by Cumbrian shepherds to count their sheep now guide you to your bedroom when staying at this 18C coaching inn; but fear not, with beds as comfortable as these, you won't need to utter a word of shepherding dialect yourself. With treats such as twice-baked 3 cheese soufflé and pan-roasted Cumbrian lamb on offer, dining is a must. They've got tasty pub classics, juicy mature steaks (including chateaubriand for two) and proper pub puddings, as well as a selection of local ales with which to wash them all down. Find a spot beside the wood-burning stove and keep an eye out for the maps of ancient Cumbria. It's well located close to Hadrian's Wall and – for those eloping – Gretna Green!

Ruleholme,
IRTHINGTON, CA6 4NF
Tel.: 01228 573686
Website: www.thegoldenfleececumbria.co.uk

6.5 mi northeast of Carlisle by B 6264 on A 689. Parking.

PRICES
Meals: a la carte £ 23/45

8 rooms:
£ 85/95

MAP: 15

CLOSING TIMES
Closed 1-7 January

SUN INN

Meat is from the butcher's two doors down

This 17C inn's hands-on owners don't have to go far to source quality produce as, with a butcher's two doors down, it's literally on their doorstep. Lunch sees a concise selection of dishes such as pork belly with pancetta, followed at dinner by the likes of chicken supreme with pea custard or Nordic sea trout with clams, gnocchi and purple carrots; lighter bar snacks are served throughout the day and could include honey and mustard glazed chipolatas or salt and pepper squid. The team are friendly and welcoming and the smart, modern bedrooms come with quality linens and thoughtful extras like homemade flapjack and fresh milk. Breakfast is well worth getting up for too, with delicious offerings including poached fruits and homemade granola.

6 Market St,
KIRKBY LONSDALE, LA6 2AU
Tel.: 015242 71965
Website: www.sun-inn.info

In the centre of town. Long stay car park in Booth Rd.

PRICES
Meals: £ 29 (dinner) and a la carte £ 26/38

 11 rooms:
£ 82/189

MAP: 16

CLOSING TIMES
Closed 25 December

PLOUGH

A cosy, homely atmosphere reigns

The Plough is set on the main road that links the Lake District to North Yorkshire and has earned itself a good reputation in the local area. There's a cosy, homely feel to the place, which is made up of a shabby-chic bar and a slightly smarter dining room with exposed beams and pink hues. The cheery, knowledgeable team serve up a pleasing mix of pub and restaurant-style dishes, so you might find Wainwright Ale battered haddock with chunky chips or an 8oz Aberdeen Angus beef burger topped with streaky bacon and Lancashire cheese, alongside the likes of rabbit rillettes with Hawkshead beetroot relish or pan-fried hake with crushed potatoes and smoked pancetta. Smart, individually styled bedrooms with roll-top baths complete the picture.

Cow Brow,
LUPTON, LA6 1PJ
Tel.: 015395 67700
Website: www.theploughatlupton.co.uk

4.75 mi northwest of Kirkby Lonsdale on A 65. Parking.

PRICES
Meals: a la carte £ 20/44

 6 rooms:
£ 85/195

MAP: 17

CLOSING TIMES
Open daily

BROWN HORSE INN

Comes with smart bedrooms and even a brewery

This simple coaching inn has always been popular with the locals; but even more so since the creation of its on-site brewery. It has a shabby-chic style, with flagged floors, antique dressers and a real mix of furniture. In one corner, a miniature model of the bar (made by one of the regulars) and a London Underground map of local pubs provide talking points; while the split-level terrace is a real draw. Seasonal menus feature produce from the fields out back and game comes from shoots they organise themselves. Dishes are designed with hungry walkers in mind; the blackboard specials are a little more adventurous and often include home-reared pork. Bedrooms are a mix of classical and boutique styles; the latter have French windows and terraces.

WINSTER, LA23 3NR
Tel.: 015394 43443
Website: www.thebrownhorseinn.co.uk

4 mi south of Windermere by A 5074. Parking.

PRICES
Meals: a la carte £ 22/49

 9 rooms:
£ 55/150

MAP: 18

CLOSING TIMES
Open daily

OLD BELL INN

They offer the world's largest selection of gins

This 18C coaching inn is set high up on the moors and is well worth a visit not just for the food but for its gins too – with over 500 different types, their selection is the biggest in the world. Food is served in both the cosy bar and the smart brasserie; choose from sharing platters, hearty pub favourites and 35 day matured steaks, including a particularly tasty veal T-bone. More modern influences feature on the set menus, with the likes of scotch egg black pudding and poached pear, followed by sea trout with beetroot fondant, finished off with chocolate, chilli and orange delice. Gin tasting boards offer three premium gins and two different tonics and they also have a great selection of real ales. Well-kept bedrooms complete the picture.

Huddersfield Rd,
DELPH, OL3 5EG
Tel.: 01457 870130
Website: www.theoldbellinn.co.uk

Between Oldham and Huddersfield on A 62. Parking.

PRICES
Meals: £ 25 (lunch and early dinner)
and a la carte £ 22/44

 18 rooms:
£ 60/125

MAP: 19

CLOSING TIMES
Open daily

ODDFELLOWS

The lamb comes from the owners' fields

The Oddfellows – or Oddies, as it is affectionately known by the locals – has a light, uncluttered feel, with wood burning stoves and an eclectic assortment of furniture adding an element of cosiness. Built into the side of a former stone quarry on a winding lane leading up into the hills, it proudly retains its identity as a pub, with its bar and hand pump beers the focal point. The appealing menu is as traditional as the surroundings, offering what they call 'British food with a modern twist' – which could include anything from a homemade burger, fishcakes or a steak and kidney pudding to sausage and mash, cottage pie or 28-day aged steak. Local suppliers are acknowledged, lamb comes from the owners' fields and bread is homemade.

Moor End Rd,
MELLOR, SK6 5PT
Tel.: 0161 449 7826
Website: www.oddfellowsmellor.com

2.5 mi northwest of Marple by Marple Bridge and minor road. Parking.

PRICES
Meals: a la carte £ 17/35

MAP: **20**

CLOSING TIMES
Closed Monday except bank holidays

WHITE HART INN

The original part of this stone-built inn dates from 1788 but with constant reinvestment from its owner, there's always something new going on here. It's a busy place, which draws a mix of locals and visitors, and its sympathetically styled extensions offer something for one and all: there's a formal restaurant, a private dining room, a large function room and smart bedrooms named after local men of note. The main pub area consists of a central bar and several smaller rooms featuring beams, open fires and photos from the owner's travels. The menu offers a good range of refined pub classics and many – such as the cep risotto and beef carpaccio – have a Mediterranean slant, the lunch and early evening menu (Mon-Thurs) draws in the crowds.

51 Stockport Rd,
LYDGATE, OLDHAM, OL4 4JJ
Tel.: 01457 872566
Website: www.thewhitehart.co.uk

3 mi east of Oldham by A 669 on A 6050. Parking.

PRICES
Meals: £ 14 (weekdays) and a la carte
£ 25/42

 17 rooms:
£ 85/165

MAP: 21

CLOSING TIMES
Closed 1 January and 26 December

EAGLE & CHILD

Superb farm shop with an on-site butcher

This 16C inn has all the characterful features you would expect to find in a proper pub, like open fires, stone floors and exposed beams fringed with hop bines; add to this locally brewed real ales and tasty, freshly prepared food and you can see why it attracts people from a distance, as well as locals with their dogs. Sit in the charmingly small snug with its four tables; there are also two rooms in the bar and an elegant candlelit restaurant in the former stables. The owner shoots game and the pub company rear their own animals and grow their own vegetables, so there's always plenty of quality seasonal ingredients with which to create the unfussy, boldly flavoured dishes. Don't leave without a visit to the delightful farm shop next door!

Maltkiln Ln,
BISPHAM GREEN, L40 3SG
Tel.: 01257 462297
Website: www.ainscoughs.co.uk

Between Ormskirk and Standish by A 5209 and B 5246. Parking.

PRICES
Meals: £ 10 and a la carte £ 21/43

MAP: 22

CLOSING TIMES
Open daily

CLOG & BILLYCOCK

Regional specialities are the draw

This popular sandstone pub was originally called the Bay Horse, before being renamed after a fashion trend often sported by the former landlord – who liked to wear the quirky combination of clog shoes and a billycock hat. The addition of a large extension means the pub is now modern and open-plan. The walls are filled with photos of their local suppliers and the extensive menus offer a strong Lancastrian slant; you might find Morecambe Bay shrimps, Port of Lancaster smoked fish or Ribble Valley beef, alongside tasty sharing platters. Most produce comes from within 25 miles and suppliers are plotted on a map on the back of the menu. Cooking is rustic and generous, prices are realistic, and the service is friendly and organised.

Billinge End Rd,
PLEASINGTON, BLACKBURN, BB2 6QB
Tel.: 01254 201163
Website: www.theclogandbillycock.com

2 mi west of Blackburn, signed off A 677. Parking.

PRICES
Meals: £ 14 (weekdays) and a la carte
£ 21/41

MAP: 23

CLOSING TIMES
Open daily

BAY HORSE INN

Food is good value and full of flavour

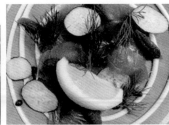

This pub is flanked by the A6 and M6, and just a stone's throw away from the main Euston to Glasgow railway line, so it's hard to believe how peaceful it is here. Burgundy walls, low beamed ceilings, a stone fireplace and a characterful corner bar provide a cosy, welcoming atmosphere, while the brighter rear dining room overlooks an attractive summer terrace and a pleasant wooded garden. Seasonal menus offer traditional, tried-and-tested dishes and, since they've been passionate about supporting regional producers here long before it became fashionable to do so, you'll always find local offerings such as Higginson's pork and leek sausages, Swainson House Farm duck liver pâté or Cumbrian beef – with the Lancashire cheeseboard a speciality.

Bay Horse Ln,
BAY HORSE, ELLEL, LA2 0HR
Tel.: 01524 791204
Website: www.bayhorseinn.com

6 mi south of Lancaster by A 6 on Quernmore rd. Parking.

PRICES
Meals: £ 20 (weekdays)/24 and a la carte
£ 20/43

MAP: 24

CLOSING TIMES
Closed Monday except bank holiday lunch
and Tuesday

WHITE SWAN

The cheeseboard is worth a try

To visitors it might be called the White Swan but to the locals this will always be the Mucky Duck – so-called because the coal miners used to stop here for a pint on their way home from work. The traditional interior points back to simpler times, with its old black and white photos and a quirky collection of animal heads mounted on the walls. It's owned by Timothy Taylor's brewery, so you're always guaranteed a perfect crystal clear pint – and the food is just as good. Concise set menus offer a daily changing selection of well-crafted, flavoursome modern dishes; maybe Gloucester Old Spot pork with liquorice sauce or poached salmon with horseradish and caviar. The cheeseboard with homemade crackers and truffle honey is well worth a try too.

300 Wheatley Lane Rd,
FENCE, BB12 9QA
Tel.: 01282 611773
Website: www.whiteswanatfence.co.uk

4.5 mi north of Burnley by A 682 and B 6248 off A 6068. Parking.

PRICES
Meals: a la carte £ 26/36

MAP: 25

CLOSING TIMES
Closed Sunday dinner and Monday

CARTFORD INN

Be sure to visit the extensive deli

The Cartford Inn stands next to small toll bridge on the River Wyre but its name refers to an earlier time, when people had to cross the ford by horse and cart. This is the kind of place that offers something for everyone, from sharing platters to steaks from the nearby Brockhole Arms auction and fish from the Fleetwood Docklands. Cooking is gutsy and satisfying and many of the tried-and-tested classics come with a twist, so you might find oxtail, beef and ale pudding accompanied by beetroot salad or duck cottage pie served with pickled figs. The owner played a big part in the interior design, particularly the bold, boutique bedrooms, which feature colourful glass fittings by a local glassblower. There's also a deli and farm shop at the rear.

Cartford Ln,
LITTLE ECCLESTON, PR3 0YP
Tel.: 01995 670166
Website: www.thecartfordinn.co.uk

7 mi east of Blackpool by A 585 and A 586. Parking.

PRICES
Meals: a la carte £ 24/39

 15 rooms:
£ 75/230

MAP: 26

CLOSING TIMES
Closed 25 December and Monday lunch
except bank holidays

THREE FISHES

Local suppliers and regional specialities

'Regional' and 'local' are the buzzwords at this behemoth of a country pub, which seems to take catering for vast numbers of people in its stride. The original in Nigel Haworth's 'Ribble Valley Inns' group, it celebrated its tenth birthday in 2014, and now has a modern style, typified by light wood and contemporary art to go with rustic features like stone walls and open fires. Produce is sourced from within 25 miles and pictorial homage is paid to their suppliers, or 'local food heroes'. Expect shrimps from Morecambe Bay, Ribble Valley beef, Goosnargh duck and Fleetwood fish, with specialities like the hotpot and the twice-baked cheese soufflé firmly rooted in the region. Sundays mean roast beef with all the trimmings; on Mondays it's BYO.

Mitton Rd,
MITTON, BB7 9PQ
Tel.: 01254 826888
Website: www.thethreefishes.com

2.5 mi northwest of Whalley on B 6246. Parking.

PRICES
Meals: £ 14 (weekdays) and a la carte
£ 22/47

MAP: **27**

CLOSING TIMES
Open daily

HIGHWAYMAN

Showcases produce from surrounding counties

It's rumoured that this sizeable 18C coaching inn with its lovely terrace was once the midnight haunt of the local highwaymen. Set on the border of three counties – Cumbria, Lancashire and Yorkshire – it makes the most of its setting, with produce so local that a meal almost constitutes a regional geography lesson. The Lancashire hotpot is a signature dish; you'll find bacon from Sillfield Farm and shrimps from Morecambe Bay; seasonal classics like asparagus from Formby in spring and game in winter; as well as hearty puds like sticky toffee pudding. The rustic, no-nonsense approach to food means dishes are well-crafted and full of flavour. Mondays mean you can bring your own wine; enjoy a pint or two of Highwayman ale any day of the week.

NETHER BURROW,
LA6 2RJ
Tel.: 015242 73338
Website: www.highwaymaninn.co.uk

2 mi south of Kirkby Lonsdale by A 65 and A 683. Parking.

PRICES   MAP: **28**
Meals: £ 14 (weekdays) and a la carte
£ 22/46

CLOSING TIMES
Open daily

213

SPREAD EAGLE

Store your bike safely in one of their pods

Very much a local pub, at the heart of the community, the Spread Eagle is stylish, characterful and has lovely river views. Eat by the fire in the cosy bar or for a touch more comfort, head for the spacious restaurant. Cooking is gutsy and flavourful with pub favourites like fish and chips available in two sizes and classic main courses such as duck breast or daube of beef, along with platters and tapas-style nibbles which are perfect for sharing. On Wednesdays they offer fish and chips for a fiver, on Thursdays it's curry night, and the locals are rewarded every day of the week with a beer loyalty card. Comfortable bedrooms have smart modern bathrooms; room 6 is one of the largest and features a mezzanine level with 'his and hers' sofas.

SAWLEY, BB7 4NH
Tel.: 01200 441202
Website: www.spreadeaglesawley.co.uk

4 mi north of Clitheroe by A 59. Parking.

PRICES
Meals: a la carte £ 20/32

 7 rooms:
£ 65/140

MAP: 29

CLOSING TIMES
Open daily

HIGHER BUCK

Desserts always include a 'tart of the day'

Waddington has earned itself the title of 'Best Kept Village in Lancashire' on several occasions and with its lovely Ribble Valley location and a babbling stream running through its centre, it's easy to see why the locals take pride in it. The Higher Buck has received a similar amount of care from its owners and a top-to-toe refurbishment has left it with pastel-painted wood panelling and a mix of modern fabric and leather chairs. Bag a spot at one of the U-shaped banquettes or find a spot on the sunny terrace overlooking the Square and dine on reassuringly robust, seasonal dishes, with the likes of steak and Thwaites Bomber Ale pudding, game or fish planks and charcoal-grilled steaks. Service is smooth and friendly and stylish bedrooms await.

The Square,
WADDINGTON, BB7 3HZ
Tel.: 01200 423226
Website: www.higherbuck.com

2 mi northwest of Clitheroe on B 6478. Parking.

PRICES
Meals: a la carte £ 22/42

 7 rooms:
£ 65/115

MAP: 30

CLOSING TIMES
Closed 25 December

FREEMASONS

Refined dishes and an elegant dining room

Until the 1950s, this building was used by the Freemasons of the borough; thankfully, you no longer need a secret handshake to get in and the friendly staff welcome all-comers to enjoy the skilful, confident cooking of chef-owner Steven Smith. Fiercely seasonal dishes are traditional with a modern, sometimes playful edge; choices might include scorched langoustines with pork belly, Yorkshire rhubarb and dashi tea or 'Anna's happy trotters': roast loin with salt-baked pineapple, black pudding and pork pie sauce. Featuring a series of nooks and crannies, the pub has a charm all of its own; the antique-furnished upstairs has an elegant feel, while downstairs, with its flagged floors, low beams and open fires is more rustic.

8 Vicarage Fold,
WISWELL, BB7 9DF
Tel.: 01254 822218
Website: www.freemasonsatwiswell.com

Signposted off A 671 east of Whalley. Some parking in the village.

PRICES
Meals: £ 25 (lunch and early dinner)
and a la carte £ 38/62

MAP: 31

CLOSING TIMES
Closed 2-14 January and Monday-Tuesday
except bank holidays

SOUTH EAST

—— England

© J. Arnold Images / hemis.fr

The south east abounds in handsome historic houses once lived in by the likes of Disraeli and the Rothschilds, and it's no surprise that during the Plague it was to leafy Chalfont St Giles that John Milton fled. It is characterised by rolling hills such as the Chilterns with their ancient beechwoods, and the lilting North and South Downs, which cut a rural swathe across busy commuter belts. The film and television worlds sit easily here: Hambleden and Turville, in the Chilterns, are as used to the sound of the autocue as to the crunch of ramblers' boots. Meanwhile, James Bond's Aston Martin glistens in Beaulieu's Motor Museum, in the heart of the New Forest. Spinnaker Tower rivals HMS Victory for dominance of the Portsmouth skyline, while in Winchester, the Great Hall, home for 600 years to the Arthurian round table, nods acquaintance with the eleventh century Cathedral.

Good food and drink is integral to the region, from Whitstable oysters and Dover sole to established vineyards.

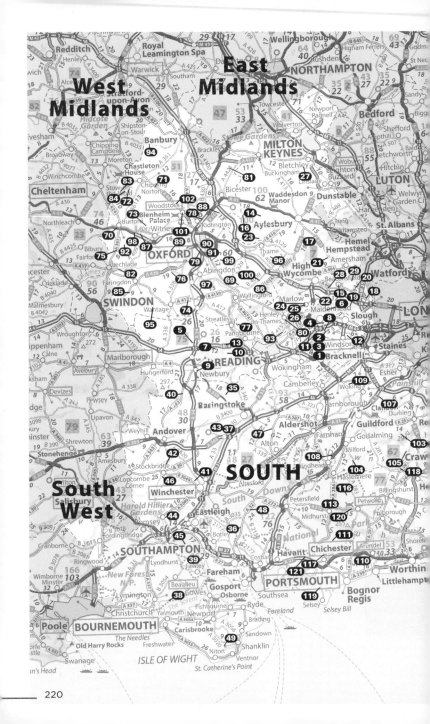

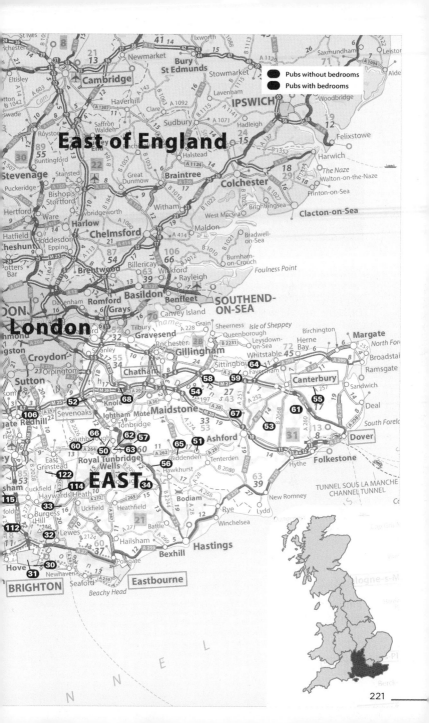

Pubs without bedrooms
Pubs with bedrooms

CROWN

Robust, flavoursome cooking

This charmingly restored 16C building began life as two cottages and an old bike shop, hence the confusion with the doors as you approach – follow your instincts and head for the middle one. Drinkers mingle with diners beside roaring fires, amongst sturdy dark oak columns and below low beams, and there are plenty of nooks and crannies in which to tuck yourself away. Cooking is robust, flavoursome and British in essence, ranging from the likes of a burger or fish and chips to more interesting dishes such as Black Angus bavette with marrowbone sauce or crispy cauliflower with cheese sauce and Henderson's relish. Ingredients are well-sourced, cooking is careful and flavours are pronounced. The covered, heated courtyard is a pleasant spot.

High St,
BRAY, SL6 2AH
Tel.: 01628 621936
Website: www.thecrownatbray.com

1.75 mi south of Maidenhead by A 308. Parking.

PRICES
Meals: a la carte £ 28/46

MAP: 1

CLOSING TIMES
Closed 25 December

HINDS HEAD

✿

Historic British dishes, wonderfully reinvented

Set in the heart of the pretty village of Bray, this charming 15C pub is full of character, with dark wood panelling, oak beams and log fires. Although situated not far from its alma mater, The Fat Duck, its menu is light years away. Down-to-earth, historic British dishes might include oxtail and kidney pudding, pea and ham soup or strawberry trifle, and although they might sound simple, these dishes have been carefully researched and redesigned to deliver the perfect balance of texture and flavour, as well as being beautifully presented. This is a proper pub and, as such, is often busy with drinkers; the bar is the most atmospheric place to sit, although they don't take bookings here. Staff are a real asset: friendly, engaging and efficient.

High St,
BRAY, SL6 2AB
Tel.: 01628 626151
Website: www.hindsheadbray.com

1.75 mi south of Maidenhead by A 308. Parking opposite the pub.

PRICES
Meals: £ 48 and a la carte £ 34/51

MAP: 2

CLOSING TIMES
Closed 25 December and Sunday dinner
booking essential

ROYAL OAK

Immensely satisfying, seasonal food

Nick Parkinson is your host and his ability to put guests at ease is clearly one family trait he's inherited from his father, Sir Michael. The Royal Oak's characterful front bar is a great spot for a drink, while the rest of the beamed room and extension are given over to dining. The menu champions all things seasonal, with top quality ingredients used to create impeccably presented, flavourful dishes like wild Berkshire rabbit haché with confit egg yolk and grain mustard sauce or navarin of Cornish spring lamb with carrots, turnips and peas. Discreet, formal service provides a sense of occasion and the garden, with its elegantly manicured herb maze and water feature, is a tranquil spot in which to enjoy a pre or post-dinner drink.

Paley Street,
BRAY, SL6 3JN
Tel.: 01628 620541
Website: www.theroyaloakpaleystreet.com

3.5 mi southwest of Bray by A 308, A 330 and B 3024. Parking.

PRICES   MAP: **3**
Meals: £ 30 (lunch) and a la carte £ 29/46

CLOSING TIMES
Closed Sunday dinner

CROWN

Refined cooking with clearly defined flavours

The Crown sits in a pretty village opposite a 300 year old oak tree and is very passionately run by the Bonwick family; dad takes charge in the kitchen, while the children keep things running smoothly in the small bar and two intimate, open-fired dining rooms. The warm bread rolls are delicious and the six deftly prepared starters, main courses and desserts are decided upon daily; the options are diverse and all are equally appealing and flavoursome – you could find anything from spiced pot-roasted pig cheek to honey-smoked trout with beetroot and horseradish grown in their garden. The experienced chef-owner takes his cooking seriously, so much so that he closes the pub on a Monday in order to go to the market and visit his suppliers personally.

BURCHETT'S GREEN,
SL6 6QZ
Tel.: 01628 824079
Website: www.thecrownburchettsgreen.com

4 mi west of Maidenhead by A 4, A 404 and Burchett's Green Rd. Parking.

PRICES   **MAP: 4**
Meals: a la carte £ 20/30

CLOSING TIMES
Closed first 2 weeks August, Sunday
dinner, Wednesday lunch, Monday and
Tuesday

CRAB & BOAR

Stylish bedrooms – some with hot tubs

This pretty part-17C inn sits just off the M4 and is the ideal stop-off point on a long journey – or a short one for that matter. It comes complete with a thatch and red tile roof, leaded windows and a lovely sunny terrace; look out for the carved blue boar from Ripley Castle, which Oliver Cromwell presented to the pub in 1644 following a very comfy night's stay. Inside, original brickwork, exposed timbers and flagged floors are offset by modern colours and studded leather banquettes. British dishes are rooted in tradition yet have a modern edge; go for one of the game or seafood specials. Grill dishes are a hit, Sunday lunch is an event and the Garden Kitchen offers pizzas and burgers outside. Many of the stylish bedrooms have hot tubs.

Wantage Rd,
CHIEVELEY, RG20 8UE
Tel.: 01635 247550
Website: www.crabandboar.com

5 mi northwest of Newbury on B 4494. Parking.

PRICES
Meals: a la carte £ 26/45

 14 rooms:
£ 110/210

MAP: 5

CLOSING TIMES
Open daily

WHITE OAK

Great value 'Menu Auberge'

Trifle – now there's a pud you want to see in a pub. Okay, so it's had a little makeover here because it comes with lavender custard and crushed meringue, but it shows that this is a pub with an inherent understanding of what its customers want. There are Aubrey Allen's finest steaks, plenty of Cornish fish, classics like shepherd's pie and other choices with more European credentials such as duck confit – all prepared with care and understanding. Look out too for the 'Menu Auberge' – a great value daily menu. One could argue about whether this is a contemporary pub or a pubby restaurant, as it's set up quite formally, but what is in no doubt is the warmth of the welcome and the affection in which the place is held by its many regulars.

Pound Ln,
COOKHAM, SL6 9QE
Tel.: 01628 523043
Website: www.thewhiteoak.co.uk

Across the common. Parking.

PRICES
Meals: £ 15/19 and a la carte £ 21/37

MAP: 6

CLOSING TIMES
Closed Sunday dinner

POT KILN

Gutsy portions in prime game country

Part of the old brickworks, The Pot Kiln originally provided refreshment for the workers digging clay from the surrounding fields. Head for the cosy bar and order a pint of Mr Chubb's or Brick Kiln beer – from the West Berkshire Brewery, which started up in their grounds – then follow the deliciously tempting aromas through to the dining area, where flavoursome British dishes arrive in unashamedly gutsy portions. Cooking is honest and straightforward and many of the vegetables come from their own garden; be sure to keep an eye out for the daily specials board. In summer come on a Sunday evening for an authentic pizza cooked in their outdoor pizza oven – where else can you have a 'Game Feast' comprising venison, pigeon and black pudding?

FRILSHAM, RG18 0XX
Tel.: 01635 201366
Website: www.potkiln.org

6 mi northeast of Newbury by B 4009 to Hermitage and minor road. Parking.

PRICES
Meals: a la carte £ 28/42

MAP: 7

CLOSING TIMES
Closed 25 December

BELGIAN ARMS

Pretty 17C inn by the village pond

This pretty 17C wisteria-clad inn is tucked away by a pond fringed with weeping willows, just off the village green, and there can be few settings more appealing than this. On warmer days, head for the terrace but if it's raining, fear not, as there's always the conservatory instead. The owners, one of whom is Nick Parkinson, have opened up the old interior and decorated it with photos of cricket and football, as well as Nick's father – Sir Michael – with his celebrated interviewees. There's no standing on ceremony here though, as this proud local has gutsy pub dishes on its menu and always plenty of events going on, from cribbage and cricket matches to barbeques, hog roasts and summer parties complete with face painting and live bands.

Holyport St,
HOLYPORT, SL6 2JR
Tel.: 01628 634468
Website: www.thebelgianarms.com

2.5 mi south of Maidenhead by A 308, just off the village green behind the telephone box. Parking.

PRICES
Meals: a la carte £ 28/39

MAP: **8**

CLOSING TIMES
Closed Monday

THE NEWBURY

Trendy pub with a lively buzz

Behind this high street pub's traditional façade lies a relaxed and trendy space. Beams, exposed bricks and flagged floors provide the requisite character for a pub of its age, while the eclectic range of art on the walls gives the place a funky, up-to-date feel. The sofas by the wood burner in the bar are a popular spot, although most people head to the dining area; if you sit on the small terrace out the back you'll share it with smokers as well as the pub's smokery. The menu offers everything from fish and chips to more interesting dishes like beetroot ravioli with goat's cheese or roasted turbot with salsa verde – or you can head upstairs for pizza fresh from the oven. There's an experienced team in charge and a lively buzz when it's busy.

137 Bartholomew St,
NEWBURY, RG14 5HB
Tel.: 01635 49000
Website: www.thenewburypub.co.uk

On the western side of the Kennett Shopping Centre.
Parking at shopping centre car park.

PRICES   MAP: **9**
Meals: a la carte £ 24/40

CLOSING TIMES
Open daily

BULL INN

Enjoy the local 'beer tapas' under 15C beams

Locals and their dogs gather beside the fire in the rustic, quarry-tiled bar of this beamed 15C inn, while those wishing to eat head for the dining rooms, with their dramatic red and silver stag antler wallpaper and trio of twinkling chandeliers. The experienced chef-owner knows what people want, so while the blackboard bar menu focuses on pub-style dishes like burgers or fish and chips, the main menu offers choices such as calves' liver, steamed hake or braised pork cheeks. There's a good range of wines, and the 'beer tapas' – which allows you to sample three of the local ales in small glasses – is a nice touch. The spacious garden plays host to alfresco diners, chickens and the annual village dog show, while bedrooms are cosy and great value.

Cock Ln,
STANFORD DINGLEY, RG7 6LS
Tel.: 0118 974 4582
Website: www.thebullinnstanforddingley.co.uk

Midway between Newbury and Theale by A 4 and Chapel Row Rd. Parking.

PRICES
Meals: a la carte £ 24/49

5 rooms:
£ 70/80

MAP: 10

CLOSING TIMES
Open daily

BEEHIVE

The specials are always a good bet

Having spent nearly nine years at the stoves of the Royal Oak in nearby Bray, Dominic Chapman decided that it was time to buy his own place and took the plunge with this traditional English pub overlooking the village cricket pitch. Although it's had a slight facelift, pleasingly, it remains a proper pub, with local drinkers in the bar and a comfy, light-filled dining room. The classically based, seasonal menu changes daily and the refined, eye-catching dishes are full of flavour and exhibit a staunch sense of Britishness. Start with a few tasty snacks like rollmops or a crunchy-crumbed, richly runny scotch egg, before moving on to dishes such as Old Spot pork and chicken liver terrine, rabbit and bacon pie or apple and rhubarb crumble.

Waltham Rd,
WHITE WALTHAM, SL6 3SH
Tel.: 01628 822877
Website: www.thebeehivewhitewaltham.com

Follow signs for Cox Green off A 404 (M). Parking.

PRICES
Meals: a la carte £ 27/45

MAP: 11

CLOSING TIMES
Closed Sunday dinner

GREENE OAK

Head for the smart sun-trap terrace

The owners of the Greene Oak call it a 'country pub and eating house' and this pretty much sums it up. It's set close the racecourse and has a subtle green interior and a rather smart sun-trap terrace. An experienced team prepare modern menus which are more akin to those of a bistro than a pub, and refined dishes show a good level of technical skill and understanding – textures and flavours are well-balanced and portions are satisfying. You might find the likes of goat's cheese mousse with pickled beetroot, hazelnut and praline crumb, followed by canon of lamb with shoulder croquette and smoked aubergine purée or an Aubrey Allen dry-aged chateaubriand steak for two. The wine list is easy to navigate and keeps prices firmly in check.

Oakley Green,
WINDSOR, SL4 5UW
Tel.: 01753 864294
Website: www.thegreeneoak.co.uk

On the western side of Windsor on B 3024 Dedworth Rd. Parking.

PRICES
Meals: a la carte £ 26/49

MAP: 12

CLOSING TIMES
Closed Sunday dinner

ROYAL OAK

A popular haunt for shooting parties

Bursting with country charm, The Royal Oak manages to pull off the tricky feat of being both a true locals pub and a popular destination for foodies. While the picture perfect village and its proximity to the M4 could account in part for the pub's attraction to visitors, it's the cooking which really gets them travelling here from a distance. Honest British dishes might include chicken livers on toast, salmon en croute or lamb and rosemary pie, with traditional puddings like cheesecake or fruit crumble to follow. The heavily beamed bar with its blazing log fires is the oldest and most characterful part of the pub and is where the action tends to happen. Country house style bedrooms are named after guns and even have their own gun cabinets.

The Square,
YATTENDON, RG18 0UF
Tel.: 01635 201325
Website: www.royaloakyattendon.co.uk

6 mi northeast of Newbury by B 4009 and minor road; in the village centre. Parking opposite and in village car park.

PRICES
Meals: £ 15 (weekday lunch) and a la carte £ 26/47

 10 rooms:
£ 95/135

MAP: 13

CLOSING TIMES
Open daily
booking advisable

THE HUNDRED OF ASHENDON

Great value dishes packed full of flavour

Back in Saxon times, shires were divided into 'hundreds' for military and judicial purposes, with each hundred comprising 100 households. This charming 17C inn is keeping this concept alive by sourcing its produce from within its 'hundred' and firmly focusing on the local community. The chef-owner, Matt, is a local lad but has spent time at London's St John – an influence which can be seen in his cooking. With its simple descriptions, the menu gives little away but you can rest assured that the great value dishes will arrive packed full of flavour, in hearty portions. Expect terrines and brandades to be followed by chops, steaks and guinea fowl, with fools and steamed puddings for dessert. The modest bedrooms are continually being upgraded.

Lower End,
ASHENDON, HP18 0HE
Tel.: 01296 651296
Website: www.thehundred.co.uk

4.75 mi southwest of Waddesdon by A41. Parking.

PRICES
Meals: £ 14 (weekday lunch) and a la carte
£ 24/35

 5 rooms:
£ 55/100

MAP: 14

CLOSING TIMES
Closed 25 December, Sunday dinner and Monday

GARIBALDI

Friendly, engaging service and local ales

This 17C inn is named after the famous Italian General Giuseppi Garibaldi, who fought for the unification of Italy and apparently once visited here. It's actually rather a good name, as unification also comes in the form of its owners – 46 shareholders from the local area, who banded together to keep their village local alive. In order to keep things running smoothly they have recruited Chris and Amanda, the experienced owners of the Cricketers at Seer Green, who have stuck to the village pub ethos by keeping the surroundings homely and the mood relaxed. Cooking is classically based and includes the likes of slow-cooked beef shin or fish and chips with scraps; Monday is seasonal pie night and on Tuesdays it's Cornish mussels and fries.

Hedsor Rd,
BOURNE END, BEACONSFIELD, SL8 5EE
Tel.: 01628 522092
Website: www.garibaldipub.co.uk

3 mi southwest of Beaconsfield by A 40 and B 4440 off A 4094. Parking.

PRICES
Meals: a la carte £ 22/35

MAP: 15

CLOSING TIMES
Closed 26 December

POINTER

The Great Train Robbery was planned here!

The butcher's shop at the side of this 18C inn sells meats from their 240 acre farm, where they raise their own rare breeds, and the rosettes displayed around the pub were won by their livestock at various shows. Sit in one of two beamed dining rooms or beside the fire in one of the smaller rooms and take time to read the menu, which explains what they are currently growing in the gardens and what is being used in the cooking (around 70 different organic ingredients throughout the year). Bread arrives in a paper bag and is followed by classic dishes such veal shin pie in puff pastry or duck breast with Anna potatoes, and if there's suckling pig, then it's decision made! It's worth checking the blackboards for their snacks and specials too.

27 Church St,
BRILL, HP18 9RT
Tel.: 01844 238339
Website: www.thepointerbrill.co.uk

6 mi northwest of Thame by B 4011. Parking around the village.

PRICES

MAP: 16

Meals: £ 18 (lunch) and a la carte £ 26/59

CLOSING TIMES

Closed first week January and Monday

RUSSELL ARMS

Flavoursome cooking has simplicity as its key

This pretty, laid-back inn started life in 1784 as the Golden Cross but was later renamed after the owners of the estate. You'll find walkers relaxing over a pint at the tables to the side and a large terrace to the rear. Daily coffee mornings are followed by a great value lunchtime 'plat du jour' and on Friday afternoons they host children's tea parties. Cooking is traditionally based and packed with flavour and the chef knows how to get the best out of his ingredients. Start with tasty bread and cold-pressed local rapeseed oil then move on to mushrooms on toast or braised pork belly – and, if they're on the menu, be sure to give the mussels a try. Proper puddings such as apple tart or perry-poached pear finish things off perfectly.

2 Chalkshire Rd,
BUTLERS CROSS, HP17 0TS
Tel.: 01296 624411
Website: www.therussellarms.co.uk

5 mi southeast of Aylesbury by A 413 and A 4010. Parking.

PRICES   MAP: **17**
Meals: a la carte £ 25/34

CLOSING TIMES
Closed 25-26 December and Monday

SWAN INN

Head for the secluded garden

Close to the A40, M40 and M25 but in a secluded little world of its own, the Swan takes up prime position in this delightful village. The Georgian red-brick building is fronted by beautiful cascades of wisteria and framed by manicured trees and there's a secluded terrace and garden to the rear; while beamed ceilings and open fires lend it a rustic air. Menus change with the seasons but their bubble & squeak and 28-day aged rib-eye steak are mainstays. Dishes are fresh and unfussy and might include confit duck with nutmeg boxty potato or fillet of hake with capers and cherry tomato, with appealing sides such as courgette fries with maple yoghurt and comforting puds like treacle and lemon sponge with fresh raspberries and vanilla custard.

Village Rd,
DENHAM, UB9 5BH
Tel.: 01895 832085
Website: www.swaninndenham.co.uk

6 mi northeast of Slough by A 412; in the centre of the village.
Small car park.

PRICES

MAP: 18

Meals: a la carte £ 23/43

CLOSING TIMES
Open daily
booking essential

BLACK HORSE

Hide in a cosy alcove or head for the terrace

Originally a lodging house for the builders of the next door church – which dates from 1610 – this whitewashed village pub is the perfect place for a pint and a meal. It's got thick walls and cosy alcoves, a wood-burning stove, a large front terrace and a gem of a garden for sunny days. The main dining area may feel quite formal and stylish, with its banquette seats and delightful portraits, but the down-to-earth staff are only too eager to help guide you through the menu. Sharing boards are a popular choice, starters might include sticky pork ribs or a hot smoked salmon fishcake, while mains could mean a steak, pork belly or a nice plump Dover sole. Uniquely styled bedrooms have spacious, modern bathrooms and Nespresso coffee machines.

Windmill Rd,
FULMER, SL3 6HD
Tel.: 01753 663183
Website: www.theblackhorsefulmer.co.uk

2 mi south of Gerrards Cross in centre of village beside St James church. Parking.

PRICES
Meals: a la carte £ 26/43

 2 rooms:
£ 120/150

MAP: 19

CLOSING TIMES
Closed 25 December and Sunday dinner

A pinch of excellence

NESPRESSO®
What else?

THREE OAKS

Great value set lunch and dinner menus

Turning into the car park and seeing all those smart cars makes you immediately aware that this isn't going to be your typical village local. Sharing the same owner as the White Oak in Cookham, this pub attracts the local 'chic' set. There's a choice of six rooms – go for the brighter one at the back as it looks out over the colourful garden where they grow their own veg and herbs. The menu changes often but keeps things British, so expect the likes of home-cured salmon, ham hock terrine, suckling pig and sticky toffee pudding. The set lunch and dinner menus offer particularly good value, they have a Steak Club every Monday with modest corkage on the BYO and enthusiastic service comes courtesy of local boys and girls dressed in black.

Austenwood Ln,
GERRARDS CROSS, SL9 8NL
Tel.: 01753 899016
Website: www.thethreeoaksgx.co.uk

0.75 mi northwest of the town by A 413 following signs for Gold Hill. Parking.

PRICES   MAP: **20**
Meals: £ 12/19 and a la carte £ 23/36

CLOSING TIMES
Closed Sunday dinner

NAGS HEAD

An original mix of French and British dishes

This traditional 15C inn is run by the same team behind the Bricklayers Arms in Flaunden and is proving just as popular, so be sure to book ahead, especially at weekends. It has been made over, yet retains a wealth of original features: the two main dining areas have thick brick walls and exposed oak beams, while an extra helping of rusticity comes courtesy of the inglenook fireplace. Original menus mix Gallic charm with British classics, so you'll find things like foie gras or mushroom feuilletté alongside eggs Benedict or sausage and mash; food is flavourful and service, cheerful and keen. Stylish modern bedrooms provide a comfortable night's sleep – number one is the best – and the tasty breakfasts ensure you leave satiated in the morning.

London Rd,
GREAT MISSENDEN, HP16 0DG
Tel.: 01494 862200
Website: www.nagsheadbucks.com

1 mi southeast by A 413 turning at Chiltern Hospital. Parking.

PRICES
Meals: £ 17 (weekdays) and a la carte
£ 26/49

 6 rooms:
£ 75/115

MAP: 21

CLOSING TIMES
Closed 25 December

QUEENS HEAD

Produce comes from local farms, forages and shoots

Head towards Little Marlow's 12C church and, tucked away down a lane opposite the village's restored cattle pound, you'll find this popular pub, with its keen owner and friendly staff. It was once a spit and sawdust sort of place; its snug bar used to be a salting room and its priest hole now makes it a popular place for filming. The garden gets into full swing during the summer months when hungry walkers gather to refuel. The light lunch menu offers a quick fix with sandwiches, ploughman's and pub classics, while the à la carte has something for everyone, from pigeon and duck liver terrine to venison Wellington, with desserts like carrot cake or crème brûlée. Menus change every few weeks and produce is from local farms, forages and shoots.

Pound Ln,
LITTLE MARLOW, SL7 3SR
Tel.: 01628 482927
Website: www.marlowslittlesecret.co.uk

3 mi east of Marlow on A 4155 by Church Rd. Parking.

PRICES
Meals: a la carte £ 25/39

MAP: 22

CLOSING TIMES
Closed 25-26 December

MOLE & CHICKEN

The garden has commanding country views

If you are struggling to get your bearings, look to the rooftops for the weather vane depicting a mole and a chicken. This remote pub was built in 1831 as part of the local farm workers' estate and later took on the role of village store. The interior is charming, with low wonky ceilings, open fires, elegant prints and two squashy sofas, but the biggest draw is the large garden, which offers commanding views over the surrounding counties. The menu features classic British dishes such as rump of local lamb or braised ox cheek, with heartwarming desserts like apple and blackberry crumble or sticky toffee pudding. Staff are friendly, the pub is understandably busy and there are five cosy, welcoming bedrooms in the adjoining house.

Easington,
LONG CRENDON, HP18 8EY
Tel.: 01844 208387
Website: www.themoleandchicken.co.uk

3 mi north of Thame by B 4011. Parking.

PRICES
Meals: a la carte £ 24/37

 5 rooms:
£ 95/125

MAP: 23

CLOSING TIMES
Closed 25 December

THE COACH

Rotisserie dishes are a speciality

The success of the Hand and Flowers means that Tom Kerridge's local guests often find it hard to get a table. His solution to the problem? Opening another great pub just down the road! It's been a hit from the start and understandably so, with its casual modern approach to dining; bookings aren't taken, so simply turn up and grab a table or a seat at the zinc-topped bar. Menus have an equally laid-back approach, with no starters or main courses, just a list of flavoursome 'Meat' and 'No Meat' dishes that arrive as they're ready and are designed for sharing – maybe venison chilli with toasted rice cream, black olive glazed neck of lamb or a speciality rotisserie dish. Start your day with a tasty breakfast or come later on for coffee and cake.

3 West St,
MARLOW, SL7 2LS
Website: www.thecoachmarlow.co.uk

On A 4155 in town centre. Pay and display parking nearby.

PRICES
Meals: a la carte £ 17/35

MAP: 24

CLOSING TIMES
Closed 25 December
bookings not accepted

HAND AND FLOWERS

High calibre cooking from a passionate chef

Many must have driven past this pretty little pub on the edge of Marlow unaware of the dedication and passion of its tenants and the calibre of the cooking. It's very much a pub, with low beams, flagged floors and a characterful lounge bar for pre and post-dinner drinks, and in keeping with this appealingly informal environment, the dishes are classical and far from pretentious. There's plenty of choice – from a glazed omelette of smoked haddock and parmesan to the popular duck breast with duck fat chips and gravy – and quality ingredients marry perfectly to turn the simple into the sublime. A few lucky souls get to eat without booking at the metal-topped bar counter; make a night of it by staying in one of the beautifully furnished bedrooms.

126 West St.,
MARLOW, SL7 2BP
Tel.: 01628 482277
Website: www.thehandandflowers.co.uk

On the western side of the town on A 4155. Parking.

PRICES
Meals: £ 20 (weekday lunch) and a la carte
£ 48/66

 8 rooms:
£ 140/190

MAP: 25

CLOSING TIMES
Closed 24-26 December
booking essential

ROYAL OAK

A popular pub with a peaceful garden

Set less than 15 minutes from the M40 and M4, this part-17C pub is the ideal escape from the busy streets of London. As you approach, pleasant scents drift up from the herb garden, gentle 'chinks' emanate from the petanque pitch and the world feels at once more peaceful. While away the warmer days on the terrace or snuggle into pretty cushions beside the wood burning stove in winter, where rich fabrics and heritage colours provide a country-chic feel, and freshly cut flowers decorate the room. Not surprisingly, it's extremely popular and the eager team are often stretched to their limit. Cooking is British-led; you might find a slow-cooked ox cheek pasty or pork chops with salt and pepper squid. Wash these down with a pint of local Rebellion ale.

Frieth Rd,
BOVINGDON GREEN, MARLOW, SL7 2JF
Tel.: 01628 488611
Website: www.royaloakmarlow.co.uk

1.25 mi west of Marlow by A 4155 and Bovingdon Green rd. Parking.

PRICES
Meals: a la carte £ 22/42

MAP: **26**

CLOSING TIMES
Closed 25-26 December

CROOKED BILLET

A charming 17C former farmhouse

This charming 17C thatched building is the last place you expect to come across as you drive around the outskirts of Milton Keynes. It was built in the 1600s using wood from an old sailing ship and started life as a farmhouse, which also provided refreshment for farmers on their way to and from work. In the 20C it evolved solely into a pub and, during the village festival, stalls and games were set up in the large garden. The same kind of community spirit remains today: they host beer festivals, comedy nights and summer BBQs, and more often than not, you'll find a cheery bunch of locals propping up the bar. Choose between pub classics on the bar menu or more modern dishes on the à la carte; the tasty meat and fish sharing platters are a hit.

2 Westbrook End,
NEWTON LONGVILLE, MK17 0DF
Tel.: 01908 373936
Website: www.thecrookedbilletmiltonkeynes.co.uk

6 mi southwest of Milton Keynes by A 421. Parking.

PRICES   MAP: **27**
Meals: a la carte £ 24/45

CLOSING TIMES
Open daily

OLD QUEENS HEAD

Turn left to sit in the characterful former barn

This pub may not be quite as old as the ancient beech woodlands that surround it but it does have a part to play in the area's history. Legend has it that Lord Penn inherited the pub when he won a game of cards against Charles II. Whether this is true or not, no one knows, but it can be proved from the 1666 deeds that it was purchased by one of the King's physicians. Find a spot on the paved terrace or take in the view from the old barn – now the dining room; the surrounding rooms may be slightly newer but they continue the rustic theme. Choose from a selection of 'small' and 'big' plates, many of which are influenced by the Med; start, perhaps, with a pork and sage scotch duck egg and follow it up with a chicken, chorizo and prawn paella.

Hammersley Ln,
PENN, HP10 8EY
Tel.: 01494 813371
Website: www.oldqueensheadpenn.co.uk

4 mi northwest of junction 2 of M 40, via Beaconsfield and B 474. Parking.

PRICES

Meals: a la carte £ 23/39

MAP: 28

CLOSING TIMES

Open daily

JOLLY CRICKETERS

Packed with cricketing memorabilia

Somehow it's hard to imagine a pub called The Jolly Footballers. Indeed, no sport does nostalgia or evokes a spirit of bonhomie quite like cricket and this charming Victorian pub certainly does its bit for the gentleman's game: there's memorabilia aplenty, including signed cricket bats and Test Match programmes, and even the menu comes divided into 'Openers, Main Play and Sticky Wicket'. But this is also a pub where people come to eat. The kitchen nicely balances classic dishes with more modern choices, so seasonal asparagus could be followed by Moroccan-spiced monkfish, then for dessert, a satisfyingly filling fruit crumble. This really is a place that brings the local community together and the live music sessions on Sundays are a hit

24 Chalfont Rd,
SEER GREEN, HP9 2YG
Tel.: 01494 676308
Website: www.thejollycricketers.co.uk

2.5 mi northeast of Beaconsfield off A 355. Parking.

PRICES   MAP: **29**
Meals: a la carte £ 25/41

CLOSING TIMES
Closed Sunday dinner
booking advisable

GINGER DOG

Cosy pub with a welcoming atmosphere

The furnishings of this charming Victorian pub are pleasingly shabby-chic and the atmosphere is suitably laid-back. As well as the canine references, keep an eye out for its original features – such as the ornately carved woodwork – which sit comfortably alongside more recent additions like the bowler hat lampshades. When it comes to the cooking, this also isn't your typical pub. Menus have a modern British style and the chef isn't afraid to use the latest techniques, so your pie might come with chicken that was hay-smoked on site and your grilled rib-eye steak could be accompanied by walnut butter and pickled mustard seed. Satisfyingly, bread and water arrive free of charge and to finish, their dessert cocktails are definitely worth a try.

12 College Pl,
BRIGHTON AND HOVE, BN2 1HN
Tel.: 01273 620990
Website: www.gingermanrestaurants.com

In heart of Kemp Town, just off Marine Parade (A 259) towards Lewes. Metered parking nearby.

PRICES
Meals: £ 13 (weekdays) and a la carte
£ 26/40

MAP: **30**

CLOSING TIMES
Closed 25 December

GINGER PIG

British dishes by the sea

Set just off the seafront, this smart building displays a mortar relief of a ship above the entrance and a beautifully restored revolving door, harking back to its former days as the Ship Inn. Its Victorian vintage is also evident in its appealing dining room and its long, wood-floored bar: the perfect setting for a cocktail or two. The extensive à la carte offers precisely prepared, flavoursome British dishes – including plenty of vegetarian options – and there's a great value set lunch menu, along with some good wine deals; order a coffee and it'll arrive with a quirky pig-shaped shortbread. They're used to being busy and service copes reasonably well under pressure, the only drawback being that it can lack a more personal touch.

3 Hove St,
HOVE, BRIGHTON AND HOVE, BN3 2TR
Tel.: 01273 736123
Website: www.gingermanrestaurants.com

Off north side of Shore Rd, Kingsway, A 259. NCP car park (2min walk) & parking meters (2hr maximum during day).

PRICES
Meals: £ 18 (weekdays) and a la carte
£ 23/44

MAP: 31

CLOSING TIMES
Closed 25 December

JOLLY SPORTSMAN

Unusual bar bites & continually evolving specials

Set in a small hamlet, down a myriad of country lanes, is this olive green pub which attracts the locals in their droves. You're greeted by a bubbly team, often even by the owner himself, along with smoky aromas from an open fire. Choose a spot in the cosy bar, the warmly decorated red room or the garden room – where concertina doors open onto a large terrace – and prepare for just as much choice when it comes to the food. There's interesting bar bites such as boquerones (anchovies) and cabezada (cured pork loin), a rustic British-based à la carte, a good value set menu, and blackboard specials which quickly come and go. Real ales are dispensed from the barrels behind the bar and there are plenty of wines, ciders and perries on offer too.

Chapel Ln,
EAST CHILTINGTON, BN7 3BA
Tel.: 01273 890400
Website: www.thejollysportsman.com

5.5 mi northwest of Lewes by A 275 and B 2116 off Novington Lane. Parking.

PRICES   MAP: **32**
Meals: £ 15 (weekday lunch) and a la carte
£ 28/41

CLOSING TIMES
Closed 25 December, Sunday dinner and Monday
booking essential

GRIFFIN INN

Wood-burning oven for summer barbecues

Under the same ownership for over 30 years, this hugely characterful red and white brick coaching inn is the kind of place that every village wishes it had. It boasts a linen-laid dining room, a traditional wood-panelled bar and a 'Club Room' adorned with cricketing memorabilia, as well as a sizeable garden and terrace – with a wood burning oven for sophisticated summer Sunday barbecues. A large freestanding blackboard in the bar offers a range of British classics with some Mediterranean influences, and there's a more structured à la carte available in the dining room. If you live locally, work it off by joining one of the pub's cricket teams; if not, follow narrow, sloping corridors to one of the individually decorated bedrooms.

FLETCHING, TN22 3SS
Tel.: 01825 722890
Website: www.thegriffininn.co.uk

In centre of village. Parking.

PRICES
Meals: a la carte £ 26/44

13 rooms:
£ 70/155

MAP: 33

CLOSING TIMES
Closed 25 December

BELL

Generous portions in a quirky 16C coaching inn

The lampshades are top hats, there are tubas in the loos and a pile of books appear to be holding up the beams: welcome to The Bell, a late 16C coaching inn which has been transformed into a quirky, shabby-chic pub with the emphasis firmly on the chic. There's a delightful snug, a bar with a vast inglenook fireplace and a dining room called 'The Stable with a Table', and the eleven rustic, individually styled bedrooms – many with their own silver birch tree – share the pub's idiosyncratic charm. Simple bar snacks might include Sussex smokies or a scotch egg, while the seasonal menus offer generous portions of proper pub food like the Bell burger alongside more adventurous dishes such as Dorset crab or pork belly with black pudding.

High St,
TICEHURST, TN5 7AS
Tel.: 01580 200234
Website: www.thebellinticehurst.com

In the centre of the village. Parking.

PRICES
Meals: a la carte £ 25/44

 11 rooms:
£ 150/295

MAP: 34

CLOSING TIMES
Open daily
booking advisable

WELLINGTON ARMS

They keep sheep, pigs, chickens and bees!

If success is dependent on the effort put into sourcing local produce and making, growing and rearing everything possible, then The Wellington is a sure-fire winner. They have herb and vegetable beds, they keep their own sheep, pigs, chickens and bees, and the rest of their meats are sourced from within 20 miles. Inside the cosy quarry-tiled, low-beamed bar you'll also find their eggs, honey and preserves for sale. Menus feature 6 dishes per course – supplemented by a selection of blackboard specials – and cooking is generous and satisfying. Dishes might include twice-baked Westcombe cheddar soufflé, venison pie or steak from the farm just over the fields. Smart, rustic bedrooms come with sheepskin rugs and big, comfy beds.

Baughurst Rd,
BAUGHURST, RG26 5LP
Tel.: 0118 982 0110
Website: www.thewellingtonarms.com

8 mi north of Basingstoke by A 339 and minor road through Ramsdell and Pound Green, on the Kingsclere / Newbury rd. Parking.

PRICES
Meals: £ 16 (weekday lunch) and a la carte
£ 22/46

 4 rooms:
£ 100/200

MAP: 35

CLOSING TIMES
Closed Sunday dinner
booking essential

BAKERS ARMS

Cosy pub serving classical fare

This traditional building houses not just a pub but also the village post office, so if you're popping in to post a letter you may well be tempted to stay for a pint or two from the nearby brewery. It's a small, cosy kind of a place with wooden beams, exposed bricks and an open fire, and whether you've come for lunch or dinner you'll find plenty of regular diners. Cooking keeps things simple and classical with the likes of pie of the day or sausage and mash, alongside maybe snails in garlic butter or trout with beetroot and horseradish. Be sure to start with some homemade bread and finish with either apple and blackberry crumble or bread and butter pudding. The midweek menu is good value and offers two courses and a glass of wine for £15.

High St,
DROXFORD, SO32 3PA
Tel.: 01489 877533
Website: www.thebakersarmsdroxford.com

6 mi north of Fareham by A 32. Parking.

PRICES   MAP: **36**
Meals: £ 15 (weekdays) and a la carte
£ 25/35

CLOSING TIMES
Closed Sunday dinner

SUN INN

Good value cooking from a young chef

From the outside, the Sun Inn doesn't look like it's got much going for it – its location on the A30 isn't ideal and it's not a particularly pretty place, but all of that pales into insignificance when you try the food. The atmosphere is suitably relaxed and you can eat anything, anywhere – whether that's sitting at a table in the dining room or on a sofa by the wood-burning stove in the bar. The young chef prepares the usual pub classics, but alongside these you'll find some more ambitious modern dishes like poached plaice with caper purée and lemon gel or slow-cooked pork belly with apricot granola and red wine jus. Good ingredients are carefully and passionately prepared and dishes are well-balanced, interesting and tasty.

Winchester Rd,
DUMMER, RG25 2DJ
Tel.: 01256 397234
Website: www.suninndummer.com

7.5 mi southwest of Basingstoke on A 30. Parking.

PRICES
Meals: a la carte £ 22/40

MAP: **37**

CLOSING TIMES
Closed 25 December and dinner
26 December, 1 January and Sunday

EAST END ARMS

Owned by John Illsley from Dire Straits

This traditional country pub is owned by John Illsley, bass guitarist of Dire Straits, and it boasts a great display of black and white photos of legendary singers, musicians and celebrities from his personal collection. When he bought the place in the late 1990s, the locals petitioned for him to keep it the same, so you'll find a slightly shabby bar with cushioned pews, an open fire and a dartboard, along with a smarter pine-furnished dining room behind. Menus are fairly concise and feature local produce in satisfying British-based dishes; you might find escabeche of mackerel, seared scallops with black pudding or local saddle of venison. Modern cottage-style bedrooms provide a smart contrast and staff are friendly and attentive.

Lymington Rd,
EAST END, SO41 5SY
Tel.: 01590 626223
Website: www.eastendarms.co.uk

3 mi east of Lymington by B 3054. Parking.

PRICES
Meals: a la carte £ 24/42

 5 rooms:
£ 85/130

MAP: 38

CLOSING TIMES
Closed dinner Sunday

BUGLE

Rustic and cosy with river views

Set in a charming spot in a quaint little village, this Grade II listed building is owned by a keen seafarer and is popular with the sailing community. With its exposed bricks and well-worn stone floors, it has a rustic, cosy feel; there's an abundance of maritime character and a private dining room with a lovely Dickensian feel, not forgetting a busy terrace with pleasant views over the River Hamble. The blackboard lists a mix of small plates and pub classics and there's a good value midweek set menu but it's the main menu that provides the most interest: choose from the likes of sea bass with chorizo, mushroom and spinach risotto or shoulder of lamb with braised carrots and mint broth. Regular quiz nights and sports events bring in the crowds.

High St,
HAMBLE-LE-RICE, SO31 4HA
Tel.: 023 8045 3000
Website: www.idealcollection.co.uk/buglehamble

7 mi southeast of Southampton by A 3024 or A 3025 and B 3397.
Pay and display parking nearby.

PRICES
Meals: £ 18 (weekday lunch) and a la carte
£ 22/36

MAP: **39**

CLOSING TIMES
Open daily
booking advisable

YEW TREE

Classic recipes are given modern twists

Just down the road from Highclere Castle – the setting for Downton Abbey – is this pretty 17C inn, where you have to stoop to enter into the rustic interior, with its low beamed ceilings and original flagstone floors. The bar with its leather sofas and roaring log fires is a great spot for a drink and a snack, while the three dining rooms with their flickering candles provide a more intimate atmosphere. The menu is divided into 'Small', 'Medium' and 'Large' dishes as well as 'The Usual Suspects' and classically based recipes are given modern twists – there are some interesting vegetarian options too. In summer, relax on the pretty rear terrace. If you fancy staying overnight, bedrooms are cosy, with good mod cons and smart wet rooms.

Hollington Cross,
ANDOVER RD, HIGHCLERE, RG20 9SE
Tel.: 01635 253360
Website: www.theyewtree.co.uk

5 mi south of Newbury on A 343. Parking.

PRICES
Meals: a la carte £ 24/49

 8 rooms:
£ 95/130

MAP: 40

CLOSING TIMES
Open daily

RUNNING HORSE

Book the cosy cabana!

You won't miss this smart, grey-painted pub: just look out for the horse running along the side and the straw-roofed cabana at the front (it's heated, very cosy and can be booked!) Sit near the log burner to the front of the shabby-chic, wood panelled bar or, for a more intimate meal, head to the rear dining area with its shelves of antique books. The menu is concise and constantly evolving and dishes are well-priced, fuss-free and big on flavour. Sharing platters include vegetarian, charcuterie and seafood options; other dishes might include home-cured gravadlax, duck liver parfait or omelette Arnold Bennett. Service is pleasingly unpretentious and the simply furnished bedrooms are arranged around the garden, motel-style.

88 Main Rd,
LITTLETON, SO22 6QS
Tel.: 01962 880218
Website: www.runninghorseinn.co.uk

2.5 mi northwest of Winchester, signed off B 3049. Parking.

PRICES
Meals: a la carte £ 23/35

 15 rooms:
£ 80/130

MAP: 41

CLOSING TIMES
Closed dinner 25 December

PEAT SPADE INN

Find a spot on the lovely terrace

In the heart of the Test Valley sits this attractive 19C inn owned by the Upham Brewery. It's popular with locals and their dogs as well as country pursuits enthusiasts and fishing has always been a focus here: they own rights on the nearby river and various fishing memorabilia adds to the cosy character of the place. When it comes to the food, you will find the requisite burger and fries and fish and chips but the core of the menu is made up of more interesting dishes such as heritage tomato salad with goat's cheese panna cotta or sea bream with dates and hazelnuts. Charming bedrooms are split between the inn and an old barn and are named after famous fishermen. In the evening, find a spot on the lovely terrace and cosy up beside the fire-pit.

Village Street,
LONGSTOCK, SO20 6DR
Tel.: 01264 810612
Website: www.peatspadeinn.co.uk

1.5 mi north of Stockbridge on A 3507. Parking.

PRICES
Meals: a la carte £ 26/43

 8 rooms:
£ 110/145

MAP: 42

CLOSING TIMES
Open daily

WHITE HART

Owned by the local Upham Brewery

Since the 18C, Overton has become known as a manufacturer of banknote paper and Overton Mill still produces banknotes today. Thankfully cost needn't be a consideration at the White Hart, as prices are kept in check to cater for the locals. Menus offer something for one and all, from a traditional chicken and mushroom pie or Punter beer-battered fish and chips through to more adventurous scallops thermidor or rack of lamb for two with thyme and goat's cheese croquettes. The lounge has a wood-burning stove in its original stone fireplace and the dining room has retained its characterful wood panelling and parquet floor, but there's now also a more modern extension for dining, an attractive rear terrace and 12 cosy boutique-style bedrooms.

London Rd,
OVERTON, RG25 3NW
Tel.: 01256 771431
Website: www.whitehartoverton.co.uk

8 mi west of Basingstoke on B 3400. Parking.

PRICES
Meals: a la carte £ 20/38

12 rooms:
£ 85/150

MAP: 43

CLOSING TIMES
Open daily

THREE TUNS

A cosy Grade II listed pub with 18C origins

After a stroll around the Norman Abbey or along the River Test, make for this cosy 300 year old building off the market square. It has a Grade II listing and its original features include exposed oak beams and a central wood bar which divides the place in two: head to the right if you're here for a drink or to the left if you're looking to dine. Cooking keeps things in the classic pub vein and dishes are generously proportioned and full of flavour: you might find a ham hock and cheddar ploughman's, a beef and bacon burger with chilli relish or a pie 'of the day' with mash, seasonal vegetables and gravy. Those only after a quick snack can choose from the likes of pork crackling with apple sauce or breaded whitebait with devilled mayonnaise.

58 Middlebridge St,
ROMSEY, SO51 8HL
Tel.: 01794 512639
Website: www.the3tunsromsey.co.uk

Towards the western end of the town, off the bypass. Parking.

PRICES
Meals: a la carte £ 23/31

MAP: **44**

CLOSING TIMES
Closed 25-26 December

ENGLAND • South East • Hampshire

WHITE STAR TAVERN, DINING AND ROOMS

All-day dining in the lively maritime district

You can't miss this striking black pub with its oversized windows and smart pavement terrace. Set in the lively maritime district, it's provided nourishment and shelter for seafarers since the 19C, although you'll find a much more diverse mix of visitors nowadays. It's a spacious place, made up of several different areas organised around a central bar, and displays an eclectic combination of furniture. The à la carte offers a good choice of modern British main courses – finished off with proper old-fashioned puddings – but there's also a selection of small plates on offer throughout the day; and they even open early for breakfast. Stylish, very comfortable bedrooms offer excellent facilities and are named after legendary yachts and liners.

28 Oxford St,
SOUTHAMPTON, SO14 3DJ
Tel.: 023 8082 1990
Website: www.whitestartavern.co.uk

Southeast of West Quay shopping centre, off Bernard Street.
Parking meters directly outside and College St car park (2min walk).

PRICES
Meals: £ 16 (lunch) and a la carte £ 23/43

 16 rooms:
£ 80/135

MAP: 45

CLOSING TIMES
Open daily

GREYHOUND ON THE TEST

Characterful pub with a mile of fishing rights

If ever there were a place close to J.R.Hartley's heart, it would have been Stockbridge: the River Test flows under the High Street and the oldest fishing club in England was founded here in 1882. This mustard-coloured pub plays its part too – head for the garden and you'll find over a mile of River Test fishing rights. At over 600 years old, it has plenty of character: low beams and wood burning stoves abound and the elegant décor gives it a French bistro feel. When it comes to the food, there's plenty to choose from, including a selection 'on toast', some modern small plates and a more classical daily menu; local game and seafood are a feature, and the chef will happily cook your catch. Homely bedrooms have large showers and quality bedding.

31 High St,
STOCKBRIDGE, SO20 6EY
Tel.: 01264 810833
Website: www.thegreyhoundonthetest.co.uk

At the western end of the High Street. Parking.

PRICES
Meals: £ 15 (weekday lunch) and a la carte
£ 22/59

 10 rooms:
£ 90/240

MAP: 46

CLOSING TIMES
Closed 25-26 December
booking advisable

HODDINGTON ARMS

Come for one of their Movie Nights

For a short time the 'Hodd' was run by some of the villagers but keeping it going alongside their everyday jobs proved a little too much, so they enlisted the help of Tom and Chris, owners of the Crown in Old Basing. When the weather's right, sit in the lovely garden – which comes complete with a wood-burning oven – or bag a spot in the smart cabana. The 17C building has plenty of rustic character and a laid-back feel: sofas sit alongside dining tables and the restored barn area is wonderfully atmospheric. Lunch offers sandwiches and the usual pub classics, while dinner sees the likes of venison scotch egg with watercress dressing, followed by slow braised lamb shoulder with potato dauphinoise, finished off with their take on a peach Melba.

Bidden Rd,
UPTON GREY, RG25 2RL
Tel.: 01256 862371
Website: www.hoddingtonarms.co.uk

6.5 miles southeast of Basingstoke sign-posted of A 339. Parking

PRICES   MAP: **47**
Meals: a la carte £ 24/42

CLOSING TIMES
Closed 26 December, 1 January and
Sunday dinner

THOMAS LORD

Named after the founder of Lord's Cricket Ground

This smartly refurbished, early 19C pub is named after the founder of Lord's Cricket Ground, who retired to and is buried in the village – which explains the bats, the county caps and the stuffed animals playing cricket above the bar. Roaring fires and friendly faces keep the atmosphere warm and welcoming and there's a lovely garden where they light a wood-burning stove on summer evenings (part of which is used to grow their own herbs and vegetables). The menu perfectly balances classic doorstop sandwiches, ploughman's lunches and risottos with dishes such as fried ham hock and black pudding or pork belly with boulangère potatoes. From time to time you'll find one of the locals having an impromptu tinkle on the piano in the bar.

High St,
WEST MEON, GU32 1LN
Tel.: 01730 829244
Website: www.thethomaslord.co.uk

9 mi west of Petersfield by A 272 and A 32 south. Parking.

PRICES
Meals: a la carte £ 28/49

MAP: **48**

CLOSING TIMES
Closed 25 December

TAVERNERS

Homemade seasonal dishes and an on-site deli

In a pretty – and often very busy – little village stands this passionately run roadside pub. It's the kind of place that's all about handmade, homemade everything and they are proud to work with the latest island ingredients. The large garden is home to herb and veg beds; various boards display food miles and tables of what's in season when; a blackboard asks for any surplus home-grown produce (in return for a local Taverners beer or two); and it even has its own deli selling homemade bread, sauces and local wares. Cooking is fresh and tasty: the main menu lists pub classics like burgers and pies but the more ambitious daily blackboard specials are ones to go for. Follow these up with a "bucket of ice cream" or "my nan's lemon meringue pie".

High St,
GODSHILL, PO38 3HZ
Tel.: 01983 840707
Website: www.thetavernersgodshill.co.uk

4 mi west of Shanklin by A 3020. Parking.

PRICES
Meals: a la carte £ 17/28

MAP: **49**

CLOSING TIMES
Closed first 3 weeks January

KENTISH HARE

It's all about the steaks from the green egg grill

The Hare and Hounds became the Kentish Hare, after it was saved from redevelopment into flats by local residents Lord and Lady Mills, of Olympic Committee, Air Miles and Nectar Card fame. A top-to-toe refurbishment followed, the talented Tanner brothers were installed to run the place, and the villagers once more had a local they could be proud of. Smart and modern, with a hare motif running through it, some quirky wallpaper and furniture, and an open kitchen, the Hare provides a great value set midweek menu, pub classics on the bar menu and dishes like roast rack of Romney lamb on the à la carte, while the speciality green egg grill section allows you to 'create your own steak', with a choice of cut, sauce and accompanying side.

95 Bidborough Ridge,
BIDBOROUGH, TN3 0XB
Tel.: 01892 525709
Website: www.thekentishhare.com

2.5 mi southwest of Tonbridge by A 26 on B 2176. Parking

PRICES
Meals: £ 22 (weekdays) and a la carte
£ 27/43

MAP: 50

CLOSING TIMES
Closed Sunday dinner and Monday except
bank holidays

THE THREE CHIMNEYS

Bedrooms open onto a garden terrace

This delightful pub dates back to 1420 and has all the character you would expect of a building its age. The low-beamed, dimly lit rooms have a truly old world feel and for sunnier days there's a conservatory, a garden and a charming terrace. Menus feature mainly British dishes, such as smoked haddock, finished off with nursery puddings like apple crumble; there are some tempting local wines, ciders and ales on offer too. The story surrounding the pub's name goes that French prisoners held at Sissinghurst Castle during the Seven Years' War were allowed to wander as far as the three lanes but were forbidden to pass the junction where the pub was sited. 'Les trois chemins' (the three roads) was then later mistranslated into 'The Three Chimneys'.

Hareplain Rd,
BIDDENDEN, TN27 8LW
Tel.: 01580 291472
Website: www.thethreechimneys.co.uk

1.5 mi west by A 262. Parking.

PRICES
Meals: a la carte £ 25/40

 5 rooms:
£ 80/180

MAP: 51

CLOSING TIMES
Open daily
booking essential

GEORGE & DRAGON

Local farm produce is the order of the day

If it's character you're after, then this 450 year old inn on the edge of the village is the place to come. Outside there's a delightful mature garden with a large terrace, a children's play area and raised herb and salad beds. Inside, there's a lovely beamed bar where they serve a huge array of cocktails, and a charming first floor dining room with a sloping ceiling and wonky floor. Looking at the menu, there's no doubting you're in England: seasonal, regional ingredients feature in dishes such as bacon, kale and chestnut soup; celeriac and celery salad with English mustard dressing; and pork belly with apple sauce. The mature, 28-day hung steaks with triple-cooked chips are a perennial favourite, along with the steak sandwiches at lunch.

39 High St,
CHIPSTEAD, TN13 2RW
Tel.: 01732 779019
Website: www.georgeanddragonchipstead.com

Located in the centre of the village. Parking.

PRICES   MAP: **52**
Meals: a la carte £ 20/39

CLOSING TIMES
Open daily

COMPASSES INN

A warm welcome is guaranteed

Just outside the village of Crundale is the even smaller, one-road hamlet of Sole Street – home to this welcoming 1420s pub, which is run by an enthusiastic young couple who are both chefs and have a genuine desire to please. The small front bar with its hop-hung beams and inglenook fireplaces is the most characterful spot but the large dining room really comes into its own in the summer when the doors are opened out onto the garden. The set price menu offers a choice of comfort dishes while the à la carte shows a little more finesse (the desserts are a highlight). They use meats from local farms, game from the Crundale Estate and fruit and vegetables from their own garden. Be sure to try one of the interesting monthly changing wines.

Sole Street,
CRUNDALE, CT4 7ES
Tel.: 01227 700300
Website: www.thecompassescrundale.co.uk

9 mi northeast of Ashford signed off A 28. Parking

PRICES

MAP: **53**

Meals: £ 18 (weekday lunch) and a la carte
£ 26/37

CLOSING TIMES
Closed Sunday dinner and Monday

THE WINDMILL

Come in the summer for weekend BBQs

The pub is a great British institution and with its giant inglenook fireplace and low-slung beams, the Windmill is as characterful as they come. You'll find tempting bar snacks like pork scratchings with apple compote, sharing roasts on Sundays and hearty British classics like fish pie – but they also offer more refined dishes too, including the likes of roast monkfish with duck egg linguine or haunch of venison with slow-cooked faggots. Drinks are by no means ignored: if you fancy a G&T, there'll be at least four different gins to choose from, while beer drinkers can enjoy Kentish ales from the local Musket Brewery. The polite young team ensure that you get what you want, when you want, and they always seem to deliver it with a smile.

32 Eyhorne St,
HOLLINGBOURNE, ME17 1TR
Tel.: 01622 889000
Website: www.thewindmillbyrichardphillips.co.uk

5.5mi east of Maidstone by A 20 and through village. Parking.

PRICES   MAP: **54**
Meals: £ 15 (weekday lunch) and a la carte
£ 27/40

CLOSING TIMES
Open daily

DUKE WILLIAM

A modern day village local

The smart grey exterior and etched windows of this 400 year old building have more of a city than a country look but the cosy interior still has a good old neighbourhood vibe. It's much larger inside than you expect: sit on fur throw covered benches by the fire in the bar, in the quieter 'den' or in the conservatory overlooking the spacious terrace and the garden beyond. The keenly priced menu is likeable for its honesty and simplicity, listing time-honoured classics that everyone knows and loves. Monday is steak night, Tuesday is wine and cheese evening and on a Friday they offer takeaway fish and chips (have some drinks in the bar while you wait!) Smart yet casual bedrooms come with cookbooks written by the chefs after whom they're named.

The Street,
ICKHAM, CT3 1QP
Tel.: 01227 721308
Website: www.thedukewilliamickham.com

6.5 mi east of Canterbury by A 257. On-street parking.

PRICES
Meals: a la carte £ 22/46

4 rooms:
£ 100

MAP: 55

CLOSING TIMES
Open daily

GLOBE & RAINBOW

Try the côte de bœuf to share

The original pub building, the White Hart, is now two private residences and the Globe & Rainbow sits to its side – look for the large decked terrace. It's run by two locals: one, a chef, who has experience in some top restaurants, the other who used to work in the wine business. The décor is modest, with pine tables and a wood-burning stove; the cooking, however, is a far cry from the surroundings. Refined dishes show a real understanding of classic techniques and prime ingredients are simply married with one or two others in order to let them shine. Lunch sees a good value set menu, while dinner offers an à la carte – keep an eye out for the 'Love Your Beef' board where they chalk up the weight and price of the local côte du boeuf to share.

Ranters Ln,
KILNDOWN, TN17 2SG
Tel.: 01892 890803
Website: www.globeandrainbow.co.uk

2.5 mi west of Goudhurst by A 262 Parking.

PRICES   MAP: **56**
Meals: £ 20 (lunch) and a la carte £ 27/40

CLOSING TIMES
Closed Sunday dinner and Monday
booking advisable

WHEELWRIGHTS ARMS

A self-taught Zimbabwean chef

What do you get if you cross a self-taught Zimbabwean chef with an early 17C Kentish former farmhouse? Very tasty food for one thing; and a genuinely warm welcome for another. Outside it's all clapboard and colourful flower baskets; inside it's rustic with a fireplace at each end, low beamed ceilings crammed with hanging hops, and photos on the wall that tell the story of the pub's past. These days, local bands perform regularly, Morris dancers wave their hankies from time to time, and the first Thursday of each month is quiz night, when they don't serve dinner. At any other time, you can expect an abundance of local, seasonal produce in classic dishes like rump and shoulder of lamb or braised beef rib with pan-roast blade and cottage pie.

The Green,
MATFIELD, TN12 7JX
Tel.: 01892 722129
Website: www.thewheelwrightsarmsfreehouse.co.uk

6 mi east of Royal Tunbridge Wells by A 264, in village centre. Parking.

PRICES   MAP: **57**
Meals: a la carte £ 22/43

CLOSING TIMES
Closed Sunday dinner and Monday

RED LION

Honest, richly flavoured Gallic and English dishes

A 'Red Lion' pub has stood on this spot since Victorian times; the current one belonging to a very capable and experienced couple, who have run numerous pubs in the area over the years. They like to get involved, so you'll find him hard at work in the kitchen and her leading the friendly, engaging service. It's a simple place, featuring a cosy, open-fired bar where the locals tend to gather and a dining room with rich red walls, benches and Lloyd Loom chairs. The menu offers a mix of Gallic and English dishes; you might find a classic bouillabaisse or a venison casserole with truffled mash; game in season is a speciality and desserts might be a lemon torte or mulled pear. In true country style, dishes are honest, wholesome and richly flavoured.

Rawling St,
MILSTEAD, ME9 0RT
Tel.: 01795 830279
Website: www.theredlionmilstead.co.uk

South of Sittingbourne signposted off the A 2. Parking.

PRICES   MAP: **58**
Meals: a la carte £ 24/42

CLOSING TIMES
Closed Sunday and Monday
booking advisable

THREE MARINERS

A great spot for walkers to refuel

If you've been negotiating the Saxon Shore Way, this 500 year old pub is a great place to refuel: it's set in a sleepy hamlet offering pleasant views over the marshes to the estuary beyond, and there's a warmth and quirkiness about it, from the roaring fires to the bright, friendly team. Constantly evolving menus offer an extensive range of British and Mediterranean-influenced dishes like garlic scallops or herb-crusted lamb rump, and the set menus represent good value: the Walkers' Lunch might include potted duck, chicken pie and homemade ice cream, and the Business Lunch, Parma ham, sea bass and artisan cheeses. Sharing dishes like 7 hour slow roast shoulder of lamb or seafood paella can be ordered 24 hours in advance.

2 Church Rd,
OARE, ME13 0QA
Tel.: 01795 533633
Website: www.thethreemarinersoare.co.uk

2.5 mi northwest of Faversham by A 2 and B 2045. Parking.

PRICES   MAP: **59**
Meals: £ 14/22 and a la carte £ 20/36

CLOSING TIMES
Closed dinner 24-25 December

LEICESTER ARMS

Sit in the garden room for a rural view

Some menus have a way with words that get your taste buds tingling in anticipation: hake here is 'pan-roasted', with 'asparagus, bacon, garden peas and baby gem'; gnocchi is 'handmade', with 'courgette, ricotta, chilli and mint' and the rabbit and cider terrine comes with 'Indian Military chutney and toasted sourdough'. Despite the rhetoric, they are essentially offering rustic and satisfying pub classics – which is as it should be, seeing as this is indeed a pub. It dates from the 16C and has been sympathetically refurbished: avoid the small front room and sit instead in the garden room – a large bright space with a lovely rural view. Bedrooms are furnished in a contemporary style; ask for Room 8, which is the biggest, with the best outlook.

High St,
PENSHURST, TN11 8BT
Tel.: 01892 871617
Website: www.theleicesterarmshotel.com

5.5 mi Southwest of Tonbridge on B 2176. Parking

PRICES
Meals: a la carte £ 23/59

 13 rooms:
£ 69/139

MAP: 60

CLOSING TIMES
Open daily

THE DUCK

Simple, satisfying, boldly flavoured cooking

Pett Bottom was the fictional home of the young James Bond and in 'You Only Live Twice' M wrote an obituary which mentioned The Duck – in fact, is it thought that Ian Fleming actually wrote the book here! Despite all this, The Duck is a pleasingly down-to-earth place, with open fires and a vast collection of cookbooks on display. It was originally built in the 17C as two farm cottages, then started trading as The Woodman's Arms, before later being renamed – supposedly due to a very low doorway with the warning to 'duck'! At lunch a set price menu is chalked on the board, while for weekday dinner, the set 4 course option represents the best value   it offers a smorgasbord platter to share, followed by soup and a choice of main course and dessert.

Pett Bottom Rd,
PETT BOTTOM, CT4 5PB
Tel.: 01227 830354
Website: www.theduckpettbottom.com

5 mi south of Canterbury by B 2068. Parking.

PRICES   MAP: **61**
Meals: £ 17/23 and a la carte £ 21/35

CLOSING TIMES
Closed dinner Sunday and Monday
booking advisable

THE BEACON

Fantastic views and great hospitality

The Beacon was built in 1895 as a private house for Sir Walter Harris, the governor of Burma, and it sits in a stunning spot – built into the stone escarpment and with fantastic views over the town. It's set over three levels and still has plenty of original decorative features, from ornate plasterwork and carved wood to pretty stained glass. Classic pub dishes are driven by the latest seasonal ingredients and have bold flavours and a comforting feel; some, such as the duck cottage pie have a more modern edge. Sit in the bar to watch the chefs at work in the kitchen or, in summer, head for the extensive terraces, which come with their own food truck and Sunday lunches cooked on a Big Green Egg. Staff are friendly and eager to please.

Tea Garden Ln,
ROYAL TUNBRIDGE WELLS, TN3 9JH
Tel.: 01892 524252
Website: www.the-beacon.co.uk

1 mi west of the town centre off A 264. Parking

PRICES
Meals: £ 17 (weekdays) and a la carte
£ 25/41

MAP: 62

CLOSING TIMES
Closed Sunday dinner and Monday

BLACK PIG

Seek out the Secret Garden

The Black Pig is a great stop-off point for weary shoppers who have spent their morning wandering around the bijou shops in the centre of town – and the Secret Garden, hidden away to the rear, is a welcome treat come summer. The black façade may feel quite austere but inside it's quite the opposite, courtesy of a friendly team, a laid-back vibe and rustic shabby-chic styling... not forgetting the tempting aromas drifting through from the kitchen. The 'PIG Heaven' section of the menu offers all manner of porcine treats ranging from crisp pig's skin with truffled mayonnaise to a Sussex pork chop with grilled hispi; alongside these you'll find meat and vegetarian sharing boards, 'Cow Corner' steaks and plenty of other gutsy, full-flavoured dishes.

18 Grove Hill Rd,
ROYAL TUNBRIDGE WELLS, TN1 1RZ
Tel.: 01892 523030
Website: www.theblackpig.net

In town centre, 2min walk from train station. Limited parking.

PRICES   MAP: **63**
Meals: £ 15 (weekdays)/30 and a la carte
£ 22/40

CLOSING TIMES
Closed 26 December and 1 January

THE SPORTSMAN

Top ingredients in well-judged combinations

Set on the edge of town, by the sea wall, the unassuming-looking Sportsman proves you should never judge a book by its cover, for while both its façade and its interior may appear rather modest, its cooking is top-notch. The constantly evolving blackboard menu is guided by what's seasonal and local, with fish coming from the local day boats and meats from Monkshill Farm down the road. Carefully prepared dishes feature just four or five complementary ingredients, flavours are well-judged and presentation is original. The bread, the butter and even the salt are homemade, and the roasted pork belly is a firm favourite. If you want to have the full tasting menu, you must request it in advance; the 5 course option can be ordered on arrival.

Faversham Rd,
SEASALTER, CT5 4BP
Tel.: 01227 273370
Website: www.thesportsmanseasalter.co.uk

2 mi southwest of Whitstable by B 2205 following the coast road. Parking.

PRICES   **MAP: 64**
Meals: a la carte £ 37/45

CLOSING TIMES
Closed 25-26 December, 1 January, Sunday
dinner and Monday
booking advisable

THE MILK HOUSE

A labour of love for a local couple

The village of Sissinghurst was without its pub for two years, so it's no wonder it's been buzzing since it reopened. Its renovation was a labour of love for local couple Dane and Sarah Allchorne and changes have included that of the pub's name, from the Bull to the Milk House, after the original name of the road on which the pub stands (Milk Street). Turn right into the bar with its soft sofas, huge fire and appetising grazing menu of nibbles like salt and pepper squid; turn left into the dining room for a seasonal list of modern British dishes such as whole grilled Dover sole. Pub classics and children's menus are available in either area and in the summer they serve wood-fired pizzas in the garden. Bedrooms are smart and contemporary.

The Street,
SISSINGHURST, TN17 2JG
Tel.: 01580 720200
Website: www.themilkhouse.co.uk

In centre of village, 2 miles northeast of Cranbrook. Parking

PRICES
Meals: a la carte £ 19/44

 4 rooms:
£ 80/140

MAP: 65

CLOSING TIMES
Open daily

GEORGE & DRAGON

Hugely characterful 13C pub serving gutsy dishes

Dating back to 1212, this black and white timbered Wealden Hall house boasts an impressive beamed ceiling and displays an unusual Queen's post in the upstairs dining room. It's thought to be the second oldest pub in the country and, in the past, provided refreshment for the soldiers returning from Agincourt. It's a hugely appealing place, with several characterful flag-floored rooms, vast inglenook fireplaces and a contrastingly modern, landscaped terrace. Cooking is generous and satisfying, and strives to keep things local and organic, with extensive menus offering a selection of pub classics alongside more elaborate British dishes such as bacon-wrapped pheasant. The Groombridge belly pork and Ashdown Forest venison are best sellers.

Speldhurst Hill,
SPELDHURST, TN3 0NN
Tel.: 01892 863125
Website: www.speldhurst.com

3.5 mi north of Royal Tunbridge Wells by A 26. Parking.

PRICES
Meals: a la carte £ 26/46

MAP: **66**

CLOSING TIMES
Open daily

PLOUGH

Impressive range of Kentish real ales

The term 'rustic' could have been invented for this rurally set 15C pub, with its thick walls, farming implements, exposed beams and hop bines. Sit at table 6 or 7 – on either side of the open fire – or go for table 10, set almost in an inglenook, where you will be able to read a verse from the farmer's poem 'God Speed the Plough' on the wall in front of you. You'll find the usual suspects on the bar snack menu: a ploughman's, fishcakes, burgers and the like, with dishes like chicken liver parfait, confit belly pork or halibut with chorizo on the à la carte. Nursery puddings such as apple crumble or sticky toffee pudding make for a pleasing end to your meal, and there's an impressive range of Kentish real ales with which to wash it down.

STALISFIELD, ME13 0HY
Tel.: 01795 890256
Website: www.theploughinnstalisfield.co.uk

7 mi southwest of Faversham by A 251. Parking.

PRICES   MAP: **67**
Meals: £ 14 (weekday lunch) and a la carte
£ 23/33

CLOSING TIMES
Closed Monday except bank holidays

Bookatable
by Michelin

Discover Restaurants You Love

Bookatable by Michelin is Europe's leading restaurant reservations website: helping millions of diners make bookings at restaurants they love. Discover **gastro pubs** and **high street favourites**, **Michelin star restaurants** and hot-off-the-press deals, and make free, instantly confirmed bookings.

www.bookatable.co.uk

THE BULL

A mix of British classics and barbecued meats

This 14C inn doesn't look much from the outside. Venture inside and it will grow on you, although you'll perhaps still think it quite plain; dine here, however, and you'll realise that you really quite like it. There are two different menus on offer: the traditional à la carte is served in the restaurant area and lists the likes of chicken risotto Bourguignon with a fried egg or slow-braised lamb shoulder with a game croquette. Most people, though, come for the Bull Pit menu, which is served in the bar and courtyard and features a host of meats cooked on the American-style BBQ, including 6-week dry-aged Welsh Wagyu steak and 8-hour oak-smoked beef rib. If you fancy staying the night, you'll find the bedrooms smart and up-to-date.

Bull Ln.,
WROTHAM, TN15 7RF
Tel.: 01732 789800
Website: www.thebullhotel.com

In centre of village, 8 mi. northeast of Sevenoaks by A 25. Parking

---

PRICES
Meals: a la carte £ 31/44

11 rooms:
£ 69/159

MAP: 68

CLOSING TIMES
Closed 1 January

CHEQUERS

Fresh flowers, candles and open fires

Following the success of their first venture – the Three Tuns in Henley – keen young owners Sandra and Mark Duggan looked to their next challenge, which presented itself in the form of this delightful 17C pub. Outside, there's a spacious garden with a children's play area; inside it's warm and welcoming, with fresh flowers and candles on the tables and warming open fires in the grates. Hearty menus list British classics such as double-baked cheese soufflé, bubble and squeak with a soft fried duck egg or ox cheek and kidney pudding – and at lunchtime they offer a good value 2 course blackboard menu with a choice of two dishes. Come on Thursday for a 'Pie and a Pint' or Friday for 'Fish and Fizz'; they also hold occasional themed evenings.

BERRICK SALOME, OX10 6JN
Tel.: 01865 891118
Website: www.chequersberricksalome.co.uk

7 mi northeast of Wallingford off A 4074. Parking.

PRICES
Meals: £ 10 (weekday lunch) and a la carte
£ 25/42

MAP: 69

CLOSING TIMES
Closed 25 December, Sunday dinner and
Tuesday

LAMB INN

A delightful spot in the Cotswolds

Cosiness is a quality for which British pubs are renowned and this delightful pub – a collection of 15C weavers' cottages – certainly has 'snug' and 'warm' down pat. A pair of sitting rooms exude charm, with comfy armchairs, oil paintings and antiques; here and in the bar an all-day menu offers anything from deli boards or a ploughman's to steaks or sausage and mash. In the elegant, candlelit dining room, things get more ambitious, with tasting menus and an à la carte displaying classic dishes like ham hock and pea soup or rack of lamb; if meat from Ruby and White butchers is listed, be sure a cut ends up on your plate. The terrace and gardens make summer extra special and comfortable bedrooms have a loveliness all of their own.

Sheep St,
BURFORD, OX18 4LR
Tel.: 01993 823155
Website: www.cotswold-inns-hotels.co.uk/the-lamb-inn

Parking at Bay Tree Hotel.

PRICES
Meals: £ 25 (lunch) and a la carte £ 28/51

 17 rooms:
£ 140/275

MAP: 70

CLOSING TIMES
Open daily

CROWN INN

Try the steak and Hooky ale pie

This 17C inn is found in among pretty mellow stone houses in a picturesque village on the edge of the Cotswolds. It boasts a welcoming slate-floored conservatory, a beamed dining room and a rustic stone-walled bar, as well as a secluded garden for sunny days. The chef-owner has built up quite a reputation for his seafood in these parts, so you'll find that some dishes – such as the fishcakes and the king scallop and bacon salad – are permanent fixtures, along with the locally renowned steak and Hooky ale pie. At lunch, the daily blackboard reads like a top ten of old pub favourites, with the likes of beer-battered cod and chips or pork sausages and mash; all of the meats, fruit and vegetables are sourced from the local farms.

Mill Ln,
CHURCH ENSTONE, OX7 4NN
Tel.: 01608 677262
Website: www.crowninnenstone.co.uk

3.5 mi southeast of Chipping Norton by A 44. Parking in village

PRICES   MAP: **71**
Meals: £ 19 (weekdays) and a la carte
£ 20/34

CLOSING TIMES
Closed 25-26 December, 1 January
and Sunday dinner

CHEQUERS

A welcoming place, popular with the locals

It may have an 'OX' postcode but this mellow limestone pub, sitting proudly at the heart of the village, is clearly in Cotswold country. It's a vital part of the local community and the owners appear to have got the formula just right; it's filled with locals playing darts and the keen serving team exude as much warmth as the roaring fire in the inglenook. The bar is well-stocked with local ales, while the counter behind is filled with enticing hams and olives, just waiting to be nibbled on. Menus are firmly rooted in tradition, with hearty dishes such as ham hock and pease pudding, calves' liver and bacon or steaks cooked on the Josper grill. It's a popular place but there are always 6 tables left unreserved, for those without a booking.

Church Rd,
CHURCHILL, OX7 6NJ
Tel.: 01608 659393
Website: www.thechequerschurchill.com

3 mi southwest of Chipping Norton on B 4450. Parking.

PRICES   MAP: **72**
Meals: £ 15 (weekday lunch) and a la carte
£ 21/40

CLOSING TIMES
Closed 25 December

LAMB INN

Top quality regional produce includes rare breeds

This pretty stone pub is set in a lovely village and is a hit with one and all, from walkers and dog-owners to those out celebrating. Roaring log fires and a friendly team welcome you into the charming bar, where old milk churns act as tables and pork scratchings and pickled onions sit temptingly behind the counter (beyond are two more rooms, both laid for dining). Expect top quality regional produce: at lunch this could include a rare breed Longhorn beef burger or Butt's Farm ham with Arlington egg and chips, while dinner might feature braised short rib of beef with caramelised artichoke purée or barbecued loin of Oxford & Sandy Black pork with smoked bacon and cider gravy. When the weather's right, they also fire-up the outdoor pizza oven.

Steep Hill,
CRAWLEY, OX29 9TW
Tel.: 01993 708792
Website: www.lambcrawley.co.uk

2 mi northwest of Witney by B 4022 (West End). Parking.

PRICES
Meals: a la carte £ 28/42

MAP: **73**

CLOSING TIMES
Closed Monday and Tuesday

EYSTON ARMS

Warm service and modern British dishes

A pub has stood on this site for many years, although it was once much smaller and adjoined by estate workers' cottages, as this characterful village was – and still is – largely owned by the local estate. Inside, original tiled floors, low beams and an inglenook fireplace remain but it's been given a typical modern dining pub makeover with scrubbed wooden tables and plenty of candles, along with caricatures of the locals and photos taken by the owner's daughter on her travels. Staff are warm and welcoming and as a result, they have gained a loyal following. The à la carte menu offers modern British dishes, Maria's blackboard lists the specials and local workers pop in for the 'business dish of the day'. Don't miss the delicious homemade puds!

High St,
EAST HENDRED, OX12 8JY
Tel.: 01235 833320
Website: www.eystonarms.co.uk

4.5 mi east of Wantage by A 417. Parking.

PRICES
Meals: a la carte £ 26/53

MAP: **74**

CLOSING TIMES
Closed 25 December

FIVE ALLS

Classical cooking and cosy, modern bedrooms

The pub's curious logo refers to the fulfilment of the 5 human needs – the lawyer pleads for all, the parson prays for all, the soldier fights for all and the farmer pays for all, while at the centre, the devil governs all. When it comes to fulfilment, they certainly seem to have it covered here: there's an open-fired bar stocked with fine ales, where they serve snacks and takeaway burgers, and three large dining rooms furnished with antiques. There's also a terrace and a garden with an Aunt Sally area and, completing the picture, some cosy, modern bedrooms; and that's before even mentioning the food! Cooking is satisfyingly traditional, offering everything from potted shrimps with melba toast to a cured meat platter and hearty steaks.

FILKINS, GL7 3JQ
Tel.: 01367 860875
Website: www.thefiveallsfilkins.co.uk

Midway between Burford and Lechlade-on-Thames. Parking.

PRICES
Meals: £ 18 (weekdays) and a la carte
£ 27/43

 9 rooms:
£ 75/150

MAP: 75

CLOSING TIMES
Closed 25 December and Sunday dinner

WHITE HART

15C chantry house with original features

This intriguing 15C chantry house displays many original features, including an inglenook fireplace in its cosy beamed bar, a minstrels' gallery, and a hall with a flagged floor and a three-storey high vaulted ceiling (now the dining room); it also boasts a pleasant terrace. They make good use of the wealth of produce on their doorstep, so you'll find meat from nearby farms or estates; flour – for the homemade bread – from the local mill; and fruit and veg from the pub's own plot or the locals' gardens. Menus offer a diverse range of dishes – from sharing boards to slow-roast pork or tempura courgette flowers – and excellent desserts. Service is slick and friendly, and the annual beer festival and hog roast always makes for a great day out.

Main Rd,
FYFIELD, OX13 5LW
Tel.: 01865 390585
Website: www.whitehart-fyfield.com

10 mi southwest of Oxford by A 420. Parking.

PRICES
Meals: £ 17 (weekday lunch) and a la carte
£ 28/41

MAP: 76

CLOSING TIMES
Closed Monday except bank holidays

MILLER OF MANSFIELD

Warm homemade bread arrives in a sack

This large 18C coaching inn sits on the banks of the Thames and its unusual name comes from a 20 verse poem called the King and the Miller of Mansfield, which tells the story of King Henry VIII losing his way in Sherwood Forest and a miller, John Cockle, who provided him with food and a bed for the night. In keeping with this tale, the pub's cheery team provide great hospitality and its bright, cosy bedrooms are named after towns on the route from Goring to Mansfield. Sit in one of two cosy bar rooms, in the smarter rear dining room or out on the terrace, and enjoy everything from homemade sausage rolls to butter-poached lobster salad. The warm homemade bread arrives in a small sack and the skilfully prepared desserts are a real highlight.

High St,
GORING, RG8 9AW
Tel.: 01491 872829
Website: www.millerofmansfield.com

In the village centre, close to the River Thames.
Parking in the village car park.

PRICES
Meals: £ 16 (weekday lunch) and a la carte
£ 29/41

 13 rooms:
£ 70/195

MAP: 77

CLOSING TIMES
Open daily

BELL AT HAMPTON POYLE

Choose something from the wood-burning oven

Tiled flooring and a bright, fresh look make the Bell seem almost Mediterranean, which is not a style one usually associates with a pub in rural Oxfordshire, but it seems to work. The owners have made the kitchen a very visual element of the operation, with its wood-burning oven and large open-plan pass, and there's a spacious main dining room and a series of small sitting rooms filled with coffee tables and books. The accessible menu covers all tastes: there's meze, homemade pizza, and seafood and charcuterie boards, as well as staples such as calves' liver and some decent steaks. They tweak it a little with the seasons and also strive to keep prices in check. Smart bedrooms are located above the bar and in a small neighbouring cottage.

11 Oxford Rd,
HAMPTON POYLE, OX5 2QD
Tel.: 01865 376242
Website: www.thebellathamptonpoyle.co.uk

9 mi north of Oxford by A 34. Parking.

PRICES
Meals: £ 10 (weekdays) and a la carte
£ 27/44

 9 rooms:
£ 95/155

MAP: 78

CLOSING TIMES
Open daily

BLACK BOY

Classic pub dishes with a Gallic edge

It's big, it's bold and it's busy – it's the Black Boy. Sit at the bar counter for cocktails and some mix and match tapas – such as fried brown shrimps, mini pea samosas or lamb koftas; or find a seat in the large, low-lit open room or small side restaurant for a proper meal. As well as having French roots, the chef did a long stint with Raymond Blanc, so it comes as no surprise that there's a Gallic edge to the essentially classical menu; but don't get the wrong idea, this is proper pub food, no messing, with unadorned mains like slow-roast pork belly or homemade chicken Kiev. The homemade bread is a great place to start and the Sunday roasts go down a storm – as do the kids' 'Sunday Kitchen' classes, which take place in the mornings.

91 Old High St,
HEADINGTON, OXFORD, OX3 9HT
Tel.: 01865 741137
Website: www.theblackboy.uk.com

East of Oxford off London Rd. On-street parking around the pub.

PRICES
Meals: a la carte £ 25/41

MAP: **79**

CLOSING TIMES
Closed 26 December and 1 January

THREE TUNS

Look out for the old coffin drop above the bar!

This pretty, red-brick, town centre pub was originally three houses, one of which used to be a mortuary and, if you take a look above the central bar, you can still see the coffin drop. The atmosphere is far from deathly in this bijoux inn, however; the best place to sit being among the drinkers in its lively, open-fired front bar (ask for table 10). The formal dining room has just four tables and is the place for a quieter, more intimate meal. There's something to please all palates on the seasonal menu, and traditional dishes like ham hock terrine or seafood pot au feu are well-presented, satisfying and full of flavour. Breads are homemade, meat comes from the butchers next door and there's an excellent value 2 course lunch menu Tues-Sat.

5 Market Pl,
HENLEY-ON-THAMES, RG9 2AA
Tel.: 01491 410138
Website: www.threetunshenley.co.uk

In the centre of town. Local pay and display parking.

PRICES
Meals: £ 12 (weekday lunch) and a la carte
£ 25/42

MAP: 80

CLOSING TIMES
Closed 25 December and Sunday dinner

MUDDY DUCK

Every village should have a pub like this one

The Muddy Duck is a labour of love and it shows. Rescued from impending closure by a local businessman, this mellow stone pub has been reinvigorated and modernised yet still manages to stay true to its traditional roots. Staff are friendly and ultra-smiley, locals gather to enjoy well-kept beer in the characterful fire-warmed bar, and people come from all around to dine on fresh, tasty food in the Malthouse Barn. The menu offers a carefully chosen mix of pub staples and more adventurous choices, with something for everyone – and the added bonus of dishes from the wood-fired oven on the terrace in summer. Unpretentious yet modish, with a very happy feel, this is the sort of pub every village should have; quite clearly, the people of Hethe agree.

Main St,
HETHE, OX27 8ES
Tel.: 01869 278099
Website: www.themuddyduckpub.co.uk

6 mi north of Bicester off A 4421 (Buckingham rd). Parking

PRICES
Meals: a la carte £ 23/60

MAP: **81**

CLOSING TIMES
Closed Sunday dinner

PLOUGH

Appealing 16C inn with stylish bedrooms

Regulars of the Five Alls were delighted when experienced restaurateur Sebastian Snow bought a second pub just 5 miles away. The Plough has 16C origins and all the character that you would expect of a pub its age, with rough stone walls, open fires and a rustic feel. The cottage-style garden is a great place to sit in summer and there's even a bar outside in the old stable block (which also functions as a private dining room). Traditional menus list dishes you'll know and love, from buck rarebit on the bar menu to twice-baked cheese soufflé, devilled lambs' kidneys and Fowey mussels on the à la carte. The bar has a mix of tables and chairs – including a pommel horse – while the dining room has a more formal feel. Bedrooms are small but stylish.

KELMSCOTT, GL7 3HG
Tel.: 01367 253543
Website: www.theploughinnkelmscott.com

5.5 mi northwest of Faringdon by A 4095. Parking in village.

PRICES
Meals: a la carte £ 27/43

 8 rooms:
£ 100/130

MAP: 82

CLOSING TIMES
Closed Monday dinner

KINGHAM PLOUGH

Well prepared, constantly evolving modern dishes

Set on the green of a beautifully unspoilt village in the Evenlode Valley, this pub boasts a rustic, fire-lit lounge-bar, a laid-back restaurant and an easy-going team. It's owned by Emily Watkins, former sous-chef at The Fat Duck, so you'll find the occasional dish that harks back to her Heston days; although the majority of dishes are rooted in a gutsy pub vein – albeit a very modern one. The snack menu offers tasty classics such as pork pie, scotched quails' eggs or Welsh rarebit, while the concise à la carte features the latest seasonal produce from foraging expeditions and nearby farms. Preparation is careful slow cooking reigns and dishes evolve throughout the evening as new ingredients arrive. For the weary, comfy bedrooms await.

The Green,
KINGHAM, OX7 6YD
Tel.: 01608 658327
Website: www.thekinghamplough.co.uk

9 mi east of Stow-on-the-Wold, signposted off A 436, in village centre. Parking.

PRICES
Meals: a la carte £ 32/44

 6 rooms:
£ 110/195

MAP: 83

CLOSING TIMES
Closed 25 December

THE WILD RABBIT

A cosy, characterful inn, full of Cotswold charm

Just down the road from the Daylesford Farm Shop is the Bamford family's lovely Cotswold pub. A subtle leporine theme runs throughout, from the inlaid stone rabbit on the floor to the name of their most delightful bedroom. The likes of sole goujons feature on the bar menu but the majority of dining takes place in the formal restaurant (the old tariff sign is from its former life as a tollgate). Cooking is modern, well-judged and has plenty of appeal – aside from the 40-day matured charcoal-grilled steak, this is restaurant food, with ingredients arranged in delicious layers of flavours. Sweetbread with Cevennes onions, tamarind, parmesan and pear might be followed by Wootton Estate mallard with crispy leg pastille and preserved elderberries.

Church St,
KINGHAM, OX7 6YA
Tel.: 01608 658389
Website: www.thewildrabbit.co.uk

9 mi east of Stow-on-the-Wold, signposted off A 436, in village centre. Parking.

PRICES
Meals: a la carte £ 38/55

 13 rooms:
£ 160/350

MAP: 84

CLOSING TIMES
Closed first 2 weeks January
booking advisable

EAGLE TAVERN

Welcoming local run by a self-taught chef

There's many a rural pub where a stranger walks through the door and the room falls silent; not so at the Eagle Tavern, where the locals welcome you with open arms. It was built in 1901 for the farmers of this sleepy hamlet and, although it might look slightly different nowadays, a convivial atmosphere still reigns. It's a spacious place with a homely bar and a dining room furnished in wood and wicker, and is run by a self-taught Slovakian chef, who cooks the kind of food he himself likes to eat. Dishes range from the simple to the ambitious and some use influences from his homeland; his keeps things local with his suppliers, however, who are all from the surrounding area. Bedrooms are cosy and worth the money – go for the four-poster.

LITTLE COXWELL, SN7 7LW
Tel.: 01367 241879
Website: www.eagletavern.co.uk

2.5 mi south of Faringdon by A 417. Parking in the village.

PRICES
Meals: £ 16 (weekday lunch) and a la carte
£ 23/36

 6 rooms:
£ 60/100

MAP: 85

CLOSING TIMES
Closed Sunday dinner and Monday

FIVE HORSESHOES

Take in delightful country views from the terrace

This charming 17C inn with delightful country views is set in the heart of walking country. When the weather's warm, head for the large garden and terrace where, on summer Fridays and Saturdays, they fire up the wood-fired oven and bespoke pizzas are the name of the game. Inside, the two intimate rooms and large conservatory are warm and welcoming and share the view; order a homemade ginger beer then seek out the small blackboard which lists the specials. The daily set lunch represents the best value and cooking is wholesome and hearty, featuring plenty of meaty dishes, game in season and proper puddings like steamed treacle sponge. They like to keep things as local as possible here, so even the wines come from a vineyard just down the road.

MAIDENSGROVE, RG9 6EX
Tel.: 01491 641282
Website: www.thefivehorseshoes.co.uk

6.25 mi northwest of Henley-on-Thames by A 4130,
B 480 and Maidensgrove rd. Parking.

PRICES
Meals: £ 13 (weekday lunch) and a la carte
£ 23/43

MAP: 86

CLOSING TIMES
Closed Monday except bank holidays

OLD SWAN

Stylish bedrooms up a winding staircase

They may be a few hundred miles apart but the Old Swan and its sister, the Cary Arms, share a few things in common, including stylish accommodation and a passion for fresh, simply cooked food. The Old Swan is just the sort of place you expect to come across in Oxfordshire, with its smart parquet floor, roaring open fires and collection of horse brasses and Toby jugs. For summer there's boules and a giant chess set in the garden – set next to large herb plots which supply the pub all year round and contribute to unfussy pub classics and tasty daily specials from the Brixham day boats. Chic bedrooms are accessed via a winding staircase and display period furnishings, quality linens and the latest mod cons – some even boast feature bathrooms.

MINSTER LOVELL, OX29 0RN
Tel.: 01993 774441
Website: www.oldswanandminstermill.com

3.5 mi west of Witney by B 4047. Parking.

PRICES
Meals: a la carte £ 25/43

 14 rooms:
£ 165/395

MAP: 87

CLOSING TIMES
Open daily

NUT TREE

Superb dishes of organic and wild produce

You want a tasty, top quality meal in good old pub surroundings: enter the Nut Tree. It's owned by a local and his wife, who have managed to retain a satisfyingly pubby feel in the cosy beamed bar, while also providing a more formal atmosphere in the smart restaurant. Appealing menus change constantly as the latest seasonal ingredients arrive and produce is organic, free range or wild wherever possible; there's always plenty of choice too, from baguettes and bar snacks to ambitious tasting selections. Breads and ice creams are homemade, salmon is smoked on-site and sausages and pork pies are for sale. Combinations are classical and satisfying, and to ensure only the freshest meats are used, they rear their own rare breed pigs out the back.

Main St,
MURCOTT, OX5 2RE
Tel.: 01865 331253
Website: www.nuttreeinn.co.uk

7 mi from Bicester by A 41 east and a minor road south; at T-junction beyond the motorway turn right. Parking.

PRICES
Meals: a la carte £ 34/59

MAP: 88

CLOSING TIMES
Closed 27 December-11 January, Sunday
dinner and Monday

RED LION

Extremely welcoming pub owned by the villagers

The Red Lion's story is one of pride and brings a whole new meaning to the term 'community spirit'. After the pub went up for sale, one of the villagers bought it, sold shares to 90 other locals, and employed an experienced young couple and a friendly team to run it. It is an extremely welcoming place where you can't help but feel at home: the rooms have a rustic modern feel; low beams, open fires and fresh flowers abound; and the menu is a great mix of pub classics and more modern daily specials, such as wood pigeon with pancetta and pickled beetroot. The passionate chef makes everything from scratch and hopes that one day the pub will be almost fully self-sufficient courtesy of the allotment out the back and the chickens roaming the grounds.

Standlake Rd,
NORTHMOOR, OX29 5SX
Tel.: 01865 300301
Website: www.theredlionnorthmoor.com

8 mi southeast of Witney by A 415; in centre of village. Parking.

PRICES
Meals: a la carte £ 23/37

MAP: 89

CLOSING TIMES
Closed Sunday dinner

THE ANCHOR

Sleek styling in the heart of Jericho

With its subtle art deco styling, tea towel napkins and black and white dining room floor tiles, The Anchor is not your typical pub. Indeed, it opens at 9am on weekdays for coffee and cakes and 10am at weekends for a leisurely brunch, while its children's menu offers choices like crudités and dip or fish pie alongside the ubiquitous burger. There is a bar, of course: popular with locals out for a drink, although this is as likely to be a cocktail as a pint of beer, and the accompanying bar snack will be rabbit rillettes or a haggis scotch egg rather than pork scratchings or a packet of crisps. The main menu changes regularly and dishes range from the dry-aged steak cooked on a Josper Grill to steamed mussels or quinoa with radicchio and fennel.

2 Hayfield Rd,
OXFORD, OX2 6TT
Tel.: 01865 510282
Website: www.theanchoroxford.com

Just north of city centre off Woodstock Rd. Limited parking.

PRICES
Meals: a la carte £ 22/69

MAP: 90

CLOSING TIMES
Open daily

311

MAGDALEN ARMS

Menus change twice a day, depending on deliveries

This battleship-grey pub is a hit with the locals: the place buzzes – even on a weeknight – and there's always something to keep you entertained, be it a board game or bar billiards. The spacious, open-plan interior boasts deep red walls, quirky lamps and an eclectic collection of 1920s posters, while huge blackboards display the twice daily changing menu. Order at the bar for a casual lunch or head through to the curtained-off dining room for table service. The experienced chef uses local ingredients to create tasty, good value dishes; perhaps pork and rabbit rillettes, braised ox cheek or seven hour lamb for five to share. The drinks selection is equally impressive; if it's a school night, stick to a glass or two of their homemade lemonade.

243 Iffley Rd,
OXFORD, OX4 1SJ
Tel.: 01865 243159
Website: www.magdalenarms.co.uk

Southeast of city centre on A 4158. On-street parking.

PRICES
Meals: a la carte £ 23/33

MAP: 91

CLOSING TIMES
Closed 24-26 December, 1 January, Monday lunch and bank holidays

ENGLAND • South East • Oxfordshire

ROSE & CROWN

Charming pub offering gutsy, good value menus

The Rose & Crown is everything you'd expect of a Cotswold village pub. 17C mellow stone walls conceal a charming interior with flickering fires, big church candles and exposed wooden beams – and the smiling owner is just as welcoming. Beside three smartly polished pumps, locals chat over an Old Hooky, a Young's Bitter or a regularly changing guest ale, while diners sit at one of a dozen or so tables spread over two cosy rooms. The owner is passionate about his pub and sources his meats from the local farms and his game from the nearby shoots. Gutsy country cooking is full of flavour and includes homemade terrines, heartwarming casseroles and delicious homemade puddings. Sunday lunch is extremely popular and prices are very reasonable.

SHILTON, OX18 4AB
Tel.: 01993 842280
Website: www.shiltonroseandcrown.com

2.5 mi southeast of Burford by A 40 off B 4020, in centre of village. Parking.

PRICES
Meals: a la carte £ 21/40

MAP: 92

CLOSING TIMES
Closed 25 December

PLOWDEN ARMS

Interesting dishes use historical recipes

This appealing pub sits close to Shiplake College and started life in the mid-18C as the Plough Hotel, but was later renamed after an eminent local lawyer. It has a delightful garden and three different rooms where open fires, flickering candles and hop bines set the scene. 1920s jazz music plays in the background and the air is one of relaxation. The experienced chef offers some interesting dishes: on the large blackboard you'll find snacks such as chicken scotch eggs or local chipolatas, alongside specials like red mullet with anchovy cream. The main menu, meanwhile, takes inspiration from old cookbooks and traditional recipes, with dishes like herrings in oatmeal or potted livers with pear chutney; their history listed alongside.

Reading Rd,
SHIPLAKE, RG9 4BX
Tel.: 0118 940 2794
Website: www.plowdenarmsshiplake.co.uk

2 mi south of Henley-on-Thames on A 4155. Parking.

PRICES   MAP: **93**
Meals: a la carte £ 24/42

CLOSING TIMES
Closed Monday except bank holidays

WYKHAM ARMS

A true village pub set down narrow lanes

If you're after a true village pub, the 17C Wykham Arms may well be it. Set down narrow lanes in the middle of the countryside, this thatched pub certainly plays its role in the community. It boasts attractive sand-coloured stone walls adorned with pretty climbing plants and a pleasant terrace with cast iron furniture. So as not to price out the locals, menus offer a range of dishes right through from light bites and bar snacks to the full three courses; so you might find Salcombe crab and mango salad or Warwickshire pork belly. Suppliers are proudly noted on the blackboard and the chef is only too happy to answer any questions. There's a good choice of wines and what better way to celebrate than with lobster and champagne on the terrace?

Temple Mill Rd,
SIBFORD GOWER, OX15 5RX
Tel.: 01295 788808
Website: www.wykhamarms.co.uk

8 mi west of Banbury by B 4035. Parking.

PRICES
Meals: a la carte £ 25/34

MAP: 94

CLOSING TIMES
Closed Monday except bank holidays

STAR INN

300 year old inn at the heart of village life

With its 300 year history, the delightful flint-walled Star Inn is at the very heart of Sparsholt village life. It was lovingly restored a few years back and now has a smart country feel and comfy bedrooms in the converted barn behind. If you're out for a meal, the restaurant overlooking the garden is the best place to be, while for those after a quick drink, the squashy sofas set around the wood-burning stove are the way to go. Menus offer an appealing mix of carefully prepared dishes, from the comforting bar menu with its fishcakes and burgers to the more adventurous à la carte which includes the likes of mallard terrine with clementine and hazelnuts, rapeseed oil poached salmon and all manner of game – maybe venison, partridge or rabbit.

Watery Ln,
SPARSHOLT, OX12 9PL
Tel.: 01235 751873
Website: www.thestarsparsholt.co.uk

3.5 mi west of Wantage off B 4507. Parking.

PRICES
Meals: a la carte £ 29/48

8 rooms:
£ 85/135

MAP: 95

CLOSING TIMES
Closed 4-11 January

SIR CHARLES NAPIER

Skilfully prepared, full-flavoured dishes

Set in a small hamlet on the hillside, this attractive 18C flint pub might just have it all. The delightful terrace and gardens buzz with conversation in the warmer months, while sculptures of beasts and figures peer out from behind bushes and lie on the lawn. Inside yet more creatures hide about the place – and all are for sale. It's worth heading to the cosy bar with its open fires and comfy sofas, although the beamed dining room adorned with flowers and art is equally charming. Cooking is refined yet unfussy, offering the likes of wood pigeon with heritage tomatoes, followed by fell-bred rack of lamb with roast sweetbreads. Dishes are skilfully prepared and capture flavours to their full. A well-chosen wine list completes the picture.

Sprigs Holly,
SPRIGG'S ALLEY, OX39 4BX
Tel.: 01494 483011
Website: www.sircharlesnapier.co.uk

2.5 mi southeast of Chinnor by Bledlow Ridge rd. Parking.

PRICES
Meals: £ 20 (weekdays) and a la carte
£ 39/56

MAP: **96**

CLOSING TIMES
Closed 24-26 December, Sunday dinner
and Monday except bank holidays
booking advisable

FISH

Its owners have brought a taste of France to Oxfordshire, so expect French pictures, French music and a largely French wine list, as well as French food and charming Gallic service. Feast on meaty terrines, escargots or moules marinière; such dishes mingle merrily with British classics like steak and kidney pie, Gressingham duck breast or fillet of lamb. L'entente cordiale continues on the dessert menu, with crème brûlée clamouring for your attention alongside treacle sponge. This is robust country cooking in its most classic form, with pretty much everything homemade using seasonal ingredients. Head to the rear of the pub for the lovely garden and conservatory, and be sure to ask Sebastian (one of the owners) for his wine recommendations.

4 Appleford Rd,
SUTTON COURTENAY, OX14 4NQ
Tel.: 01235 848242
Website: www.thefishatsuttoncourtenay.co.uk

Between Abingdon and Didcot on B 4016. Parking.

PRICES
Meals: £ 16 (weekdays)/19 and a la carte
£ 27/48

MAP: 97

CLOSING TIMES
Closed January, Monday except bank
holidays and Sunday dinner

SWAN INN

Charming in every respect!

Booking is a must at this delightful pub, set on the banks of a meandering river. Its honey-coloured walls are covered in wisteria and its lovely garden filled with fruit trees, while the interior boasts an open oak frame and stone walls covered with old lithographs and handmade walking sticks. A well-versed team serve tasty dishes from the daily menu, which features the latest seasonal produce from nearby farms and estates. Cooking is fairly modern in style, with some dishes a contemporary take on older recipes; you might find roe deer carpaccio with truffled mayonnaise, fillet of bream with tandoori potatoes or baked ginger pudding with hot spiced treacle. Well-appointed bedrooms have a luxurious feel; riverside rooms have the best view.

SWINBROOK, OX18 4DY
Tel.: 01993 823339
Website: www.theswanswinbrook.co.uk

3 mi east of Burford by A 40 and minor road north. Parking.

PRICES
Meals: a la carte £ 25/44

 11 rooms:
£ 110/195

MAP: 98

CLOSING TIMES
Closed 25-26 December

MOLE INN

Attractive interior and lovely landscaped terrace

The Mole has made quite a name for itself in the area and deservedly so. Beautiful landscaped gardens and a pleasant terrace front the building, while inside, attractive beamed ceilings and exposed brick walls create a warm and welcoming atmosphere. The menu is equally appealing, catering for all tastes and appetites; you might find sautéed squid with linguine and chorizo, followed by twice-cooked belly of pork with gratin dauphinoise. Sourcing is a serious business and it's a case of 'first come, first served' if you want the full choice. The Tuesday grill and Friday fish night menus are decided the day before, so if there's something you've set your heart on, it's worth calling to reserve your dish. Service remains smooth under pressure.

TOOT BALDON, OX44 9NG
Tel.: 01865 340001
Website: www.themoleinn.com

6 mi southeast of Oxford off A 4074. Parking.

PRICES   MAP: **99**
Meals: £ 23

CLOSING TIMES
Closed 25 December
booking advisable

FAT FOX INN

Run with integrity by experienced owners

This pub was originally called the Fox and Hounds but there were so many other pubs of the same name in the surrounding villages that it became a little confusing; so the owners decided to hold a renaming competition and the Fat Fox was born. It's in the heart of a busy market village and dates from the 1800s and, although it's nothing fancy, is run with honesty and integrity by its experienced owners. The menu reflects what they themselves like to eat in a pub and covers all bases from potted mackerel or local rabbit broth to filling pheasant pie. Fight the cats for a spot on the sofas by the wood burning range in the buzzy bar or make for the slightly more formal dining room; afterwards, settle in for the night in one of the cosy bedrooms.

13 Shireburn St,
WATLINGTON, OX49 5BU
Tel.: 01491 613040
Website: www.thefatfoxinn.co.uk

9 mi southwest of Thame by B 4012, A 40 and B 4009. Parking.

PRICES
Meals: a la carte £ 25/35

 9 rooms:
£ 65/119

MAP: 100

CLOSING TIMES
Closed dinner 25 December and 1 January

CROWN

Bedrooms are beautifully appointed

It might have 18C origins and a Grade II listing but inside, the Crown is not your typical coaching inn. An impressive makeover by the team who own the Anchor in Oxford has left it with a cosy bar, a comfy lounge and a bright, airy, almost greenhouse-style dining room with an attractive Belgian tiled floor and plenty of potted plants; for warmer days there's also a pleasant courtyard. Fresh, light cooking takes its influences from the Med and makes good use of the wood-fired oven. Homemade focaccia is followed by dishes in 2 sizes – maybe butternut squash and spelt risotto, Provençal fish stew or octopus with tomatoes, capers and dill. They open in the morning for coffee and cake and on Sundays the roast lunches are followed by £5 pizzas.

31 High St,
WOODSTOCK, OX20 1TE
Tel.: 01993 813339
Website: www.thecrownwoodstock.com

In centre of town, on-street parking.

PRICES
Meals: a la carte £ 20/32

 5 rooms:
£ 175/250

MAP: 101

CLOSING TIMES
Open daily

KILLINGWORTH CASTLE

Interesting dishes follow the seasons

This pub's name is slightly odd... first of all, it's nowhere near Killingworth, and secondly, there's no castle nearby! It's a large building dating from the 1500s and, after a year standing derelict, was taken over by the Alexanders, who soon returned it to proper pub status. Open fires, thick stone walls and old mix and match furniture provide a rustic feel, and black and white photos depicting its past adorn the walls. The chatty staff clearly know what they're doing and the food is great value, especially the dish of the day. The main menu follows the seasons and provides plenty of interest, offering the likes of sticky pork belly or lamb with truffle mash. Retire to one of the spacious, comfy bedrooms feeling suitably fortified.

Glympton Rd,
WOOTTON, OX20 1EJ
Tel.: 01993 811401
Website: www.thekillingworthcastle.com

3.5 mi northwest of Woodstock by Hensington Rd and Banbury Rd on B 4027. Parking.

PRICES
Meals: a la carte £ 20/49

 8 rooms:
£ 99/180

MAP: 102

CLOSING TIMES
Closed 25 December

ABINGER HATCH

An outside bar and kitchen for summer BBQs

This attractive 18C pub is found in a charming spot at the centre of a small hamlet on the Wotton Estate, deep in walking country, and with its low beams, cosy corners and roaring log fires it oozes country gentility. It's open throughout the day, offering snacks and drinks, sharing boards, starters like potted shrimps or a scotch egg with soldiers, and comforting main courses such as the 'pie of the day'. In the winter you'll often see the local hunt in for lunch, while on summer Saturdays the outside bar and kitchen really comes into its own and dishes from the barbecue are the order of the day. After lunch grab a picnic mat and a board game or head for the boules pitch at the end of the garden for a spot of friendly competition.

Abinger Ln,
ABINGER COMMON, RH5 6HZ
Tel.: 01306 730737
Website: www.theabingerhatch.com

Between Guildford and Dorking off A 25 in village centre. Parking.

PRICES   MAP: **103**
Meals: a la carte £ 23/30

CLOSING TIMES
Closed 25 December

SWAN INN

Make for the three-tiered terraced garden

With its part-whitewashed, part tile-hung exterior, the Swan Inn certainly catches the eye of those passing through this charming village. The nearby green was once home to eleven different glass works, which supplied many of the country's finest buildings – including St Stephen's Chapel – but it's now every bit a perfect English village scene. It might be over 200 years old but the Swan has a modern feel and its 11 bedrooms are equally stylish. The extensive menu changes a little each day and offers a mix of pub and restaurant style dishes, so alongside beer-battered haddock and shoestring fries you'll find the likes of pan-seared cod with sauce vierge and fennel-crushed potatoes. On sunny days, the stepped rear terrace is a popular spot.

Petworth Rd,
CHIDDINGFOLD, GU8 4TY
Tel.: 01428 684688
Website: www.theswaninnchiddingfold.com

On A 283 on the eastern side of the village. Parking.

PRICES
Meals: a la carte £ 22/45

 11 rooms:
£ 74/195

MAP: 104

CLOSING TIMES
Open daily

PARROT INN

Characterful 17C pub on the village green

After 30 years working in the food industry, the Gotto family decided it was time to do something about the lack of good quality meat being served, so they bought a farm and started rearing cows, pigs and sheep. Another 20 years on and the family business is thriving: they serve their own meats in the pub; they have a farm shop in the car park (which also sells their homemade bread, cakes and preserves); and they even run their own butchery courses! Well-priced, generously proportioned dishes include tasty terrines and raised pastry pies, and you'll always find some lesser cuts alongside the prime ones as beasts are utilised to the full. The 300 year old pub interior oozes character, courtesy of low beams, flagged floors and open fires.

FOREST GREEN, RH5 5RZ
Tel.: 01306 621339
Website: www.theparrot.co.uk

8 mi south of Dorking by A 24, A 29 and B 2126 west. Parking.

PRICES   MAP: **105**
Meals: a la carte £ 22/36

CLOSING TIMES
Closed 25 December and Sunday dinner

THE PENDLETON IN ST JOHNS

A smart, buzzy, food-focused pub

A buzzing atmosphere and friendly service are guaranteed at this smart, contemporary pub just south of Redhill. Unsurprisingly, it's a popular place both with the locals and those from further afield, so make sure you book ahead. One side of the bar gives a view into the kitchen, while the other is next to a counter displaying breads and charcuterie. The serve lunch and dinner Wednesday to Saturday and, on Tuesday evenings, pizzas and bar snacks. Menus have plenty of South American influences courtesy of the Brazilian chef and on warm summer evenings, pizzas are served on the terrace from the van outside. While the food is the main attraction, drinks are in no way neglected: the wine list is well chosen and cocktails are a popular choice.

26 Pendleton Rd,
ST JOHNS, REDHILL, RH1 6QF
Tel.: 01737 760212
Website: www.thependleton.co.uk

1 mi south of Redhill by A 23 and Pendleton Rd. Parking.

PRICES   MAP: **106**
Meals: a la carte £ 25/39

CLOSING TIMES
Closed 25 December-2 January, Sunday
dinner, Monday
bookings advisable at dinner

ANCHOR

Interesting dishes burst with flavour

It's not an unusual name for a pub, but it begins to seem so when you find out that the pub in question is actually nowhere near any water. However, it is near a cycle route which was known in the 19C as 'The Mecca of all good cyclists', and this explains the number of bicycle-themed objects therein. Originally constructed as almshouses for the poor, the inn is reputed to be over four hundred years old; today it has a smart yet rustic feel with polished slate floors and on-trend grey walls, along with a lovely courtyard terrace. The cooking moves with the times too, so instead of classic pub dishes you could find pan-roast pork chop with caponata and confit tomato or, for dessert, elderflower panna cotta with apple and gin sorbet.

High St,
RIPLEY, GU23 6AE
Tel.: 01483 211866
Website: www.ripleyanchor.co.uk

In the centre of the village. Parking.

PRICES
Meals: £ 19 (weekday lunch) and a la carte
£ 24/39

MAP: 107

CLOSING TIMES
Closed Monday

THREE HORSESHOES

Owned by the locals, with a homely, lived-in feel

This is the sort of pub where a line of locals turn away from their drink to look at you as you come through the door – but we can forgive them this, as not only are they very welcoming, the fact of the matter is that without them, there would be no pub: following a five year period of closure, they clubbed together to save it – and it has been at the heart of the community ever since. This local success story is as much about the food as the beer, with hearty, traditional meals served daily – high on flavour yet low on price – and everything, including bread and ice cream, homemade. Real fires, fresh flowers, books and village info give the place a homely, lived-in feel. Head for 'Brian's Corner': the cosy snug at the back.

Dye House Rd,
THURSLEY, GU8 6QD
Tel.: 01252 703268
Website: www.threehorseshoesthursley.com

Between Farnham and Godalming, signed off B 3001. Parking.

PRICES
Meals: a la carte £ 23/44

MAP: **108**

CLOSING TIMES
Closed Sunday dinner

THE INN WEST END

A lively atmosphere and genuine hospitality

Its lively atmosphere and genuine hospitality are two reasons why this recently refurbished pub is always so busy. Another big draw here is the food: there's something for everyone on the menu, from sandwiches and pub classics like sausage and mash to dishes like lobster Caesar salad and deep-fried poached egg; with fish specials and plenty of game in season. Portions are generous and flavours robust, with global influences, good quality ingredients and some original touches. The owners also have a wine shop in the car park, which focuses on Europe, so it comes as no surprise to find an interesting list of well-chosen wines, strong on pinot noir and claret. Twelve smart, well-equipped boutique bedrooms complete the picture.

42 Guildford Rd,
WEST END, GU24 9PW
Tel.: 01276 858652
Website: www.the-inn.co.uk

2.5 mi southeast of junction 3 of M 3 on A 322. Parking.

PRICES
Meals: £ 16 (weekday lunch)/28
and a la carte £ 25/49

 12 rooms:
£ 125/150

MAP: 109

CLOSING TIMES
Open daily

THE GEORGE AT BURPHAM

Beams, fires and a smugglers' wheel

This pub was on the brink of closure when a local consortium headed by three local businessmen stepped in and saved it. It has been given a smart new look, a new name and a new tagline which sums up the spirit of its reincarnation: 'By the locals, for the locals, of the locals… and a very warm welcome to everyone'. Dogs are patently included within the 'everyone', with dog biscuits provided on the bar, and whether you're a hungry walker back from the South Downs or a thirsty cricketer fresh from the adjacent pitch, you'll be given cheery treatment from the friendly, long-standing staff. The seasonal menu is full of tasty, popular classics; and beams, fires and a smugglers' wheel on the ceiling add character to the modern interior.

Main St,
BURPHAM, BN18 9RR
Tel.: 01903 883131
Website: www.georgeatburpham.co.uk

3 mi northeast of Arundel by A 27.

PRICES   MAP: **110**
Meals: a la carte £ 25/43

CLOSING TIMES
Closed 25 December

FOX GOES FREE

Oozes traditional English charm

Set in the beautiful South Downs countryside, close to Goodwood, this charming 17C flint pub was once the haunt of William III and his Royal Hunting Party. It boasts a superb garden and terrace with lovely outlooks and retains most of its original features, including exposed stone walls, low beamed ceilings, brick floors, inglenook fires and even an old bread oven. There are three dining areas, two with table service and one where you order at the bar; behind which you'll find a good selection of hand-pulled ales. Dishes range from simple pub classics on the bar menu to an à la carte featuring local pork chops, braised venison shank or steak and kidney pie for two. Bedrooms are clean and unfussy; those above the pub have low ceilings.

CHARLTON, PO18 0HU
Tel.: 01243 811461
Website: www.thefoxgoesfree.com

Midway between Chichester and Midhurst off the A 286. Parking.

PRICES
Meals: a la carte £ 21/44

 5 rooms:
£ 70/180

MAP: 111

CLOSING TIMES
Open daily

GINGER FOX

The first thing you notice is the pub's charming thatch – spot the fox running across it and you know you've come to the right place. The play area in the garden is a reassuring sight for parents; base yourself in 'the den' and you can keep an eye on your children as you eat. A monthly changing menu offers good value, flavoursome dishes; there's the occasional pub classic like beef and ale pie, but dishes are generally more akin to those served in a restaurant; perhaps crispy lamb sweetbreads, scallops with onion purée, roast partridge or wild halibut with sprouting broccoli. The vegetarian tasting plate will please any herbivores in your party and desserts are a highlight, so save space for some doughnuts or a slice of Bakewell tart.

Muddleswood Rd,
ALBOURNE, HENFIELD, BN6 9EA
Tel.: 01273 857888
Website: www.gingermanrestaurants.com

3 mi southwest of Henfield on A 281. Parking.

PRICES
Meals: £ 15 (weekday lunch) and a la carte
£ 25/45

MAP: 112

CLOSING TIMES
Closed 25 December

DUKE OF CUMBERLAND ARMS

Sit by the stream in the pretty tiered gardens

A hidden gem affectionately known as The Duke, this 16C hillside pub nestles in pretty tiered gardens with trickling streams, trout ponds and a splendid view over the South Downs. The pub's interior is as enchanting as the garden, with a cosy beamed, fire-lit bar and a more modern dining area which opens onto a terrace. Appealing menus offer carefully prepared seasonal dishes: lunch sees hearty pub classics, with choices like Cornish day boat fish and chips or braised oxtail and horseradish mash; dinner shifts things up a gear and might include Selsey crab thermidor with truffled chunky chips, confit free-range pork bolly with apple and Calvados glaze or oven-roasted trio of English lamb – neck, steak and rack – with pommes sarladaise.

HENLEY, GU27 3HQ
Tel.: 01428 652280
Website: www.dukeofcumberland.com

2.75 mi north of Midhurst off A 286. Parking.

PRICES
Meals: a la carte £ 28/51

MAP: 113

CLOSING TIMES
Closed 25-26 December and dinner
Sunday-Monday

CROWN INN

A renowned local chef cooks classic dishes

Having survived untouched since the 16C, this pub was nearly destroyed in a fire caused by lightning in 2003 and remained closed for over five years. Finally restored to its former glory in 2009, it entered a new era in early 2013 with the arrival of renowned local chef Mark Raffan, who not only brought with him his many years of experience, but also his army of loyal followers. With its exposed brick, wooden beams and feature inglenook, the front bar is full of character, while the smart dining room houses a grand piano, played on Friday nights. Classical dishes form the core of the menu, while the more ambitious blackboard specials embrace the seasons. Simple bedrooms have views of the village green; Room One has a four-poster bed.

The Green,
HORSTED KEYNES, RH17 7AW
Tel.: 01825 791609
Website: www.thecrown-horstedkeynes.co.uk

West of Danehill, signposted off A 275. Parking.

PRICES
Meals: a la carte £ 25/44

 4 rooms:
£ 75/110

MAP: 114

CLOSING TIMES
Closed Sunday dinner and Monday
January-June

CRABTREE

A family-run affair with a cosy, lived-in feel

Having had new life breathed into it, this pub is back once more at the heart of community, serving everything from bar snacks to feasts of several courses. A family-run affair, it has a cosy, lived-in feel, helped along by warming fires and cheery, helpful staff. Various rooms provide a characterful backdrop to your meal: there's the Garden Room which is light and airy; the Pass Room which allows you to see into the kitchen, and the tiny Smithy Room, which was once – you guessed it – the village smithy. Traditional English dishes like rump of Sussex lamb come with a touch of refinement and plenty of flavour and the wine list is well-priced and full of helpful information, including which wines are suitable for vegetarians and vegans.

Brighton Rd,
LOWER BEEDING, RH13 6PT
Tel.: 01403 892666
Website: www.crabtreesussex.com

5 mi south of Horsham on A 281. Parking.

PRICES
Meals: £ 15 (weekdays) and a la carte
£ 25/40

MAP: 115

CLOSING TIMES
Closed Sunday dinner

Q60

INDULGE YOURSELF

INFINITI

EMPOWER THE DRIVE

NOAH'S ARK INN

Watch the local cricket team from the garden

This quintessentially English pub is found in a picturesque location next to the church on the village green and its large garden overlooks the cricket pitch. Rumour has it that the pub was once accessed by a narrow path over a moat, where visitors had to go in two-by-two, hence its unusual name. The gloriously rustic interior features a bar – which offers a good selection of real ales; a large baronial-style room with cosy sofas, a tiled floor, exposed beams and a wood-burning stove; and 'The Restaurant' with its scrubbed wooden tables and large inglenook fireplace. Generously sized dishes keep things in the traditional vein with the likes of cream of cauliflower soup, battered haddock and chips and, to finish, rhubarb trifle with custard.

The Green,
LURGASHALL, GU28 9ET
Tel.: 01428 707346
Website: www.noahsarkinn.co.uk

Between Petworth and Chiddingfold off the A 283. Parking.

PRICES
Meals: a la carte £ 25/36

MAP: 116

CLOSING TIMES
Open daily

EARL OF MARCH

British dishes and views of the South Downs

This 18C inn offers the perfect blend of contemporary styling and relaxed country character. Sit on cosy sofas beside the wood burning stove, find a spot in the smarter restaurant or head for the terrace which affords amazing views of the South Downs (the Goodwood race circuit is hidden opposite amongst the trees). The owner previously spent time as executive head chef at The Ritz, so expect good quality seasonal produce and British-based dishes. Start with maybe asparagus, slow-cooked egg and hollandaise or cured pork, salsify and raspberry, then for mains, lamb rump with samphire and heritage tomatoes or pan-fried polenta cake with wild mushroom and nettle butter. Desserts keep things traditional with crumbles and sticky puddings.

MID LAVANT, PO18 0BQ
Tel.: 01243 533993
Website: www.theearlofmarch.com

3 mi north of Chichester on A 286. Parking.

PRICES   MAP: **117**
Meals: £ 22 (lunch and early dinner)
and a la carte £ 30/40

CLOSING TIMES
Open daily

CHEQUERS INN

The chef-owner likes to track game and forage

As you step inside this pub, you're instantly surrounded by the oaky aroma of an open fire and the murmur of the day's tales being recounted by cheery locals. The origins of the inn can be traced back to the 15C, which comes as no surprise when you look around the charming stone-floored bar, but there's also a slightly unusual corrugated dining room extension (formerly the village hall), a large paved terrace and a spacious garden. The experienced chef-owner loves the hands-on approach, so he's often out in the woods foraging for wild mushrooms and tracking down game, or out in the garden gathering the latest yield; maybe artichokes, pears or greengages. Classically based menus display a good understanding of how best to prepare ingredients.

ROWHOOK, RH12 3PY
Tel.: 01403 790480
Website: www.thechequersrowhook.com

3 mi west of Horsham by A 281. Parking.

PRICES
Meals: a la carte £ 26/41

MAP: 118

CLOSING TIMES
Closed 25 December and Sunday dinner

CRAB & LOBSTER

Located within the Pagham Harbour Nature Reserve

This historic inn is superbly located within the striking landscape of Pagham Harbour Nature Reserve, a marshy haven for wildlife, particularly birds. Sympathetically modernised, it retains a flagged floor, open fires and the odd beam – there are a few tables for drinkers but being a dining pub, most tables are laid up for eating. Well-presented dishes are very much at the restaurant end of the scale; perhaps saffron-scented seafood risotto with seared scallops and crab mascarpone or poached fillet of halibut on a sweetcorn and spring onion chowder – although lunch also sees lighter options like sandwiches and salads. Comfortable bedrooms have a modern, minimalist style; two-roomed Crab Cottage has a garden and an open-fired stove.

Mill Ln,
SIDLESHAM, PO20 7NB
Tel.: 01243 641233
Website: www.crab-lobster.co.uk

5 mi south of Chichester by B 2145, then turn right into Rookery Lane. Parking.

PRICES
Meals: £ 27 (weekday lunch) and a la carte £ 31/52

 5 rooms:
£ 90/300

MAP: 119

CLOSING TIMES
Open daily
booking advisable

HORSE GUARDS INN

Chatty young staff add to the charm

In an elevated spot in the heart of a quiet village sits this pretty mid-17C inn with views over the Rother Valley and the South Downs from its lovely lavender-filled garden. Happily, it's equally charming inside, with its low beams, fireplaces, period features and fresh flowers. The names of suppliers are chalked up on the blackboard and dishes are a good mix of rustic, like wild mushrooms on toast, and more elaborate, like stone bass with roast fennel. Local seafood is handled with skill and some of the vegetables and salads come from their own patch. The staff are young, chatty and willing, and contribute greatly to the appeal. There are also three charmingly understated bedrooms available (family groups can book the cottage next door).

Upperton Rd,
TILLINGTON, GU28 9AF
Tel.: 01798 342332
Website: www.thehorseguardsinn.co.uk

Just off A 272 in heart of the village. Unrestricted on-street parking.

PRICES
Meals: a la carte £ 21/38

3 rooms:
£ 100/150

MAP: 120

CLOSING TIMES
Closed 25-26 December

RICHMOND ARMS

Luxurious bedrooms at the foot of the South Downs

This appealing, laid-back country pub is found in a lovely little village at the foot of the South Downs, opposite the duck pond; keep an eye out for the colourful decoy ducks. In warmer weather, try for one of the handful of tables outside amongst the colourful hanging baskets; otherwise, head inside, where you'll find fresh flowers and a blackboard listing enticing nibbles such as halloumi chips or ham cut on an antique slicing machine. The menu offers plenty of appeal; game comes from the family estate in Anglesey, and there's a delightful rotisserie and a Japanese robata grill used to cook local mature steaks. Two luxurious bedrooms are above – and on Friday and Saturday there's a vintage Citroën van selling pizzas in the car park.

Mill Rd,
WEST ASHLING, PO18 8EA
Tel.: 01243 572046
Website: www.therichmondarms.co.uk

4.5 mi northwest of Chichester, located on far side of village pond.
Parking.

PRICES
Meals: a la carte £ 22/44

 2 rooms:
£ 115/145

MAP: 121

CLOSING TIMES
Closed Christmas-New Year, last week
July, first week November, Sunday dinner,
Monday and Tuesday

CAT INN

Very much a village pub and a hit with the locals

Set in an idyllic village and only four centuries younger than the 11C church it overlooks, The Cat is very much a village pub, where you'll find locals relaxing by the inglenook with a pint. There are beamed ceilings, pewter tankards, open fires and plenty of corners in which to get cosy; one of these even contains a surprisingly deep well. Run by an experienced owner who cut his teeth at Gravetye Manor just down the road, it can get very busy; but, full or not, the friendly service doesn't falter. Cooking focuses on tasty pub classics and is carefully executed and good value; dishes might include roast belly of pork, Rye Bay lemon sole or steak, mushroom and ale pie. Four tastefully decorated bedrooms complete the picture.

Queen's Sq,
WEST HOATHLY, RH19 4PP
Tel.: 01342 810369
Website: www.catinn.co.uk

Between East Grinstead and Haywards Heath off B 2028; follow signs for the church. Parking.

PRICES
Meals: a la carte £ 23/42

 4 rooms:
£ 95/165

MAP: 122

CLOSING TIMES
Closed 25 December and Sunday dinner

343

SOUTH WEST

—— **England**

Six hundred miles of relentlessly breathtaking coastline pound the majestic South West, assuring it of a dramatic backdrop whatever the season. Its prestige is bolstered by four UNESCO World Heritage sites: one of them is Dorset's spectacular Jurassic Coast, which includes the 180 billion pebbles of Chesil Beach. Further north, Dartmoor and Exmoor embody the region's untamed beauty. The built environment may be of a more recent time line, but examples are still impressive, ranging from thirteenth century Lacock, home of many a filmed costume drama, to Elizabethan Longleat with its Capability Brown designed parkland, and late Victorian Lanhydrock, "the great house of Cornwall". The same county boasts its very own "theatre under the stars", The Minack, where the drama of nature collides with the drama of the written word.

Days out in this unforgettable region come complete with pasties and a pint of local ale, or freshly caught lobster, scallops or mussels enjoyed along the quay.

CHANNEL ISLANDS

France

SOUTH

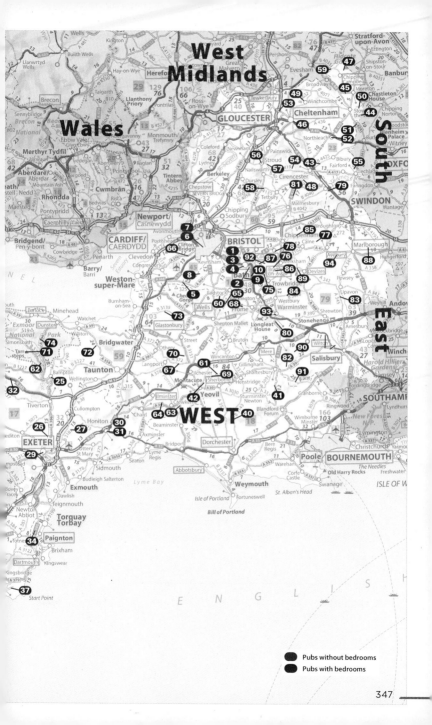

Pubs without bedrooms

Pubs with bedrooms

CHEQUERS

Sophisticated cooking and elaborate presentation

Set in a residential street amid elegant Georgian terraces, the Chequers isn't far from its sister, the Marlborough Tavern. They may look similar from the outside but cross their thresholds and you'll see each has something different to offer. The Chequers has some pubby character with its simple tables, parquet floor and central bar but it's also been smartened up with a bright paint job. The cooking is fairly sophisticated and the presentation, elaborate, so alongside a few robust pub favourites you might find pigeon with seeds, pickled walnuts and red cabbage or pork belly, cheek and tenderloin with faggots and black pudding. The homemade breadboard is a highlight, as are the creative desserts, which offer something a little different.

50 Rivers St,
BATH, BA1 2QA
Tel.: 01225 360017
Website: www.thechequersbath.com

Close to The Royal Crescent, off Upper Church St.
On-street pay & display parking.

PRICES
Meals: a la carte £ 23/46

MAP: 1

CLOSING TIMES
Closed 25 December

HARE & HOUNDS

Modern versions of classic dishes and great views

This is a huge place, attracting large numbers of people – so not the best choice for a quiet, romantic evening – but for a birthday celebration or a night out with friends, it's ideal. There has been a property here since the 16C, when a hunting lodge was built; over the years it's been an inn and a hotel but it's now very much a local pub. Its hillside location near the racecourse affords superb views over the Bath countryside, and its gardens and large terrace come into their own in the warmer months. Inside it's light and airy: choose a seat with a view in the conservatory, cosy up by the fire or watch the chefs hard at work in the kitchen pass. Menus are appealingly pithy and offer modern versions of classic dishes.

Lansdown Rd,
BATH, BA1 5TJ
Tel.: 01225 482682
Website: www.hareandhoundsbath.com

1.5 mi north of the city centre on Lansdown Rd. Parking.

PRICES
Meals: a la carte £ 25/40

MAP: 2

CLOSING TIMES
Open daily

MARLBOROUGH TAVERN

Smart, cosy pub near the Royal Crescent

On the eastern edge of Victoria Park, only a stone's throw from the Royal Crescent, sits this 18C pub, surrounded by grand terraced properties. Despite its traditional outer appearance, it's surprisingly chic and fashionable inside, boasting a modern, open-plan interior, boldly patterned wallpaper and contemporary art; not forgetting a rather pleasant walled terrace to the rear. At lunch they offer sandwiches, pub classics and a good value set menu, while dinner steps things up a gear with some interesting specials; there might be potted Wiltshire game, followed by south coast plaice with Cornish samphire and, to finish, iced coffee and honeycomb parfait with hot apple spring roll and blackberry and apple fool.

35 Marlborough Buildings,
BATH, BA1 2LY
Tel.: 01225 423731
Website: www.marlborough-tavern.com

East side of Royal Victoria Park. On-street pay & display parking.

PRICES
Meals: £ 16 (lunch) and a la carte £ 25/42

MAP: 3

CLOSING TIMES
Closed 25 December

WHITE HART

Shows the value of good sourcing

Situated close to the railway, just over the river, The White Hart has a real neighbourhood feel. It attracts a loyal local following, so get here early or book ahead as it fills up quickly. Food-wise, the mantra here is 'keep it simple', with the sourcing of ingredients afforded paramount importance. Portions are large and cooking, hearty, with dishes like baked fillet of pork wrapped in bacon, breast of chicken with lentils or whole baked sea bass with lime, ginger and chilli butter. Most people have a main dish and share a side and a dessert, but the smaller tapas plates are also very popular. The pub has a rustic feel, with scrubbed wooden floors and worn wooden tables and the rear terrace is a great spot in warmer weather.

Widcombe Hill,
BATH, BA2 6AA
Tel.: 01225 338053
Website: www.whitehartbath.co.uk

On southern side of the city just off A 36. On-street parking.

PRICES   MAP: **4**
Meals: £ 13 (weekday lunch) and a la carte
£ 30/40

CLOSING TIMES
Closed 25-26 December, 1 January, Sunday
dinner and bank holidays
booking essential at dinner

SEYMOUR ARMS

Come on a Friday for fish & chips or moules frites

The country cousin of the Albion Public House and Dining Rooms sits in a small village in the Mendip Hills, overlooking Blagdon Lake. There's plenty to do around these parts, from visiting the Wookey Hole caves and Cheddar Gorge to fishing, pony trekking and potholing. The less adventurous, however, can hole up beside the wood-burning stove of this modern pub with a pint of Butcombe Bitter – brewed just down the road. The regularly changing menus are refreshingly concise and the unfussy, confidently prepared dishes have a modern British style. Don't miss the homemade ice creams and West Country cheeses, and keep an eye out for the seasonal bar deal, usually £10 for a pint and a burger or pie. Up-to-date bedrooms are simply furnished.

Bath Rd,
BLAGDON, BS40 7TH
Tel.: 01761 462279
Website: www.theseymourarmsblagdon.co.uk

14 mi southwest of Bristol by A 38 on A 368. Parking.

PRICES
Meals: a la carte £ 24/40

 5 rooms:
£ 77/105

MAP: 5

CLOSING TIMES
Closed Monday lunch

KENSINGTON ARMS

Assured cooking and a friendly team

It might be painted 'stealth' grey but this smart neighbourhood pub stands out a mile for its warm atmosphere and great food. It's the kind of place that could have been teleported over from London, with a bustling bar (where they leave scotch eggs and sausage rolls on the counter from 6pm) and a high-ceilinged dining room with red leather banquettes – its Victorian style accentuated by oil paintings and a collection of copper pans on the walls. Daily changing menus have a strong British base and tick both the local and seasonal boxes. Open with duck hearts on toast or smoked haddock rarebit, then move on to hogget with potato terrine or rib of beef for two to share. Puddings follow the traditional route, with the likes of tarts and crumbles.

35-37 Stanley Rd,
BRISTOL, BS6 6NP
Tel.: 0117 944 6444
Website: www.thekensingtonarms.co.uk

In city centre. Unrestricted parking outside pub and in nearby streets.

PRICES
Meals: a la carte £ 20/39

MAP: 6

CLOSING TIMES
Closed 25-26 December

PUMP HOUSE

Victorian former pumping station by the docks

Standing proudly on the quayside, this cavernous Victorian building was once a pumping station for the adjacent docks; evidence of which can be seen in the form of exposed stone walls, quarry tiled floors and original pipework. When the sun's out, sit on the terrace and watch the boats; on colder days head for the large bar or one of the many tables or sofas dotted about over the various different levels. Dishes change with the seasons and focus on a selection of modern classics, including the likes of braised lambs' hearts and coddled egg with marmite soldiers From Weds-Sat they offer a tasting menu of more refined dishes; you can have any menu anywhere, but the latter is perhaps best suited to the linen-laid mezzanine restaurant.

Merchants Rd,
BRISTOL, BS8 4PZ
Tel.: 0117 927 2229
Website: www.the-pumphouse.com

On the eastern side of the docks. Parking.

PRICES   MAP: **7**
Meals: a la carte £ 22/44

CLOSING TIMES
Closed 25 December

PONY & TRAP

✿

Skilfully crafted classical dishes and rural views

This pub's name conjures images of a rural idyll and that's exactly what you'll find here – ask for a table in the rustic rear room or on the terrace, where you can enjoy the wonderful countryside views; at the front is a cosy, characterful bar with stone walls, church pews and an old range laden with pans. Brother and sister team Josh and Holly Eggleton took on this pub almost a decade ago when they were barely out of their teens and have made a real success of it. She runs the service with aplomb while he's hard at work in the kitchen, creating tasty, classical British dishes, with pub favourites at lunch and the occasional innovative touch at dinner. It takes skill to make something as simple as, say, a faggot look and taste quite so good.

Knowle Hill,
NEW TOWN, CHEW MAGNA, BS40 8TQ
Tel.: 01275 332627
Website: www.theponyandtrap.co.uk

1.5 mi south of the village; follow signs for Bishop Sutton. Parking.

PRICES
Meals: a la carte £ 25/44

MAP: 8

CLOSING TIMES
Closed 25 December, dinner 26,
31 December and 1 January, Monday except December
and bank holidays booking essential

WHEATSHEAF

Characterful 1576 farmhouse with a modern look

The Wheatsheaf began life as a farmhouse in 1576. Centuries and several seamless additions later it boasts modern styling, typified by pink flock wallpaper and vivid artwork, and a relaxed atmosphere helped on its way by open fires, low sofas and an abundance of books and magazines – not forgetting the pub's friendly resident spaniels. The flavourful, seasonal food is presented in a contemporary style – often on slates – and dishes might include cottage pie of Wiltshire venison with spiked blackberries or fillet of Somerset pork wrapped in black pudding and prosciutto; with desserts such as chocolate and praline cheesecake or glazed lemon curd. Bedrooms follow the pub's lead, with their spacious, modern feel; Buttercup is the largest.

COMBE HAY, BA2 7EG
Tel.: 01225 833504
Website: www.wheatsheafcombehay.com

Signposted off A 367, 5 mi south of Bath. Parking.

PRICES
Meals: £ 20/23 and a la carte £ 26/48

 3 rooms:
£ 100/150

MAP: 9

CLOSING TIMES
Closed 10 days January, Sunday dinner and Monday except bank holidays

WHEELWRIGHTS ARMS

A place to relax and unwind

If you fancy a change of pace then you've come to the right place; no one is in a rush here and it feels like you have all the time in the world. It's tucked away in a hamlet in a beautiful valley and, apart from the sound of birdsong, peace and quiet reigns. The place is made up of two open-fired stone buildings: one of which was originally a carpenter's workshop where they used to make waggon wheels – hence the pub's name. For the large part, cooking is in the traditional vein, although you will find the occasional contemporary twist; the blackboard specials are always worth a look and whatever you choose, it will arrive presented in an attractive modern manner. There's a sunny terrace for warmer days and bedrooms are warm and welcoming.

Church Ln,
MONKTON COMBE, BA2 7HB
Tel.: 01225 722287
Website: www.wheelwrightsarms.co.uk

2 mi southeast of Bath city centre by A 3062. Parking.

PRICES
Meals: £ 12 (weekday lunch) and a la carte £ 23/36

 7 rooms: £ 85/160

MAP: 10

CLOSING TIMES
Closed dinner 25-26 December and 1 January

FLEUR DU JARDIN

Island seafood and a heated outdoor pool

Set in a small hamlet, not far from the sea, this attractive, personally run inn started life as several stone cottages. The first thing you'll notice is the stylish terrace and lovely landscaped garden with its heated outdoor pool; pleasingly, the interior lives up to every expectation too, with its series of charming, adjoining rooms, rustic beams, exposed stone walls and open fires. When it comes to dining, the regularly changing menu ranges from homemade burgers or pulled pork to lamb shank in a red wine jus or sea bass with pesto potatoes; specials feature tasty island seafood and every dish is prepared with care and a lightness of touch. Completing the picture are stylish New England themed bedrooms with luxury bathrooms.

Grand Moulins,
KINGS MILLS, GUERNSEY, GY5 7JT
Tel.: 01481 257996
Website: www.fleurdujardin.com

In the centre of the village. Parking.

PRICES
Meals: £ 13 (lunch and early dinner)
and a la carte £ 20/37

 13 rooms:
£ 62/189

MAP: 11

CLOSING TIMES
Closed dinner 25 December and 1 January

SWAN INN

An enthusiastic Frenchman at the helm

With its smart, bottle-green façade, this pub wouldn't look out of place in London, although its tightly packed, shabby-chic interior might not go down so well. It's very passionately and personally run by a gregarious French owner, and his enthusiasm can be felt throughout the place. On the ground floor there's a traditional bar complete with a coal fire; above, there's a more sedate dining room with polished wood tables and leather chairs. Both the choice of dishes and the portions themselves are large and, tempting as it may be, you're unlikely to make it through all three courses. Although there might be few Asian influences on the menu, dishes tend to be tried-and-tested pub classics; the most popular being the 100% Guernsey beef burger.

St Julian's Ave,
ST PETER PORT, GUERNSEY, GY1 1WA
Tel.: 01481 728969

St Julian's Ave is opposite South Quay. Parking on South Quay (50yds).

PRICES
Meals: a la carte £ 21/30

MAP: 12

CLOSING TIMES
Closed 25 December, Sunday and Monday

BASS AND LOBSTER

Oysters and seafood after a walk on the beach

This bright, modern pub, set close to the sandy beach, has smartly laid wooden tables, a mock wooden floor, some banquette seating and a small decked terrace. Having lived and worked on the island for many years, the experienced owner has built up a network of local suppliers and uses these whenever possible. Fresh seafood and shellfish dominate the seasonal menu, with starring roles given to the eponymous bass and lobster, and dishes are simply cooked, satisfying and immensely flavourful: try the Chancre crab linguine with prawns, some fantastic steely oysters or a side dish of wonderfully earthy Jersey Royals. Along with the food, the prices also bring a smile to one's face, as does the smooth service from a friendly European team.

Gorey Coast Rd,
GOREY, JERSEY, JE3 6EU
Tel.: 01534 859590
Website: www.bassandlobster.com

On the coast road. Parking.

PRICES   **MAP: 13**
Meals: £ 16/19 and a la carte £ 29/56

CLOSING TIMES
Closed 26 December, 1 January, Monday
and Sunday lunch May-November

ROZEL

In summer head for the lovely garden

For many years, the owners of the Chateau La Chaire hotel watched as tenants came and went at their neighbouring pub – and as the residents of this small coastal hamlet cried out for a place to meet – so, eventually, they decided to take it over themselves. With its three small rooms, including one with an old bar billiards table, the ground floor is a cosiest place to be, although the larger upstairs dining room does have distant sea views; in summer, though, head for the lovely garden, with its terraces cut into the valley walls. Traditional, homely dishes have an appealing 'no-fuss' honesty about them and include the likes of toad in the hole and mac and cheese. Alongside island ingredients you'll find ales from the Liberation Brewery.

Rozel Valley,
ROZEL BAY, JERSEY, JE3 6AJ
Tel.: 01534 863438
Website: www.rozelpubanddining.co.uk

On the approach to Château La Chaire. Parking.

PRICES
Meals: a la carte £ 22/31

MAP: **14**

CLOSING TIMES
Open daily

HALSETOWN INN

'Real pub, thoughtful food' is their strapline and it sums up this endearingly quirky place pretty well. It's a bit scruffy from the outside and fairly modest inside but it's got character and more importantly, it's got soul. There are various little areas where you can eat – find a spot in front of the bar or on the back terrace, which is a real suntrap. Menus change every 6-8 weeks and offer an interesting selection of dishes enlivened with some global flavours, with a particular nod towards Asia, so you'll find the likes of Nasi Goreng or Pad Thai alongside cider-roasted gammon and wild harbour fish of the day. They plough their own furrow on Sundays when, in lieu of a traditional lunch, they operate their own burger van in the car park.

HALSETOWN, TR26 3NA
Tel.: 01736 795583
Website: www.halsetowninn.co.uk

1.5 mi southwest of St Ives on B 3311. Parking.

PRICES
Meals: £ 16 (weekday lunch) and a la carte
£ 23/38

MAP: 15

CLOSING TIMES
Closed January and Sunday dinner

MEXICO INN

Come at the weekend for brunch

It's a slightly unusual name for a pub – a reference to the Cornish miners who travelled out to Mexico – but at least it gets itself noticed! It's run by a local couple, Tom and Amy, who have worked in some of the South West's best-known pubs and restaurants – and Amy's three sisters are all involved too. The interior has a touch of the shabby-chic about it, with a wood-burner in the main bar and a sunnier room to the rear; there's a lovely suntrap terrace too and it's only a few minutes' walk from the beach. Start your meal with nibbles such as whitebait with harissa mayonnaise before moving on to gutsy, flavourful dishes like crispy smoked ham hock or Barnsley chop with broad beans, followed by carrot cake with homemade marmalade ice cream.

4 Riverside,
LONGROCK, TR20 8JD
Tel.: 01736 710625
Website: www.themexicoinn.com

3.5 mi northeast of Penzance by A30 off A30/A394 roundabout.
Small car park to rear and on street parking

PRICES
Meals: a la carte £ 20/28

MAP: 16

CLOSING TIMES
Closed 1 week early February, Sunday
dinner and Monday

TOLCARNE INN

Local seafood is the star of the show

Having been flooded a number of times over the years, this unremarkable looking but refreshingly unaffected 18C pub is now protected by a tall sea wall – it's a shame it hides the view of Mount's Bay but at least it keeps the wind off the terrace. Inside the family-run inn things are cosy and traditional, with a wood-burner at one end keeping the drinkers warm and the rest of the place laid out for eating. The chef-owner is an experienced chap who cooks with intelligence and care. Being in Newlyn, and within a literal stone's throw from the boats, it's no surprise that fish and shellfish are the stars of the show. The blackboard changes daily and you can always expect wonderfully fresh and uncomplicated dishes that deliver plenty of flavour.

Tolcarne Pl,
NEWLYN, TR18 5PR
Tel.: 01736 363074
Website: www.tolcarneinn.co.uk

By the sea wall in the centre of town. Parking.

PRICES
Meals: a la carte £ 23/38

MAP: 17

CLOSING TIMES
Open daily

VICTORIA INN

Plenty of fish from nearby Newlyn

The previous owners worked hard to establish this pink-washed pub, which sits in the small seaside village of Perranuthnoe – and its current owner, Nikolaus, looks set to uphold its name. He is originally from Cornwall but left to spend time in London learning his trade, before returning home to settle down in a place of his own; and many members of the pub's old team have stayed on to help him. Save for a couple of international dishes, the menu sticks with the classics and, due to its proximity to Newlyn, fish is in abundance. Sundays see plenty of choice, with everything from roast beef to garlic roast lobster, and be sure to save room for one of the delicious puddings. Simply furnished bedrooms are bright and cosy, with a seaside feel.

PERRANUTHNOE, TR20 9NP
Tel.: 01736 710309
Website: www.victoriainn-penzance.co.uk

3 mi east of Marazion, south of A 394. Parking.

PRICES
Meals: a la carte £ 25/41

 2 rooms:
£ 75/85

MAP: 18

CLOSING TIMES
Closed 25 December and 1 January

MARINERS

Take in stunning views of the Camel Estuary

Two of Cornwall's top ambassadors have come together to run the Mariners. Local brewery Sharp's – known countrywide for their Doom Bar ale – own the place and chef Nathan Outlaw, who has become synonymous with the Cornish cooking scene, runs the show in the kitchen. The menu is short and simple and dishes are satisfying – as you would expect, fresh local seafood is a feature but there are also top quality meats from Warren's Farm. Bookings are only taken for Sunday lunch and blackboard specials are just that, so once they're gone, they're gone. Ask for advice if you'd like to pair your dish with a real ale. Sit on the terrace for stunning views over the Camel Estuary, and if you're out in Padstow jump on the foot ferry for the short ride over.

Slipway,
ROCK, PL27 6LD
Tel.: 01208 863679
Website: www.marinersrock.com

Close to the Padstow ferry. Pay and display parking 200 yards away.

PRICES

Meals: a la carte £ 25/43

MAP: 19

CLOSING TIMES
Closed 25 December

ST KEW INN

Superb cask beers and a lovely garden

The St Kew Inn was built in the 15C to serve the masons who were constructing the neighbourhood church and it boasts flagged floors, stone walls and wooden beams. It sits in a quintessentially English location and its attractive front garden is as much of a draw as the pub itself; a massive electric umbrella means that summer showers aren't a problem and there are heaters too should it turn nippy. Cooking is fresh and tasty, with a wide range of appealing, good value dishes; lunch means choices like Fowey mussels, Welsh rarebit and a range of sandwiches, while dinner is similar with the addition of perhaps some grilled lemon sole or pan-fried lamb's liver. Be sure to order one of the beers from the casks behind the bar – they are divine.

ST KEW, PL30 3HB
Tel.: 01208 841259
Website: www.stkewinn.co.uk

3 mi northeast of Wadebridge by A 39 and minor road north. Parking.

PRICES
Meals: a la carte £ 24/36

MAP: 20

CLOSING TIMES
Closed 25-26 December

ST TUDY INN

Unfussy, good value cooking

There are three key components to this pretty Cornish village – a Norman church, a community shop and this lovingly restored pub. Inside there's a labyrinth of cosy rooms with a mix of open fires and log-burning stoves. Fresh flowers sit on scrubbed wooden tables and the place has a rustic, modish overtone. Food is unfussy, seasonal and satisfying and arrives beautifully presented. Cornish produce includes meats from Launceston and seafood from Padstow and suppliers are proudly listed on the menu. The 3 course midweek menu is good value and unusually includes the blackboard specials too – you might find chilled almond soup topped with figs, followed by monkfish with saffron, cream and rocket. The chef is passionate and service is friendly.

ST TUDY, PL30 3NN
Tel.: 01208 850656
Website: www.sttudyinn.com

6 mi northeast of Wadebridge off A39 in village centre. Parking.

PRICES
Meals: a la carte £ 25/36

MAP: 21

CLOSING TIMES
Closed 25-26 December

SPRINGER SPANIEL

Sister to the Treby Arms in Devon

Following the success of the Treby Arms, South African born Anton Piotrowski decided to cross the border into Cornwall. The unassuming-looking Springer Spaniel is set on the roadside in a small hamlet and has three cosy rooms filled with scrubbed wooden tables. It's very much the village local and each week hosts 'Thirsty Thursday', where the villagers come together to catch up. What is a little out of the ordinary here is the food; expect bold flavours, colourful combinations and more ingredients than the menu suggests. For fish lovers the 'Seafood Wreck' offers a selection of the day's catch, for those celebrating there's a 7 course tasting menu and for those with a sweet tooth they serve the renowned "Treby's Gone Carrots" dessert.

TREBURLEY, PL15 9NS
Tel.: 01579 370424
Website: www.thespringerspaniel.org.uk

5 mi south of Launceston on A 388. Parking.

PRICES   **MAP: 22**
Meals: £ 20 (weekdays) and a la carte
£ 20/43

CLOSING TIMES
Closed Monday

SHIP INN

The oldest public house in town

This 16C inn was originally owned by a shipbuilding family and it is one of the oldest public houses in town. Pleasingly, it has a real community feel – particularly on the regular wine, backgammon and folk music evenings. Grab a seat in one of the three cosy, low-beamed rooms or continue through to the brighter former workshop. The menu offers something for everyone by mixing pub classics with more modern dishes. Simply prepared fish comes from the Looe and Newlyn day boats; hotdogs arrive in brioche buns; burgers come with the choice of beef, fish or the filling of the week; and puddings are of the proper old-fashioned variety. Tuesday burger night features 'guest' burgers and Thursday steak night includes cuts for two to share.

Gonvena Hill,
WADEBRIDGE, PL27 6DF
Tel.: 01208 813845
Website: www.shipinnwadebridge.com

Northeast of town centre after crossing River Camel. Limited parking.

PRICES
Meals: a la carte £ 21/33

CLOSING TIMES
Closed Sunday dinner in winter.

GURNARD'S HEAD

Shabby-chic and dog friendly

Surrounded by nothing but fields and livestock, the Gurnard's Head provides a warm welcome that sets you immediately at your ease. It's dog-friendly, with stone floors and shabby-chic décor, and its blazing fires and brightly coloured walls help to create a relaxed, cosy feel. Menus include a good value set lunch and rely on regional produce, including some locally foraged ingredients. Dishes might include pigeon with celeriac purée and mushroom jus or gurnard with braised fennel and scallop velouté – and be sure to save room for one of the delicious homemade ice creams. The wine list includes a very interesting selection by the glass and service is calm and friendly. Compact bedrooms feature good quality linen and colourful throws.

Treen,
ZENNOR, TR26 3DE
Tel.: 01736 796928
Website: www.gurnardshead.co.uk

7.5 mi west of St Ives on B 3306. Parking.

PRICES
Meals: £ 19 (weekday lunch)/23
and a la carte £ 26/32

 7 rooms:
£ 95/230

MAP: 24

CLOSING TIMES
Closed 24-25 December and 4 days early
December
booking advisable

SWAN

Run by a relaxed, friendly team

The Swan's history can be traced back to 1450, when it provided accommodation for craftsmen working on the charming village church. The original inglenook fireplace and bread oven remain in situ – along with exposed wooden beams – but the open-plan layout gives it an up-to-date feel; if you fancy a more intimate experience, head for the upstairs dining room. When it comes to the food, the menu sticks to unfussy pub classics, with the likes of homemade soup or whitebait, followed by pies or liver and bacon, finished off with comforting old school desserts like treacle pudding. Dishes arrive neatly presented, with fish originating from Devon and Cornwall and steaks from nearby Waterhouse Farm. Smart, modern bedrooms are found on the 2nd floor.

Station Rd,
BAMPTON, EX16 9NG
Tel.: 01398 332248
Website: www.theswan.co

6 mi north of Tiverton by A 396 and B 3190. Public car park opposite.

PRICES
Meals: a la carte £ 22/36

3 rooms:
£ 70/90

MAP: 25

CLOSING TIMES
Closed 25 December

LAZY TOAD INN

The local shoots supply game in season

It's well worth navigating the winding lanes for a visit to this sweet Grade II listed pub in a pretty village near the River Exe. In winter, sit under a lovely oak-beamed ceiling beside an inviting log fire; in summer, head for the beautiful walled garden or the charming cobbled courtyard (the latter was once used by the local farrier and wheelwright), and keep an eye out for the odd toad or two! Nibble on snacks like ham hock fritters while you choose from the regularly changing list of hearty British dishes such as seared corn-fed chicken breast with swede and apple mash or roast cod with lemon and chive cream. Produce comes from the garden and polytunnel behind the pub and they use their own fruit and berries to make summer cordials.

BRAMPFORD SPEKE, EX5 5DP
Tel.: 01392 841591
Website: www.thelazytoad.com

5 mi north of Exeter by A 377. Parking.

PRICES
Meals: a la carte £ 16/38

MAP: 26

CLOSING TIMES
Closed 1 week January, Sunday dinner
and Monday

FIVE BELLS INN

Pretty 16C thatched pub serving great value food

Narrowly saved from conversion into houses by the present owners, this pretty thatched 16C pub deep in the Devon countryside had the locals tirelessly campaigning for its survival during its closure. In appreciation of their efforts, the table opposite the front door has been named a 'Stammtisch' or 'locals' table' – so whatever you do, don't sit there! The experienced chef uses the finest local ingredients to create well-balanced dishes with real clarity of flavour. There's a blackboard of pub favourites and a small à la carte offering more creative dishes – though the chef's classical roots are clearly evident. The set lunch menu offers excellent value for money and, on Sunday, roasts take centre stage. Service is smooth and friendly.

CLYST HYDON, EX15 2NT
Tel.: 01884 277288
Website: www.fivebells.uk.com

4.5 mi south of Cullompton by B 3181 and minor road east, turning right just before village sign. Parking.

PRICES   MAP: **27**
Meals: £ 15 (weekday lunch) and a la carte
£ 30/42

CLOSING TIMES
Open daily
bookings advisable at dinner

RAMS HEAD INN

You'll be welcomed like an old friend

The Rams Head Inn is the first solo venture for Simon Hunt and its transformation from run-down boozer to smart country inn has obviously been a labour of love. It's divided into three main areas and sports a mix of stripped wood and flagged flooring which gives it a cosy, characterful feel. Enjoy a drink by the inglenook fireplace in the large beamed bar or head for the traditional dining room for a quieter meal. Dishes are a mix of old favourites such as local Exe mussels or rump steak, and more restaurant-style dishes like brill with watercress or smoked haddock risotto. There are dishes to share – maybe a retro cheese fondue with cider – and the daily changing suet puddings are a real hit. Simply furnished bedrooms have a modern feel.

South St,
DOLTON, EX19 8QS
Tel.: 01805 804255
Website: www.theramsheadinn.co.uk

15 mi north of Okehampton signposted off A 386, in centre of Village. Parking.

PRICES
Meals: a la carte £ 23/35

 9 rooms:
£ 50/99

MAP: 28

CLOSING TIMES
Closed February and lunch Monday

RUSTY BIKE

Nose-to-tail dining in a bohemian atmosphere

This small backstreet boozer was closed for 7 years before larger-than-life owner Hamish skilfully transformed it into a bohemian-style dining pub. It's made up of three rustic rooms filled with reclaimed furniture and an eclectic mix of art, and to pass the time there are magazines, board games and a vintage table football game. When it comes to the cooking, it's hearty, satisfying and follows a traditional British nose-to-tail approach: produce is sourced from within 20 miles; rare breed pigs are butchered on-site; they make their own bread and pasta; and they smoke their own bacon and cure their own bresaola and hams. Alongside your potted Ruby Red beef or Dexter beef shank hash, try a home-brewed cider or specially commissioned beer.

67 Howell Rd,
EXETER, EX4 4LZ
Tel.: 01392 214440
Website: www.rustybike-exeter.co.uk

On northern edge of city centre. On-street parking.

PRICES
Meals: a la carte £ 28/41

MAP: 29

CLOSING TIMES
Closed 24-25 December, 1 January
and Sunday dinner
dinner only and Sunday lunch

HOLT

Very passionately run and family-owned

This is a family owned and run pub, where the passion for food and drink is almost palpable. Angus McCaig oversees goings-on in the Holt's kitchen, while brother Joe works out front; their parents meanwhile run the well-known Otter Brewery down the road. Sustainable, regional produce is the central tenet of their ethos with everything cooked in-house and meats and fish cured and smoked on-site. Oft-changing, eco-friendly menus are printed on paper made from recycled hops and list rustic dishes like slow-roasted pork belly or seared lamb rump, with tapas and sandwiches also available at lunch. The pint of smoked prawns is a real winner – and try the tasting rack: a third of a pint of three Otter Brewery ales, matched with recommended dishes.

178 High St,
HONITON, EX14 1LA
Tel.: 01404 47707
Website: www.theholt-honiton.com

At lower end of High Street. Dowell Street car park (2min walk).

PRICES   MAP: **30**
Meals: a la carte £ 27/35

CLOSING TIMES
Closed 25-26 December, 1 January, Sunday
and Monday

RAILWAY

This smart, modern pub offers authentic Mediterranean cooking at affordable prices; a combination patently pleasing the people in this East Devon market town. Touches like the Bibendum statues and various cookery books dotted around suggest a serious approach, underlined by the open kitchen and the pub's strap-line, 'Every plate a picture of freshness and flavour'. Nibble on olive oil dipped bread while you read the menu, where classics like fritto misto sit alongside homemade pastas, brick-fired pizzas and steaks; the warm Sicilian tart is a house favourite and specials might include seared scallops or wild boar terrine. An eclectic wine list and an olive oil top-up service add to the fun and comfortable bedrooms complete the picture.

Queen St,
HONITON, EX14 1HE
Tel.: 01404 47976
Website: www.therailwayhoniton.co.uk

2 min off the High Street, via New Street. Parking.

PRICES
Meals: £ 16 (weekday lunch) and a la carte
£ 24/34

 3 rooms:
£ 85/110

MAP: 31

CLOSING TIMES
Closed 25-26 December, Sunday and
Monday

MASONS ARMS

Charming service and sophisticated dishes

This pretty thatched inn sits in a secluded village in the beautiful foothills of Exmoor. It was built in the 13C by the masons who constructed the village church and with its cosy beamed bar and inglenook fireplace, exudes plenty of rural charm. The food is more sophisticated than you'd expect to find in a pub, with canapés and petit fours served alongside attractively presented British and French classics. Cooking is refined and flavours are pronounced and assured; the chef is experienced and employs the finest local produce. Dine beneath a celestial ceiling mural in the bright rear dining room and enjoy delightful views over the rolling hills towards Exmoor. Charming, attentive service is a perfect match for the food.

KNOWSTONE, EX36 4RY
Tel.: 01398 341231
Website: www.masonsarmsdevon.co.uk

7 mi southeast of South Molton by A 361; opposite the village church. Parking.

PRICES
Meals: £ 25 (lunch) and a la carte £ 40/50

MAP: **32**

CLOSING TIMES
Closed first week January, 1 week mid-February, 10 days August-September, Sunday dinner and Monday booking essential

DARTMOOR INN

A pub might have a snazzy new look or a barrel-load of special offers on but it's the feel of a place which dictates whether you'll want to spend time there – this rustic pub being a case in point. The exterior is rather non-descript but the owners offer a genuinely warm welcome, the local staff are friendly and there's a buzzing air of satisfaction. The numerous rooms are decorated in a shabby-chic style; low ceilings add a cosy feel, while artwork provides a modern touch. Classic dishes like liver and onions or slow-cooked belly pork are satisfying and full of flavour; there is an emphasis on local produce and Devon Ruby Red beef and dishes from the charcoal grill are the specialities. Spacious, elegant bedrooms have a French feel.

Moorside,
LYDFORD, EX20 4AY
Tel.: 01822 820221
Website: www.dartmoorinn.com

8.5 mi northeast of Tavistock on A 386. Parking.

PRICES
Meals: £ 13 (weekdays)/27 and a la carte
£ 21/46

 3 rooms:
£ 65/140

MAP: 33

CLOSING TIMES
Closed Sunday dinner and Monday

CHURCH HOUSE INN

Seasonal dishes inspired by the Mediterranean

The Church House Inn was originally built in the 14C to provide accommodation for stone masons constructing the nearby church; it was rebuilt in the 18C and still displays some of its eye-catching Strawberry Gothic windows. Inside, it's fresh and simple, with a formally laid restaurant and a bar offering locally brewed beer; there are beams, open fires and plenty of nooks and crannies in which to settle, and local art hangs on the walls. The multitude of menus can be a little confusing, with different blackboards offering everything from tapas and sharing plates to vegetarian dishes and wines by the glass, but once you've decided what to go for, you'll find the cooking hearty and comforting and the service friendly and helpful.

Village Rd,
MARLDON, TQ3 1SL
Tel.: 01803 558279
Website: www.churchhousemarldon.com

Between Torquay and Paignton off A 380. Parking.

PRICES   MAP: **34**
Meals: a la carte £ 24/38

CLOSING TIMES
Closed 25 December and dinner
26 December

THE HORSE

Tasty, unfussy cooking with Italian influences

It's hard to believe that this pub, in the heart of rural Dartmoor, was semi-derelict when its owners took it on. While locals gather in the bar to watch the sport, diners head for rustic, flag-floored rooms created from the converted stable and barn; or out to the sunny, Mediterranean-style courtyard. With an actor-turned-chef at the helm you might expect some melodrama in the kitchen; you won't get this, but you will get tasty, unfussy dishes with more than a hint of Italy. Frittata, panini, sandwiches and pizza are served at lunch, with dishes like crab linguine or gnocchi on the menu at dinner. Authentic, thin crust pizzas come from a custom-built oven, while desserts such as burnt toffee panna cotta finish your meal off with a flourish.

7 George St,
MORETONHAMPSTEAD, TQ13 8PG
Tel.: 01647 440242
Website: www.thehorsedartmoor.co.uk

In heart of village. Two car parks within 1min walk.

PRICES
Meals: a la carte £ 18/37

MAP: 35

CLOSING TIMES
Closed 25 December and Monday lunch

SHIP INN

Seafaring memorabilia and wonderful water views

Wonderful waterside views are one of the main attractions of this fine pub, set in a peaceful spot on the south side of the Yealm Estuary. It's well run, large and very busy, with friendly staff who cope admirably under pressure. Its oldest part dates from the 18C and its characterful interior features wooden floors and open fires, while its collection of maritime memorabilia, including numerous old photographs, gives a tangible sense of seafaring history. The menu offers pub classics such as rib-eye steak or sausage and mash, followed by tried-and-tested desserts like bread and butter pudding. The wine list is well-presented, with a good selection by the glass. Be careful where you park your car because time and tide wait for no man!

NOSS MAYO, PL8 1EW
Tel.: 01752 872387
Website: www.nossmayo.com

10.5 mi southeast of Plymouth; signed off A 379; turn right onto B 3186. Restricted parking, particularly at high tide.

PRICES
Meals: a la carte £ 22/33

MAP: **36**

CLOSING TIMES
Closed 25 December

MILLBROOK INN

The olive oil is from their farm in Andalucía

You'll find this characterful, appealingly worn pub squeezed in between the houses on a narrow village street. Low beamed ceilings and an open fire create a cosy atmosphere and two terraces provide a pleasant alternative come summer. It's very passionately run: they use olive oil from their farm in Andalucía and sell fresh local produce 24hrs a day in the 'Veg Shed'. Cooking is traditional and hearty with some Mediterranean influences; you might find potted South Devon crab, bouillabaisse or Chateaubriand with pommes pont neuf and béarnaise sauce. The blackboard offers a good value set menu and if you're in a group, you can order 72 hrs ahead for a whole roast suckling pig. They host regular live music nights to keep the locals entertained.

SOUTH POOL, TQ7 2RW
Tel.: 01548 531581
Website: www.millbrookinnsouthpool.co.uk

5.5 mi southeast of Kingsbridge off A 379.
On-street parking in the village.

PRICES   **MAP: 37**
Meals: a la carte £ 26/50

CLOSING TIMES
Open daily

TREBY ARMS

It's a popular spot, so book ahead

A quotation chalked on the timbers warns that 'you can't please all of the people all of the time' but they seem to be doing a pretty good job of it here! Chef-owner Anton is a past winner of 'MasterChef: The Professionals' and Plympton residents were no doubt relieved when he chose to return to the stoves rather than chasing the bright lights of stardom. His carefully prepared, clearly flavoured modern dishes are visually appealing and often feature a playful twist; the 'Taster' menus best demonstrate his considerable talent. The place was built by Brunel in the 1950s to serve workers constructing the Devon-Cornwall train bridge and to this day it maintains a loyal following – as evidenced by the locals' pint jugs hanging above the bar.

SPARKWELL, PL7 5DD
Tel.: 01752 837363
Website: www.thetrebyarms.co.uk

10 mi east of Plymouth signposted off A 38. Parking.

PRICES
Meals: £ 18 (weekday lunch)/80
and a la carte £ 30/55

MAP: 38

CLOSING TIMES
Open daily
booking essential

CORNISH ARMS

Sophisticated desserts are worth saving room for

It might have been refurbished but the Cornish Arms is still a pleasingly traditional pub. It's run in partnership by the St Austell brewery and local lad John Hooker, and has a warm, welcoming feel. The quarry-tiled bar is usually filled with regulars playing darts, watching the football or sitting at simple wooden tables snacking on homemade sausage rolls or fishcakes; a few steps up is the equally relaxed restaurant. The talented, ambitious chef prepares both carefully crafted classics – like braised ox cheek with horseradish, mash and beef gravy – and more elaborate offerings such as fillet of stone bass with potted shrimp bisque and braised lettuce. Desserts are sophisticated and a treat for both the eyes and the stomach.

15 West St,
TAVISTOCK, PL19 8AN
Tel.: 01822 612145
Website: www.thecornisharmstavistock.co.uk

In the centre of town. Limited parking at the rear.

PRICES   MAP: **39**
Meals: a la carte £ 20/40

CLOSING TIMES
Closed dinner 24 December

NEW INN

Stylish bedrooms and a large orchard garden

In the main street of the delightful village of Cerne Abbas, in the shadow of the famous Chalk Giant, stands this 16C part-flint inn. It's a charming place, with a relaxed ambience; antler chandeliers and framed guns remind you that you're in the country, black and white village photos evoke bygone days, and the collection of clocks reminds you to slow down and enjoy yourself. Menus are a mix of the modern and the traditional, so you might find smoked mackerel pâté with Melba toast and cucumber gazpacho, followed by Gressingham duck breast with a duck and a foie gras sausage roll and creamed Savoy cabbage. Spacious, stylish bedrooms are split between the pub and the courtyard; some are duplex suites and have a freestanding bath in the room.

14 Long St,
CERNE ABBAS, DT2 7JF
Tel.: 01300 341274
Website: www.thenewinncerneabbas.co.uk

In the centre of the village. Parking.

PRICES
Meals: £ 16 (weekday lunch) and a la carte
£ 24/42

 12 rooms:
£ 85/170

MAP: 40

CLOSING TIMES
Closed 25-26 December

FONTMELL

Pleasingly different from the norm

This stylish, modern pub is set in a small hamlet and features a comfy bar – complete with an open fire and a piano – and a spacious dining room, which straddles the brook below. Sit in the latter of the two rooms, surrounded by shelves filled with books, knick-knacks and wine bottles, and keep an eye out for the visiting otters. The concise daily menu offers an eclectic mix of carefully executed dishes, ranging from homely pub classics to those that display Mediterranean and even some Thai influences. You might find Dorset lamb and black pudding suet pudding or Sicilian-style linguine alla Norma, and on Sundays, the likes of kedgeree and eggs Benedict on the simpler 'Supper' menu. Smart bedrooms are named after butterflies; one has a roll-top bath in the room.

FONTMELL MAGNA, SP7 0PA
Tel.: 01747 811441
Website: www.thefontmell.com

4.75 mi south of Shaftesbury on A 350 in centre of village. Parking.

PRICES
Meals: a la carte £ 25/46

 6 rooms:
£ 95/185

MAP: 41

CLOSING TIMES
Closed 26 December

ROSE & CROWN

Warm and welcoming, with plenty of character

This pretty part-thatched pub dates back to the 14C, when it was built to house workers constructing the adjacent church spire. It's run by two experienced locals, who have brought plenty of warmth to the place and this, coupled with roaring open fires, beamed ceilings and quarry tiled floors, has turned out to be a winning formula. The main bar is often packed with the local shoots, so if you're looking to eat head for the characterful 'Buffs Bar' or the bright conservatory which opens out onto the garden. Tasty country cooking is the order of the day – bypass the pub classics and go for the likes of crispy pig's head with apple purée or calves' liver with sage fritters and smoked bacon. Bedrooms come with patios overlooking the countryside.

TRENT, DT9 4SL
Tel.: 01935 850776
Website: www.theroseandcrowntrent.co.uk

4 mi northwest of Sherborne signposted off B 3148. Parking.

PRICES
Meals: a la carte £ 24/39

 3 rooms:
£ 65/125

MAP: 42

CLOSING TIMES
Closed 25-26 December

VILLAGE PUB

Stylish, cosy country pub with a heated terrace

With an interior straight out of any country homes magazine, the Village Pub has that cosy, open-fired, village pub vibe down to a tee. Four small, intimate rooms are set around a dimly lit copper-topped bar and there's a carefully manicured terrace complete with patio heaters to the rear. The menu exudes modern appeal; nibbles like sea trout blinis are an irresistible teaser, there are starters like homemade country terrine, mains like shoulder of venison with braised red cabbage and comforting desserts such as treacle tart. Meat comes from within a 30 mile radius, with charcuterie often from Highgrove and vegetables from partner Barnsley House just up the road. Bedrooms have a similarly tasteful style; number Six has a four-poster bed.

BARNSLEY, GL7 5EF
Tel.: 01285 740421
Website: www.thevillagepub.co.uk

4 mi northeast of Cirencester on B 4425. Parking.

PRICES
Meals: a la carte £ 23/40

6 rooms:
£ 89/169

MAP: 43

CLOSING TIMES
Open daily
booking essential

KINGS HEAD INN

Dine next to the inglenook fireplace in the bar

Sitting on a picturesque village green, bisected by a stream filled with bobbing ducks, this charming 16C former cider house provides the perfect backdrop for a holiday snap. The interior doesn't disappoint either: the large, heavily beamed bar with its vast inglenook fireplace, the solid stone floors and the comfortable, laid-back feel create a wonderful atmosphere, and the cosy bedrooms – split between the pub and the courtyard – finish it all off perfectly. Appealing bar snacks might include spiced whitebait or pheasant in a basket, while the main menu offers pub classics like steak or fish and chips alongside some interesting modern dishes such as vodka and tonic soft shell crab or beef carpaccio with orange and juniper reduction.

The Green,
BLEDINGTON, OX7 6XQ
Tel.: 01608 658365
Website: www.kingsheadinn.net

4 mi southeast of Stow-on-the-Wold by A 436 and B 4450. Parking.

PRICES
Meals: a la carte £ 25/40

 12 rooms:
£ 75/130

MAP: 44

CLOSING TIMES
Closed 25-26 December

HORSE & GROOM

Good selection of wines by the glass

Having grown up working in their parents' pub, brothers Will and Tom jumped at the chance to start their own venture when this listed Georgian building came on the market. Built from honey-coloured Cotswold stone, it's set on the main street of a pretty village high on the hillside, and features stone walls and open fires as well as five stylish, contemporary bedrooms. Study the daily blackboard menu and then order at the bar, but bear in mind that it's a popular place, so you'll need to have booked or be willing to wait. The food is good value, fresh and flavoursome; expect the likes of parmesan and rosemary crumbed sardine fillets, pan-roast skate wing or braised blade of Dexter beef, with classic puddings such as steamed lemon curd sponge.

BOURTON ON THE HILL, GL56 9AQ
Tel.: 01386 700413
Website: www.horseandgroom.info

2 mi west of Moreton-in-Marsh on A 44. Parking.

PRICES
Meals: a la carte £ 22/37

 5 rooms:
£ 80/170

MAP: 45

CLOSING TIMES
Closed 25, 31 December and Sunday dinner
except bank holidays
booking essential

ROYAL OAK

Large garden with heaters and a skittle alley

The 'Pavilion' may sound like a strange name for their skittle alley and function room but it all becomes clearer once you learn that batting legend Tom Graveney was a previous landlord. Turn left and you'll discover a bar with a worn floor, a wood burning stove and plenty of framed sporting prints; turn right and you'll find a dark wood-furnished dining room with an open fire, red walls filled with an array of jugs and vessels, and several blackboards announcing the month's events. Lunch offers tasty, satisfying dishes such as kedgeree or duck hash with bubble and squeak, while dinner steps things up with the likes of goat's cheese and beetroot terrine or rump of lamb with baby onions. The large garden, with its patio heaters, is a hit.

The Burgage,
PRESTBURY, CHELTENHAM, GL52 3DL
Tel.: 01242 522344
Website: www.royal-oak-prestbury.co.uk

Follow signs from the city to the racecourse via Prestbury Rd and New Barn Ln. On-street parking.

PRICES   MAP: **46**
Meals: a la carte £ 23/45

CLOSING TIMES
Closed 25 December

EBRINGTON ARMS

Ales are brewed to their own recipes

This 17C inn sits in a charming chocolate box village in the glorious Cotswold countryside; its beamed, flag-floored bar with a blazing log fire providing the hub from which locals and visitors come and go, while owners Claire and Jim oversee proceedings with humour and grace. The characterful dining rooms provide an intimate atmosphere for a meal, while the delightful sloping garden is the place to be in warmer weather. Choose from pub classics on the blackboard or more elaborate dishes on the monthly à la carte, maybe ham hock terrine, rump of lamb or roast breast of guinea fowl, with fresh fruit and veg supplied by village farms. Comfortable bedrooms come with countryside views and plenty of thoughtful extras; Room 3 has a four-poster bed.

EBRINGTON, GL55 6NH
Tel.: 01386 593223
Website: www.theebringtonarms.co.uk

2 mi east of Chipping Campden signposted off B 4035. Parking.

PRICES	5 rooms:	**MAP: 47**
Meals: a la carte £ 26/41	£ 100/150	

CLOSING TIMES
Closed 25 December

WILD DUCK

The duck for two is a hit!

The Wild Duck is a charming place, both inside and out. As you approach you're greeted by antique signs and a clock with ducks flying over it – maybe to remind you of how time flies when you're having fun. If dining alfresco is your thing then there's a lovely terrace concealed behind the thick vegetation; on colder days, open fires and beams hung with hop bines welcome you in and various snug seating areas provide an intimate feel. If you're making a flying visit, snack on some charcuterie sliced on the ornate slicer behind the bar; if you're here for a meal, choose a healthy option such as soy-glazed mackerel or really push the boat out with The Wild Duck's Duck for two with pancakes, damson plum sauce, red cabbage slaw and straw potatoes.

Drakes Island,
EWEN, GL7 6BY
Tel.: 01285 770310
Website: www.thewildduckewen.com

4 mi southwest of Cirencester by A 429. Parking.

PRICES
Meals: £ 15 (weekday lunch) and a la carte
£ 22/38

MAP: **48**

CLOSING TIMES
Open daily

ROYAL OAK

Watch the steam trains chug past from the garden

There's no doubt that the selling point of this pub is its large garden: aside from being a great place to sit and eat – especially in barbecue season – it offers plenty to keep you occupied. Children are kept busy watching the chickens or in the play area, while those of more mature years can sit back and appreciate the chug of the trains passing by on the Gloucestershire-Warwickshire Steam Railway; sporty individuals can even don their shorts and make for the tennis court! Inside, there's a nice bar and two snug dining rooms but head for the conservatory to be rewarded with the best views. The experienced owner has good local connections when it comes to sourcing his produce and the dishes are honest and traditionally based.

GRETTON, GL54 5EP
Tel.: 01242 604999
Website: www.royaloakgretton.co.uk

On the edge of the village, 2 mi northwest of Winchcombe. Parking.

PRICES   **MAP: 49**
Meals: a la carte £ 24/42

CLOSING TIMES
Open daily

FOX INN

Creeper-clad and quintessentially English

Lying at the heart of a peaceful Cotswold village is this creeper-clad, quintessentially English pub. Well-regarded locally and often busy, it's as characterful inside as its exterior suggests, with beamed ceilings, solid stone walls, flagged floors and plenty of cosy nooks and crannies. The lovely garden has plenty of seating for long, sunny summer afternoons, while the wood burning stoves make cold winter days desirable. Wherever you sit, Mr Fox is never too far away, be he a wall-mounted head, a cartoon or a cuddly toy, as featured in the individually furnished, comfortable bedrooms. The regularly changing menu keeps things fresh, with the focus on carefully prepared, tasty British classics like local steak, calves' liver or Dover sole.

LOWER ODDINGTON, GL56 0UR
Tel.: 01451 870555
Website: www.foxinn.net

3 mi east of Stow-on-the-Wold signposted off A 436. Parking.

PRICES
Meals: a la carte £ 20/43

 3 rooms:
£ 85/100

MAP: 50

CLOSING TIMES
Closed Sunday dinner and Monday
booking essential

FEATHERED NEST

Superb views and over 200 wines!

Set in a small hamlet, this pub has really come into its own under its latest owners, who spent several years in Portugal gaining experience in the hospitality industry. It's the type of place that offers something for everyone, with its laid-back bar, rustic snug, casual conservatory and formal dining room. Sit on quirky bar stools made from horse saddles and sample unfussy dishes from the daily blackboard menu or head through to elegant antique tables for more complex offerings such as grouse with celeriac pudding or halibut tempura with charred squid – not forgetting a list of over 200 wines. Once fully sated, make for one of the comfy bedrooms complete with antique furnishings, quality linens and a smart roll-top bath. The views are superb.

NETHER WESTCOTE, OX7 6SD
Tel.: 01993 833030
Website: www.thefeatherednestinn.co.uk

Signposted off A 424 southeast of Stow-on-the-Wold. Parking.

PRICES
Meals: £ 25 (weekday lunch) and a la carte
£ 44/65

 4 rooms:
£ 195/260

MAP: 51

CLOSING TIMES
Closed 1 week February, 1 week July,
1 week October, 25 December Monday and
Tuesday

WHEATSHEAF INN

Furnished with interesting French market finds

The owners of this smart, 17C coaching inn also own the old cottage next door, where you'll find stylish, contemporary bedrooms with some quirky touches; some have baths in the rooms and most are furnished with interesting finds from French flea markets. The pub has a stone-floored, open-fired bar in the centre and a traditional, clubby dining room on either side – look out for the semi-private 'Poker Table' in the alcove – and the pretty tiered terrace provides plenty of extra space when the weather's good. The same menu is available throughout, offering classical dishes and something to suit every taste: maybe pappardelle of braised beef or cheese soufflé to start and slow-cooked pork belly or confit duck leg with cassoulet to follow.

West End,
NORTHLEACH, GL50 3EZ
Tel.: 01451 860244
Website: www.cotswoldswheatsheaf.com

In centre of town. Parking.

PRICES
Meals: £ 13 (weekday lunch) and a la carte
£ 24/46

 14 rooms:
£ 120/220

MAP: 52

CLOSING TIMES
Open daily

GLOUCESTER OLD SPOT

Rare breed pork is their speciality

There's no denying that British pub names are a varied and interesting bunch. This little beauty used to be called the ubiquitous 'Swan' but now its moniker has more meaning, as its owners specialise in rare breed pork; enjoy such delights as crispy Old Spot pig's cheeks, rolled and boned belly pork, or pork T-bone steak. If you don't fancy pig, fret not: there are plenty of other tasty offerings on the seasonal menu, from a crusty lunchtime cob filled with roast lamb and mint & cucumber relish to pan-fried sea bass with seared squid and prawns. The atmosphere is cosy and relaxing and the staff, cheery and welcoming – although it was not ever thus: there used to be a hanging post in the garden where many miscreants met their demise.

Tewkesbury Rd,
PIFF'S ELM, GL51 9SY
Tel.: 01242 680321
Website: www.thegloucesteroldspot.co.uk

4 mi northwest of Cheltenham on A 4019. Parking.

PRICES
Meals: £ 14 (weekday lunch) and a la carte
£ 25/40

MAP: 53

CLOSING TIMES
Closed 25-26 December

THE BELL

Bring your dog or even your horse!

The team at this charming Cotswold pub have considerable local experience and when they took over, they wisely decided not to change too much of the villagers' beloved local. Flagged floors, exposed stone and an abundance of beams lend character while the open fires add cosiness and warmth. Four rooms are served by the central bar and all-comers are equally welcome, whether here for a pint or a three course meal. Menus are the same at lunch and dinner, and offer the expected burger or fish and chips as well as dishes which allow a little more creativity from the chef, like curried day boat seafood stew or braised pork belly with cheek croquette. Dogs are welcome and there's even 'horse parking' for those who'd rather ride than drive.

SAPPERTON, GL7 6LE
Tel.: 01285 760298
Website: www.bellsapperton.co.uk

5 mi west of Cirencester by A 419. Parking.

PRICES
Meals: a la carte £ 23/39

MAP: 54

CLOSING TIMES
Closed 25 December and Sunday dinner

SWAN

British cooking showcases produce from the garden

There are few more charming Cotswold villages than Southrop and it's here you'll find the equally delightful Swan. This 17C Virginia creeper covered inn comes with characterful beamed dining rooms, open fires and modern artwork. It also plays a key role in the community; you'll always find plenty of locals in the snug bar and there's even a skittle alley at the back. Cooking is firmly British based and features produce from the extensive gardens; you might find brawn with pickled artichokes or roast breast of guinea fowl with pea purée. If you're feeling particularly inspired after your meal, you can always enrol at the owners' cookery school, and if you fancy staying a little longer, they also own three delightful cottages just down the road.

SOUTHROP, GL7 3NU
Tel.: 01367 850205
Website: www.theswanatsouthrop.co.uk

3 mi northwest of Lechlade-on-Thames on Eastleach rd.
On-street parking around the village.

PRICES
Meals: £ 16 (weekdays) and a la carte
£ 24/47

MAP: 55

CLOSING TIMES
Closed 25 December

BELL INN

Sit on the terrace for amazing views

Great food seems to taste even better when accompanied by a great view. Set high above the busy streets of Stroud, this Grade II listed stone inn dates back to the 16C, and its delightful terrace and airy conservatory look out across the countryside. Interesting modern dishes showcase produce from the chef-owner's allotment – including vegetables, herbs and berries – and there's a great vegetarian selection. Start with a salmon fishcake with red onion and sweet chilli, then move on to pan-fried parmesan polenta with roasted vegetables or smoked haddock with wilted spinach and a poached egg; save room for dessert though, as there might be a pistachio soufflé or a thick treacle tart. Make a night of it by staying in one of the homely bedrooms.

Bell Ln,
SELSLEY, STROUD, GL5 5LY
Tel.: 01453 753801
Website: www.thebellinnselsley.com

2 mi southwest of Stroud by A 419 and on B 4048. Parking.

PRICES
Meals: a la carte £ 20/32

2 rooms:
£ 90

MAP: 56

CLOSING TIMES
Closed Sunday dinner

BISLEY HOUSE

Stroud's oldest pub sports a bright, modern look

Stroud's oldest pub, the former brewery-owned Bisley House, is hidden away on a residential side street and has been given a new lease of life by Rorie Scott and family. It now sports a surprisingly bright, modern look, with tiled floors, white walls – and not a beam or a horse brass in sight! The menu changes almost daily and offers an interesting range of dishes, from moules marinière or chicken liver parfait, to braised ox cheek with horseradish mash, duck leg with mustard sauce or Moroccan-spiced lamb stew. The cooking is simple, fresh and tasty – and the locals clearly love it. Service is friendly and attentive, the soundtrack's a good'un, and if you venture out the back, you'll find a suntrap of a terrace built into the hill.

Middle St,
STROUD, GL5 1DZ
Tel.: 01453 751328
Website: www.bisleyhousecafe.co.uk

Turn right onto Nelson St at the mini roundabout opposite Police Station on Cornhill. On-street parking adjacent.

PRICES   MAP: **57**
Meals: a la carte £ 23/33

CLOSING TIMES
Closed Monday

GUMSTOOL INN

Flexible dining and a contemporary country style

This converted farm outbuilding – now an attractive country pub – is set in the grounds of the stylish Calcot Manor Hotel and Spa, on a 700 year old estate. With its wood-panelled walls, flag flooring and mustard-coloured walls, it successfully combines a classic country style with a more contemporary edge, and the copper-topped bar and open fire – complete with a chargrill – are great features. The flexible menu offers snacks and two sizes of starter, followed by a selection of rustic, hearty main courses; the extensive selection of daily specials provides some interesting choices and meat from the chargrill is always a good choice. It's warm and cosy in winter, bright and airy in spring and the paved terrace is the perfect spot in summer.

Calcot,
TETBURY, GL8 8YJ
Tel.: 01666 890391
Website: www.calcot.co

3.5 mi west of Tetbury on A 4135, in grounds of Calcot Manor Hotel.
Parking.

PRICES
Meals: a la carte £ 21/41

 35 rooms:
£ 174/364

MAP: 58

CLOSING TIMES
Open daily

SEAGRAVE ARMS

Refined dishes of produce from the local larder

This handsome Grade II listed Cotswold stone building, with its elegant Georgian façade, was built as a coach house and converted into a pub in 1840. Smaller inside than the exterior leads you to believe, it has a cosy fire-warmed bar and two traditional dining rooms, while the large terrace provides a good spot for an alfresco meal in the warmer months. Classical bedrooms are split between the inn and an annexe; one has a four-poster bed and the suite has a spacious bathroom and a roll-top bath. Attractively presented, refined modern dishes use well-judged combinations of ingredients from the local larder; expect Cotswold lamb, Gloucester Old Spot pork and vegetables from the Vale. Start with a freshly baked mini loaf and farmhouse butter.

Friday St,
WESTON-SUB-EDGE, GL55 6QH
Tel.: 01386 840192
Website: www.seagravearms.co.uk

3 mi northwest of Chipping Campden. Parking.

PRICES
Meals: £ 15 (lunch and early dinner)
and a la carte £ 30/42

 8 rooms:
£ 70/165

MAP: 59

CLOSING TIMES
Open daily

REDAN INN

Choose pub classics or more modern dishes

At one time there were 7 pubs in the village, so when the last pub standing was put on the market, the villagers banded together to form the 'Friends of the Redan'. They needn't have worried though, as it was soon taken over by the experienced owners of the Pump House and the Bird In Hand near Bristol. The Redan was built in 1840 and named after a battle which took place during the Crimean War and, although it's now been smartly refurbished, it still displays an impressive selection of old curios and enamel signs. The concise weekly menu offers an enticing mix of accomplished dishes. They cure their own meats, make their own sausages and use apples from the garden for their chutney. Service is relaxed and engaging and bedrooms are stylish.

Fry's Well,
CHILCOMPTON, BA3 4HA
Tel.: 01761 258560
Website: www.theredaninn.co.uk

3.75 mi southwest of Radstock by A 367 and B 3139. Parking.

PRICES
Meals: £ 15/20 and a la carte £ 23/44

 8 rooms:
£ 80/170

MAP: 60

CLOSING TIMES
Open daily

QUEENS ARMS

The events at this hub-of-the-village pub include everything from a game and wine evening and a winter film night to a brewing course hosted by the local brewery. Sit beside a roaring fire at one of the hotchpotch of tables – the glass-topped cartwheel is a favourite – and keep an eye out for 'Bertie the Bull', who appeared in Carry On Cowboy! The menu lists food 'metres' rather than food 'miles' and much of the produce is from their nearby smallholding; choose from small plates, pub classics and some more elaborate dishes like venison saddle with faggots and pickled walnuts. The bar is topped with tempting treats, the apple juice list is worth a look and they also do a roaring trade in afternoon tea. Plush bedrooms complete the picture.

CORTON DENHAM, DT9 4LR
Tel.: 01963 220317
Website: www.thequeensarms.com

3 mi north of Sherborne by B 3145 and minor road west. Parking.

PRICES
Meals: a la carte £ 26/43

 8 rooms:
£ 90/135

MAP: 61

CLOSING TIMES
Open daily
booking advisable

WOODS

Try the meat from the owner's farm

It doesn't look much like a pub – in fact, with its shop window still in situ, it looks more like the bakery it once was – but its cosy, hugely characterful interior soon allays any doubts: a fire blazes in the hearth, locals prop up the bar and wooden beams abound, while the walls are lined with rustic oddments ranging from agricultural implements to hunting paraphernalia and even a pair of antlers. Carefully prepared, tasty dishes offer more than the usual pub fare: you might find seared steak or pancetta and black pudding salad at lunch, and the likes of scallops with cauliflower purée or chicken ballotine with wild garlic mousse at dinner. Provenance is taken seriously here, with quality local produce including meat from the owner's farm.

4 Banks Sq,
DULVERTON, TA22 9BU
Tel.: 01398 324007
Website: www.woodsdulverton.co.uk

In the centre of the town. Pay and display parking close by.

PRICES
Meals: a la carte £ 23/33

MAP: 62

CLOSING TIMES
Closed 25 December, dinner 26 December
and 1 January
bookings advisable at dinner

WHITE HORSE

Gallic dishes made with South West produce

With dried hops hung on exposed beams, a mix of wood and flagged floors, and a fire at either end, the White Horse is every bit a traditional village pub. In summer, the small side terrace fills up quickly and every Friday you'll find the locals out in force for a drink and a chat. Owners Rebecca and Richard worked in London before swapping the bustling streets for the more sedate pace of village life and influences from their time in the city can be seen on the menu. The majority of produce comes from within 50 miles and, alongside British classics, you'll find dishes with Gallic and Mediterranean leanings – maybe Dorset snails Bourguignon, followed by Devon chicken with Alsace bacon and mushroom duxelles, finished off with crème caramel.

North St,
HASELBURY PLUCKNETT, TA18 7RJ
Tel.: 01460 78873
Website: www.thewhitehorsehaselbury.co.uk

8.5 mi southwest of Yeovil, village signposted off A 30.
Limited parking at pub.

PRICES   MAP: **63**
Meals: £ 17 and a la carte £ 21/36

CLOSING TIMES
Closed Sunday dinner and Monday

LORD POULETT ARMS

Charming pub run by a friendly team

Lord Poulett, a former local landowner, would no doubt have been pleased to put his name to this honey stone pub. It oozes character, courtesy of open fires, beams fringed with hop bines and antique wooden chairs – and outside it's just as charming, with a lavender-framed terrace, a boules pitch, a secret garden and even a pelota wall built by Basque monks in the 16C. Creative cooking has a British base but it also displays more wide ranging influences, so you might find wild boar scotch egg, duck breast with braised leg fritter or fava bean chilli with polenta chips, followed by blackcurrant bavarois with cassis ice cream or a selection of West Country cheeses. Stylish bedrooms come with feature beds and have Roberts radios instead of TVs.

High St,
HINTON ST GEORGE, TA17 8SE
Tel.: 01460 73149
Website: www.lordpoulettarms.com

3 mi northwest of Crewkerne signposted off A 356. On-street parking.

PRICES
Meals: £ 16 (lunch and early dinner) and a la carte £ 26/38

 4 rooms:
£ 60/95

MAP: 64

CLOSING TIMES
Closed 25-26 December and 1 January

HOLCOMBE INN

Cosy beamed inn with luxurious bedrooms

Set deep in the heart of the Somerset countryside, on the edge of a small village, the 17C Holcombe Inn provides all the charm you'd expect of a building its age, with exposed beams, flag floors and cosy open fires. Come summer, the large garden with its lovely southerly aspect makes a great place to sit and as you unwind, you feel as if you really have escaped to the middle of nowhere. Satisfyingly, this is a place that has a good reputation for its food too, with menus offering quite a range of dishes, from good old pub classics like homemade pie of the day to more sophisticated offerings like ballotine of local chicken or pork belly with black pudding. Bedrooms are luxuriously appointed and some boast views over Downside Abbey.

Stratton Rd,
HOLCOMBE, BA3 5EB
Tel.: 01761 232478
Website: www.holcombeinn.co.uk

4.25 mi southwest of Radstock by A 367; on the western edge of the village on Stratton-on-the-Fosse rd. Parking.

PRICES
Meals: a la carte £ 29/44

 10 rooms:
£ 75/145

MAP: 65

CLOSING TIMES
Open daily

BIRD IN HAND

Tiny, quirky and very good value

When the owner of the Pump House pub found out his own local was going to close, he did what any panicking regular would like to do – he bought the place! This tiny country pub, with its three small, simply but smartly decorated rooms, is a complete contrast to his first venture and boasts quirky touches like an antelope's head, cast iron advertising signs and walls covered with pages from Mrs Beeton's Book of Household Management. Equal attention has been paid to the appealing menus, which offer dishes like onglet steak with oxtail and bone marrow or roast fillet, faggot and belly of suckling lamb. Cooking is tasty, carefully executed and keeps things simple, letting the seasonal British ingredients speak for themselves.

17 Weston Rd,
LONG ASHTON, BS41 9LA
Tel.: 01275 395222
Website: www.bird-in-hand.co.uk

2.5 mi southwest of Bristol city centre, well signposted off the A 370.
Parking on the High Street.

PRICES   MAP: **66**
Meals: a la carte £ 25/31

CLOSING TIMES
Open daily
booking essential at dinner

DEVONSHIRE ARMS

Bedrooms are modern and well-furnished

The Devonshire Arms is a striking Grade II listed former hunting lodge that sits overlooking the village green, but despite its outward appearance, this is a place that keeps up with the times. Inside it's had a contemporary makeover: wing-back leather chairs sit by an open fire, lanterns hang above comfy banquettes and blue panelled walls are broken up by boldly printed wallpaper. When the weather's good, grab a pint of Moor Beer or Harry's Cider – both brewed in the village – and head for the tiered garden or courtyard terrace. Menus follow the seasons and offer an appealing range of dishes: choose something Mediterranean such as duck confit or aubergine involtini or stick with British classics like organic sausages and mustard mash.

LONG SUTTON, TA10 9LP
Tel.: 01458 241271
Website: www.thedevonshirearms.com

4 mi east of Langport by A 372. Parking.

PRICES
Meals: a la carte £ 25/36

 9 rooms:
£ 90/155

MAP: 67

CLOSING TIMES
Closed 25-26 December

TALBOT INN

Food is full of flavour; staff go the extra mile

This 15C coaching inn on the Mells Estate, sister to the Beckford Arms at Tisbury, has been given a shake-up style-wise but thankfully without losing any of its substantial charm. A cobbled courtyard leads through to a series of rustic rooms featuring stone floors and painted panelling; there's a cosy sitting room with an open fire, a snug bar offering real ales and the elegantly dressed Coach House Grill Room to keep carnivores happy at weekends. Food is seasonal, modern and full of flavour, with gutsy main courses like braised roe deer with creamed mash or roasted partridge with celeriac purée. Delightful, understated bedrooms are comfortable and well-priced – and the staff may be casually attired but their manner is anything but.

Selwood St,
MELLS, BA11 3PN
Tel.: 01373 812254
Website: www.talbotinn.com

3 mi northwest of Frome by A 362. On-street parking.

PRICES
Meals: a la carte £ 24/34

 8 rooms:
£ 100/160

MAP: 68

CLOSING TIMES
Open daily

WHITE POST

Stunning West Country views

This pub sits on the Dorset/Somerset border, with stunning views of the West Country. Back in the days when different counties had different licencing hours, the pub used to have two bars – one in each county – and when time was called in one room, the locals would simply move to the other room to continue drinking. These days the focus is more on dining than drinking: local chef Brett Sutton is known for his flamboyant cooking displays, but there are plenty of pub classics on the menu alongside his more imaginative creations and quirky touches like piggy nibbles – pulled pork, chorizo and glazed sausage – and the Sunday roast board: surely every carnivore's dream dish? Bedrooms are simply furnished: ask for Dorset, which has the best views.

RIMPTON, BA22 8AR
Tel.: 01935 851525
Website: www.thewhitepost.com

On B 3148 between Marston Magna and Sherbourne. Parking.

PRICES
Meals: a la carte £ 26/46

3 rooms:
£ 80/95

MAP: 69

CLOSING TIMES
Closed Sunday dinner and Monday

WHITE HART

Seasonal cooking using the wood-burning oven

This 16C inn hasn't just had a makeover, it's had a facelift, some Botox and some fillers too. Sister to the Swan at Wedmore, it sits on the main market square of this pretty Somerset village; a beautiful parquet-floored entrance leading to six characterful rooms, including 'the barn' where you can watch the chefs at work. Seasonal food centres around the wood-burning oven, with flavourful dishes like Old Spot pork belly or dry-aged flat-iron steaks and there's a special pizza menu on Sunday nights. Desserts could include baked vanilla cheesecake with poached rhubarb and the delicious homemade ice creams come in flavours like salted caramel or hazelnut brittle. Stylish bedrooms have a cosy feel; Room 3, with a bath centre stage, is the best.

Market Pl,
SOMERTON, TA11 7LX
Tel.: 01458 272273
Website: www.whitehartsomerton.com

8 mi northwest of Yeovil by A 37, B 3151 on B 3153. On-street parking.

PRICES
Meals: a la carte £ 22/33

 8 rooms:
£ 85/135

MAP: 70

CLOSING TIMES
Open daily

TARR FARM INN

Idyllically located by a sparkling river

Arrive on the wrong side of the river and you might get a shock – you'll be able to see the pub but, unless you have a 4x4, contending with the water isn't an option. That said, if you've travelled by foot then there's no better way to approach than by crossing the 17 spans of the charming 1000 BC, stone-slab clapper bridge. The setting is nothing short of idyllic: birds sing in the trees and cool, clear water gurgles under the bridge. If the sun's out, head for the garden for a spot of afternoon tea; if the rain's lashing down, make for the narrow, beamed bar or the cosy restaurant. Menus provide plenty of choice, from potted shrimps or gravadlax through to rack of Exmoor lamb or Devon Red Ruby steak. Bedrooms are comfy and well-equipped.

TARR STEPS, TA22 9PY
Tel.: 01643 851507
Website: www.tarrfarm.co.uk

Signed off B 3223 Dulverton to Exford road. Limited parking.

PRICES
Meals: a la carte £ 23/41

 9 rooms:
£ 75/150

MAP: 71

CLOSING TIMES
Closed 1-13 February

BLUE BALL INN

Sit in the lovely tiered garden

This characterful thatched barn is located in the beautiful Quantock Hills; it dates from the 15C and boasts a cosy, rustic feel, courtesy of exposed rafters, open fires, tartan carpets and mounted stags' heads. Lunchtime sandwiches, 'posh' ploughman's and classics like sausage and mash or guinea fowl and mushroom pie provide fuel for passing walkers; while dinner sees well-presented, modern dishes with a touch of originality – perhaps linguine with hare bolognese or pork cutlet with braised cheek – and the bacon and black pudding scotch egg is a favourite at either sitting. Behind the pub, you'll find a lovely tiered garden, and the pretty thatched cottage alongside contains comfortable, rustic bedrooms named 'Pheasant', 'Hind' and 'Stag'.

TRISCOMBE, TA4 3HE
Tel.: 01984 618242
Website: www.blueballinn.info

Between Taunton and Williton off A 358. Parking.

PRICES
Meals: a la carte £ 23/35

 3 rooms:
£ 65/95

MAP: 72

CLOSING TIMES
Closed 25 December, dinner 1 January and Sunday dinner

SWAN

Seasonal British ingredients and unfussy cooking

If good British ingredients that match the seasons and unfussy, flavoursome dishes are your thing, then this 18C coaching inn is the place for you. Portions are generous: expect the likes of stuffed Cornish sardines or ham, cheddar and parsley croquettes, followed by braised pheasant with juniper and thyme or orange-marinated Orchard Farm pork T-bone with fennel. Inside it's spacious and airy: there's a large bar with bare floorboards and simple wooden tables; a cosy little area with rugs and leather furniture; and, past the open kitchen and display of home-baked breads, a comfortable dining room – be sure to book, as it's a rightly popular place. Stylish bedrooms complete the picture; those at the top of the stairs can be noisy.

Cheddar Rd,
WEDMORE, BS28 4EQ
Tel.: 01934 710337
Website: www.theswanwedmore.com

In the centre of the town. Parking.

PRICES	7 rooms:	**MAP: 73**
Meals: a la carte £ 23/39	£ 85/125	

CLOSING TIMES
Closed 25 December
booking essential

ROYAL OAK INN

Delightful 12C farmhouse down country lanes

Mind the pheasants as you navigate the winding lanes of Exmoor towards this charming little village. Beside the ford, you'll see a delightful 12C former farmhouse and dairy, which is one of the country's most photographed pubs. Turn left into the dining room or right into the rustic bar, where you'll find a small gathering of locals and their dogs and a wood-furnished dining area. The menu changes every 3 months and offers a mix of pub dishes and British classics; there's also a selection of daily specials chalked on a board above the fire. Dishes are tasty, satisfying and well-executed – the desserts, in particular, are very tempting. Spacious country bedrooms come with huge bathrooms and rain showers; most of them have four-poster beds.

Halse Ln,
WINSFORD, TA24 7JE
Tel.: 01643 851455
Website: www.royaloakexmoor.co.uk

5 mi north of Dulverton off B 3223. Parking.

PRICES
Meals: a la carte £ 23/35

 8 rooms:
£ 75/140

MAP: 74

CLOSING TIMES
Open daily

BUNCH OF GRAPES

French bric-a-brac adds to the appeal

The Bunch of Grapes is an apt name for this collaboration between five friends, who have all spent time living in the South West of France and love nothing better than to eat good food and drink good wine. Rustic cooking relies largely on the wood-fired Bertha oven, which uses oak and apple wood to add smoky flavours. There are aperitif plates for sharing, tartines and pissaladières, and generous main courses like wood pigeon cassoulet and duck à l'orange. Wines are imported directly from French vineyards and the concise list champions Bordeaux and Languedoc-Roussillon. The friendly team welcome you as much for coffee and cake or a cocktail as they do for a 3 course dinner, and the whole place has an appealingly bijou, brocante feel.

14 Silver St,
BRADFORD-ON-AVON, BA15 1JY
Tel.: 01225 938088
Website: www.thebunchofgrapes.com

On B 3107 heading northeast out of town centre. Pay and display car park in town centre just over Town Bridge.

PRICES   MAP: **75**
Meals: £ 16/22 and a la carte £ 24/42

CLOSING TIMES
Closed 25-26 December

THE FOX

Cooking uses what's in the garden

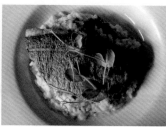

Raising the profile of this pub, both locally and farther afield, has been a labour of love for its young owner, Alex, who has given it one of those clever refurbishments that cost a lot of money but make everything look largely unchanged. It is set in front of the village hall and lies very much at the heart of the community. There's always a great choice of beer on draught but the real surprise is out back: there are raised beds of salad leaves, rhubarb, herbs and fruits, and behind these, you'll find chickens and a pigsty. In a move towards self-sufficiency, the kitchen also makes its own sausages and dries its own meat for the excellent charcuterie dishes. And what does Alex do on his day off? He goes foraging for more local produce.

The Street,
BROUGHTON GIFFORD, SN12 8PN
Tel.: 01225 782949
Website: www.thefox-broughtongifford.co.uk

Between Bradford-on-Avon and Melksham off B 3107. Parking.

PRICES   MAP: 76
Meals: £ 18 (weekday lunch) and a la carte
£ 22/46

CLOSING TIMES
Closed 2-8 January and Monday

WHITE HORSE INN

Regular BBQs and food and wine evenings

The White Horse Inn dates back over a century and a half and is named after the hillside carving at Cherhill Down. Until shortly before the First World War, it also functioned as a grocer's shop and a bakery, at which point the owner decided to concentrate all his efforts into running it as a pub. The cosy bar is where you'll find the regulars, while most diners head for the rustic room next door. For traditionalists there's the pub classics menu, which offers homemade burgers and fish battered to order; for those with more adventurous tastes there's the à la carte, which lists the likes of Cornish hake with risotto nero or braised shoulder of Wiltshire lamb with ratatouille. Beyond the large garden are 8 snug, simply furnished bedrooms.

COMPTON BASSETT, SN11 8RG
Tel.: 01249 813118
Website: www.whitehorse-comptonbassett.co.uk

4 mi east of Calne signposted off A 4. Parking.

PRICES
Meals: £ 15 (weekday lunch) and a la carte
£ 21/49

 8 rooms:
£ 75/110

MAP: 77

CLOSING TIMES
Closed 25 December, Sunday dinner and
Monday

424

METHUEN ARMS

Try the good value weekday lunch menu

The Methuen Arms started life as a 14C nunnery but was converted into a coaching inn and brewery in 1608. It's a substantial place, set over three storeys, with a columned porch and a pleasant courtyard terrace. Before choosing what to eat, there's the choice of where to sit – the 'Little Room' by the bar, the flag floored 'Nott Room' or the characterful restaurant with its French doors onto the garden. Once that decision's been made it's on to the appealing menus, which offer modern British dishes with a focus on flavour and feature the likes of confit guinea fowl or venison and mushroom puff pastry pie. If you're staying the night in one of the boutique bedrooms, it's the perfect excuse to sample their breakfast and afternoon tea too!

2 High St,
CORSHAM, SN13 0HB
Tel.: 01249 717060
Website: www.themethuenarms.com

In the centre of the town. Parking.

PRICES
Meals: £ 20 (weekdays) and a la carte
£ 27/47

14 rooms:
£ 90/175

MAP: 78

CLOSING TIMES
Closed 25 December

RED LION

Meats and fish smoked and ales brewed on-site

Just off the Thames path, you'll find this traditional 17C inn. With a cosy, low-beamed interior crammed full of bric-a-brac, it looks like a proper pub; and pleasingly, it adopts a good old English attitude too. The bar serves 10 different ales – some of which are brewed in-house – as well as 30 speciality bottled beers, which can be sampled while tucking into a pub classic, dog at your feet. Next door is a small but airy stone-walled dining room with a beautiful carved slab. Here you'll find slightly more refined classics such as oysters, venison stew and treacle tart. Produce is fresh and extremely local – and if you're down a pound or two, they'll accept some home-grown fruit or veg as payment. Comfy, modern bedrooms are in the old stables.

74 High St,
CRICKLADE, SN6 6DD
Tel.: 01793 750776
Website: www.theredlioncricklade.co.uk

At the eastern end of the High St. Unrestricted parking on the High St.

PRICES
Meals: a la carte £ 22/36

 5 rooms:
£ 85

MAP: 79

CLOSING TIMES
Open daily

BATH ARMS

Plenty of country appeal and outdoor space

The Bath Arms offers a warm welcome, open fires, plenty of country appeal and a wealth of outdoor space. Once part of the Longleat Estate, it is run with a passion by local boy Dean Carr, who returned from his culinary experiences in the Big Smoke to put some love back into this community pub. The menus offer something for everyone, from filled baguettes or shepherd's pie to dishes such as fillet of red mullet with fennel salad or slow-braised rabbit with polenta and bacon; not forgetting favourites like the fishcakes or the now legendary sticky beef with braised red cabbage. Traditional desserts like tarte Tatin round things off nicely – and there are two ultra-spacious, contemporary bedrooms should you wish to stay the night.

Clay St,
CROCKERTON, BA12 8AJ
Tel.: 01985 212262
Website: www.batharmscrockerton.co.uk

2 mi south of Warminster just off A 350 on Shearwater rd. Parking.

PRICES
Meals: a la carte £ 24/33

2 rooms:
£ 80/110

MAP: 80

CLOSING TIMES
Closed Sunday dinner in winter

POTTING SHED PUB

A relaxed feel and an unusual horticultural theme

Despite its contemporary décor, the Potting Shed is very much a proper pub, where locals gather for a pint and a chat. Situated opposite its sister establishment, the Rectory Hotel, it consists of five spacious, light-filled rooms, with open fires and a relaxing feel. The pub's large gardens provide it with an abundance of fresh, seasonal herbs and vegetables – and the horticultural theme continues inside, with trowel door knobs, wheelbarrow lights and fork and spade pump handles. Monthly changing menus offer fresh, satisfying dishes like local trout, wild rabbit fettuccine, and apple and blackberry crumble. Lollipops on the bar ensure that the kids are kept happy, while dog biscuits do the same for your four-legged friends.

The Street,
CRUDWELL, SN16 9EW
Tel.: 01666 577833
Website: www.thepottingshedpub.com

4 mi north of Malmesbury by A 429. Parking.

PRICES
Meals: a la carte £ 25/32

MAP: 81

CLOSING TIMES
Open daily

THE FORESTER

Worth finding for its classic country cooking

Hidden down narrow lanes in a delightful Wiltshire village, this 13C thatched pub has a gloriously rustic feel. Exposed stone walls feature throughout and vast open fires ensure that it's always cosy. There's a lovely bar crammed with cookery books, and two main dining areas – one in a cleverly added extension that's perfectly in keeping. The experienced owners take a very hands-on approach and, along with the chef, are passionate about using good country ingredients, with meats coming from local farms and estates and fish from the Brixham day boats. Menus change with the seasons and there's always a daily 3 course set selection dedicated to seafood. Dishes are well-prepared and flavoursome, with a classical country base and a refined edge.

Lower St,
DONHEAD ST ANDREW, SP7 9EE
Tel.: 01747 828038
Website: www.theforesterdonheadstandrew.co.uk

5 mi east of Shaftesbury by A 30, taking Tisbury and Donhead rd. Parking.

PRICES
Meals: £ 19 (weekdays) and a la carte
£ 27/47

MAP: 82

CLOSING TIMES
Closed Sunday dinner and Monday except
bank holidays

RED LION FREEHOUSE

Book the glass-walled private dining room

The Red Lion sits on the edge of Salisbury Plain and although it's not a spot for passing trade, its owners needn't worry, as it's become a real destination in itself. With its thatched roof and welcoming look, it immediately draws you in; although you'll probably want to stay out in the pretty garden if the weather's right. The daily à la carte is a roll-call of carefully prepared classics which arrive fully garnished and packed with flavour; these could include herb-roast guinea fowl with hot Caesar sauce or rib of Wiltshire beef for two. The midweek lunch is great value and the well-chosen wine list offers a good selection by the glass. Smart, well-equipped bedrooms are set opposite and have private terraces overlooking the river.

EAST CHISENBURY, SN9 6AQ
Tel.: 01980 671124
Website: www.redlionfreehouse.com

Between Pewsey and Amesbury off the A 345. Parking.

PRICES
Meals: £ 24 (weekday lunch) and a la carte
£ 34/50

 5 rooms:
£ 130/250

MAP: 83

CLOSING TIMES
Open daily
booking advisable

THREE DAGGERS

Produce from the owner's farm down the road

Originally named after the local landowners, this pub has been refurbished and reborn as the 'Three Daggers' – a reference to the insignia on the Paulet family's coat of arms. It's an attractive place, with a large conservatory overlooking the garden, and the original beams and flagstones are still in place, so the character quotient remains high. When it comes to the food, there's something for everyone: a homemade soup, the 'pie of the day' or a local lamb burger; and the sharing plates – the Huntsman's and the Fisherman's – prove extremely popular. They have their own farm shop and brew their own beers too, so are pretty self-sufficient. Charming bedrooms feature bespoke oak furnishings and you're given free rein of the farmhouse kitchen.

47 Westbury Rd,
EDINGTON, BA13 4PG
Tel.: 01380 830940
Website: www.threedaggers.co.uk

4 mi east of Westbury on B 3098. Parking.

PRICES
Meals: a la carte £ 23/41

 3 rooms:
£ 85/165

MAP: 84

CLOSING TIMES
Open daily

FOXHAM INN

The regular gourmet nights are a hit

Located in a sleepy Wiltshire village, the family-run Foxham Inn is a secret that the locals have clearly been trying to keep to themselves. For pleasant views over the fields and paddocks, bag a seat on the semi-covered terrace; on colder days, make for the cosy bar with its scrubbed pine tables, old church pews and wood burning stove, or if you fancy some live cooking action, head through to the airy extension, where you can look into the kitchen. The menu offers a good range of dishes at a uniform price for each course, along with sandwiches and panini at lunch. Everything from the condiments to the ice creams is homemade and flavours are clear and defined. The regular gourmet nights are a hit and two homely bedrooms complete the picture.

FOXHAM, SN15 4NQ
Tel.: 01249 740665
Website: www.thefoxhaminn.co.uk

7 mi northeast of Chippenham signposted off B 4069 in west end of village. Parking.

PRICES
Meals: a la carte £ 27/42

 2 rooms:
£ 75/90

MAP: 85

CLOSING TIMES
Closed 2 weeks early January, Sunday dinner and Monday
booking advisable

TOLLGATE INN

Cheery, attentive service sets it apart

If there was an award for the most welcoming pub, then this village inn would surely be crowned the winner. With their wide smiles and easy rapport, the attentive staff pitch things just right; from the cheery hello as you enter, to the personal touches provided for those staying in the cosy bedrooms – no wonder the place is buzzing! The menu keeps things simple, as befits a pub; with hearty, flavoursome dishes like slow-braised pork belly or Cumberland sausages with sweet potato gratin alongside steaks, the fish of the day and a daily changing lunchtime quiche. Beef is from Broughton Gifford, fish comes from Lyme Bay and the vegetables are from Bristol; much of the game is brought in by the villagers, who are rewarded with a beer or two.

Ham Grn,
HOLT, BA14 6PX
Tel.: 01225 782326
Website: www.tollgateinn.co.uk

Midway between Bradford-on-Avon and Melksham on B 3107. Parking.

PRICES
Meals: a la carte £ 18/41

 5 rooms:
£ 50/120

MAP: 86

CLOSING TIMES
Closed 25 December and Sunday dinner

MUDDY DUCK

Smart bedrooms and a switched-on team

The Muddy Duck is thought to be Wiltshire's most haunted pub and with its far-reaching history, it could well be: there's been an inn on this site since the 17C and before that, a house dating back to the reign of Henry VIII. From the outside it looks like a manor house and inside it's full of character, with a giant inglenook fireplace in the bar and a stylish, rustic dining room. Concise menus offer mainly classic British dishes such as Wiltshire lamb with asparagus, Gloucestershire beef with garlic and herb butter or South Coast hake with crab crushed potatoes. Bedrooms are smart – those in the converted barn are duplex and come with a snug decked out with a wood burning stove – and nothing is too much trouble for the switched-on team.

42 Monkton Farleigh,
MONKTON FARLEIGH, BA15 2QN
Tel.: 01225 858705
Website: www.themuddyduckbath.co.uk

7 mi east of Bath signposted off A 363. Parking.

PRICES
Meals: £ 15 (weekday lunch) and a la carte
£ 24/44

 5 rooms:
£ 100/250

MAP: 87

CLOSING TIMES
Open daily

BELL

Pub favourites and ambitious, accomplished dishes

Despite an extensive refurbishment, this charming 16C building has managed to retain plenty of its original pubby character, particularly in the open-fired bar, where you'll find hop-covered beams and a menu of old pub favourites. If you're looking for the bell the pub's named after, you'll find it hanging in the fireplace of the crisply laid dining room. Here you can sit on smart tartan banquettes and enjoy a more sophisticated atmosphere, dining on ambitious, accomplished dishes such as crispy fried duck egg with chorizo and tomato salsa, followed by local estate venison with carrot and celeriac purées. At the back, 'Café Bella' is a popular meeting place for the locals, while stylish, well-appointed bedrooms welcome those staying over.

The Square,
RAMSBURY, SN8 2PE
Tel.: 01672 520230
Website: www.ramsbury.com

4 mi northwest of Hungerford signposted off B 4192. Parking.

PRICES
Meals: a la carte £ 25/52

 9 rooms:
£ 110/170

MAP: 88

CLOSING TIMES
Closed 25 December

GEORGE & DRAGON

It's all about seafood from St Mawes

This 16C coaching inn has a rustic feel throughout; its cosy inner boasting solid stone floors, wooden beams and open fires. There's a strong emphasis on seafood, with fish delivered daily from Cornwall to ensure it arrives on your plate in tip-top condition. That the menu is written anew each day also speaks volumes about the pub's take on food; seafood dishes could be a plate of fishy hors d'oeuvres, pan-fried cod with bacon or a whole grilled lemon sole; more meaty choices might include rack of lamb or roast fillet of beef. Some dishes come in two sizes and can be taken as either a starter or a main course. There is also a good value set three course menu. Old-world charm meets modern facilities in the individually designed bedrooms.

High St,
ROWDE, SN10 2PN
Tel.: 01380 723053
Website: www.thegeorgeanddragonrowde.co.uk

2 mi northwest of Devizes on A 342. Parking.

PRICES
Meals: £ 20 and a la carte £ 26/43

 3 rooms:
£ 75/125

MAP: 89

CLOSING TIMES
Closed Sunday dinner

BECKFORD ARMS

Sunday is film night at this charming inn

Set next to the 10,000 acre Fonthill Estate, this charming 18C inn offers a delightful terrace and a large garden – complete with hammocks, a petanque pitch and a dog bath – as well as a beamed dining room, a rustic bar and a lovely country house sitting room, where films are screened on Sunday nights. Tasty, unfussy cooking relies on excellent ingredients, with the daily menu offering classics and country-style fare such as roast partridge or pork with Morteau sausage, while for a snack, the homemade pork scratchings are a hit. Tastefully furnished bedrooms offer thoughtful comforts, while two smart duplex suites are a few minutes' drive away. The charming young team will gladly provide hampers and arrange fishing and shooting trips.

Fonthill Gifford,
TISBURY, SP3 6PX
Tel.: 01747 870385
Website: www.beckfordarms.com

Between Shaftesbury and Warminster signposted off A 350. Parking.

PRICES
Meals: a la carte £ 24/35

 10 rooms:
£ 95/130

MAP: 90

CLOSING TIMES
Closed 25 December
booking essential

KING JOHN INN

Built in 1859 and a hit with shooting parties

The creeper-clad King John Inn sits in a small village on top of Cranborne Chase and is so-named because the area once served as King John's hunting grounds. Modern black and white hunting photos line the walls of the open-plan interior and provide a clue both to the pub's cooking and its main clientele. The short daily menu is printed on brown paper and each dish lists the origin of its ingredients; be sure to start with some of the tasty homemade bloomer bread. Dishes are modern in the main but have classical roots. The likes of burger and fries vie with lemon sole ravioli; Portland crab on toast and 28-day aged rump steak are perennial favourites; and, unsurprisingly, local game is a highlight. Comfortable bedrooms complete the picture.

TOLLARD ROYAL, SP5 5PS
Tel.: 01725 516207
Website: www.kingjohninn.co.uk

5 mi southeast of Shaftesbury on B 3081. Parking.

PRICES
Meals: £ 22 (weekday lunch) and a la carte
£ 26/51

 8 rooms:
£ 90/190

MAP: 91

CLOSING TIMES
Closed 25 December

LONGS ARMS

Traditional British fare and home-smoked produce

The appetite for British food shows no sign of abating, particularly in British pubs. How apt it is to see traditional dishes like goats' scrumpets or crispy tongue and pickles in a pub like this – named after local landowners, the Long family, in whose manor house Sir Walter Raleigh allegedly smoked the first tobacco in England. The only smoking that goes on nowadays is that of meat and fish in the pub's own smokehouse. Meat is hung and butchered on-site, there's a kitchen garden and everything is made in-house, including bread, ice cream, feta cheese, faggots, black pudding and haggis. Service is warm and friendly and the pub itself is bursting with character; think exposed Bath stone walls, bay windows, a wood-burner and flagged floors.

UPPER SOUTH WRAXALL, BA15 2SB
Tel.: 01225 864450
Website: www.thelongsarms.com

3 mi north of Bradford-on-Avon by A 363, signed off B 3109. In centre of village opposite the church. Parking.

PRICES
Meals: a la carte £ 17/42

MAP: 92

CLOSING TIMES
Closed 3 weeks January,1 week September,
Sunday dinner and Monday
booking essential

WEYMOUTH ARMS

Immensely characterful with charming bedrooms

If you fancy a slice of history with your lunch, you won't be disappointed. This Grade II listed building started life as a private home (round the back, an archway is inscribed with '1771 D.C.', as the house once belonged to Daniel Capel, a well-known clothier); in the 19C it became a lodging house and, a century later, was turned into a public house. It's immensely characterful, displaying wood panelling, antiques and lithographs, as well as two fireplaces originally intended for nearby Longleat House (Lord Weymouth of Longleat was once a frequent visitor). Cooking is fittingly traditional, with fresh ingredients featuring in dishes such as chicken liver pâté and apple and pear crumble. Cosy bedrooms have charming original fittings.

12 Emwell St,
WARMINSTER, BA12 8JA
Tel.: 01985 216995
Website: www.weymoutharms.co.uk

In centre of town just off George St. Pay and display parking adjacent.

PRICES
Meals: a la carte £ 21/45

 6 rooms:
£ 70/95

MAP: 93

CLOSING TIMES
Closed Monday-Wednesday lunch

BELL

Relax on the spacious south-facing terrace

One way to improve any walk, apart from having proper shoes and fair weather, is to end up at a decent pub. If you've been out on the Cherhill Downs, then pop into the Bell at West Overton. The pub was rescued by a local couple, who realised a dream by buying it, but who were also sensible enough to hire an experienced pair to run it. The same menu is served in the bar and restaurant, and the latter is far from stuffy as they don't want to scare anyone away; there's also a large, south-facing terrace out the back, perfect for alfresco lunches. The menu offers an appealing blend of pub classics and dishes of a Mediterranean bent, such as Cornish bream with chorizo and olives. Presentation is modern but not at the expense of flavour.

Bath Rd,
WEST OVERTON, SN8 1QD
Tel.: 01672 861099
Website: www.thebellwestoverton.co.uk

4 mi west of Marlborough on A 4. Parking.

PRICES
Meals: a la carte £ 23/40

MAP: 94

CLOSING TIMES
Closed Sunday dinner and Monday except
bank holidays

WEST MIDLANDS

England

The names Gas Street Basin, Custard Factory and Mailbox may not win any awards for exoticism, but these are the cutting edge quarters fuelling the rise of modern day Birmingham, at the heart of a region evolving from its grimy factory gate image. Even the Ironbridge Gorge, the cradle of the Industrial Revolution, is better known these days as a fascinatingly picturesque tourist attraction. The old urban landscapes dot a region of delightful unspoilt countryside with extensive areas of open moorland and hills, where stands Middle Earth, in the shape of Shropshire's iconic Wrekin hill, true inspiration of Tolkien. Shakespeare Country abounds in pretty villages, such as Henley-in-Arden, Shipston-on-Stour and Alcester, where red-brick, half-timbered and Georgian buildings capture the eye.

Taste buds are catered for courtesy of a host of local specialities, not least fruits from the Vale of Evesham and mouth-watering meats from the hills near the renowned gastro town of Ludlow.

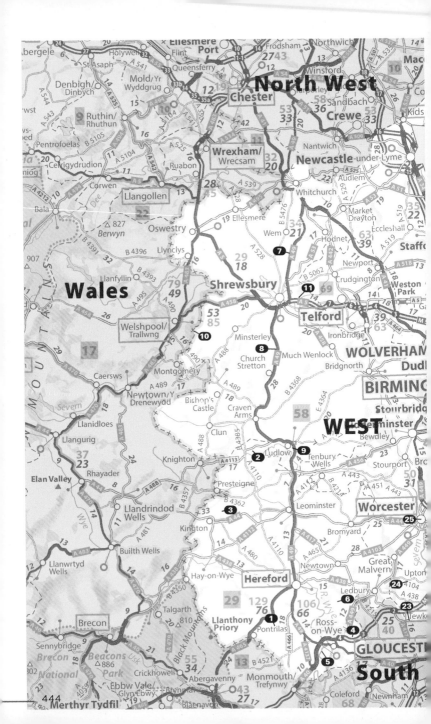

445

KILPECK INN

Impressive green credentials

The former Red Lion narrowly escaped being turned into private housing thanks to the villagers' valiantly fought 'Save Our Pub' campaign. Refurbished and reborn as the Kilpeck Inn, it serves pub classics, locally sourced meats like braised beef or slow-roasted pork belly and old fashioned English puddings like those of the sticky toffee or rice varieties. Any carbon emissions generated on your journey are sure to be offset by the pub's green credentials: with measures such as solar panels and a rainwater recovery system, it must be one of the country's most environmentally friendly eateries. Ecological efficiency does not come at the expense of style, however, and the spacious interior and four bedrooms are smart, modern and characterful.

KILPECK, HR2 9DN
Tel.: 01981 570464
Website: www.kilpeckinn.com

The village is signposted off A 465, 10 mi southwest of Hereford. Parking.

PRICES
Meals: a la carte £ 20/35

 4 rooms:
£ 70/110

MAP: 1

CLOSING TIMES
Closed 25 December

THE LION

Relaxed and stylish, with river views

This 18C inn stands on the banks or the River Teme, next to an attractive medieval bridge, and is owned by local mineral water company Radnor Hills. An extensive refurbishment has created a relaxed, stylish environment: there's a proper bar with a wood-burning stove and a selection of real ales, and a slightly smarter dining room with river views. The same menu is served wherever you sit, offering everything from a beef and thyme burger to lemon-marinated chicken with Thai spiced greens, and from a gypsy tart to rhubarb parfait. Dishes are nicely presented and local produce plays a big part – you'll find a list of their suppliers on the back of the menu. Smart bedrooms have up-to-date facilities and some look out across the water.

LEINTWARDINE, SY7 0JZ
Tel.: 01547 540203
Website: www.thelionleintwardine.co.uk

10 mi west of Ludlow by A 49 on A 4113. Parking.

PRICES
Meals: a la carte £ 20/36

8 rooms:
£ 75/120

MAP: 2

CLOSING TIMES
Closed 25 December

STAGG INN

Delightfully cosy, passionately run pub

Situated at the meeting point of two former drovers' roads, this part-medieval, part-Victorian pub was once called 'The Balance', as it marked the point where farmers would stop to weigh their wool. Inside, it's delightfully cosy; one room was once a butcher's shop and another still displays an old bread oven. Seasonal menus offer tried-and-tested combinations and local meats, fish and cheeses all feature, alongside eggs from their hens and ingredients foraged from the hedgerows. The owners are keen to promote the area and serve local beers, ciders and perries, along with some unusual vodkas – such as marmalade or rhubarb flavour – from the Chase Distillery. Bedrooms in the pub are snug but can be noisy; opt for one in the old vicarage.

TITLEY, HR5 3RL
Tel.: 01544 230221
Website: www.thestagg.co.uk

3.5 mi northeast of Kington on B 4355. Parking.

PRICES
Meals: a la carte £ 32/42

 6 rooms:
£ 60/140

MAP: 3

CLOSING TIMES
Closed 1-4 January, 1-8 March, 1-17 November,
25-27 December, Monday and Tuesday booking essential

MOODY COW

More traditional than its name might suggest

Allegedly named by a previous landlord following his less than amicable divorce, the Moody Cow is a more traditional pub than its moniker might suggest, with a hop-covered wooden bar, deep sofas, a warming wood burning stove and a barn-style dining room. The food matches the surroundings with a range of classic dishes like chicken liver parfait, sausage and mash, pan-fried fillet steak or slow-roasted pork belly and, what it may lack in originality, it makes up for with its quality ingredients, careful cooking and distinct flavours. Just make sure you leave room for the crème brûlée! The friendly owners run this pub with real commitment and passion and even grow some of the ingredients themselves in their kitchen garden.

UPTON BISHOP, HR9 7TT
Tel.: 01989 780470
Website: www.moodycowpub.co.uk

3 miles northeast of Ross-on-Wye signposted off the A 40. Parking.

PRICES
Meals: a la carte £ 22/40

MAP: **4**

CLOSING TIMES
Closed 1-14 January, Sunday dinner
and Monday

MILL RACE

Try the steaks from the charcoal oven

This isn't the kind of place you'd expect to find in a small country village but the locals aren't complaining. It doesn't really look like a pub, either outside or in, save for the bar counter; you enter via a Gothic-style door, pass a board pinpointing their suppliers and head towards the chefs hard at work in the semi open-plan kitchen. You'll find regulars standing around the bar, pint in hand, and local families out for the night in the darker, slate-floored areas. Cooking is fairly simple, showcasing plenty of produce from their estate and farm and letting the ingredients speak for themselves, and regular theme nights include the likes of 'game' and 'pudding'. The small team flit about, coping well when it's busy – which it usually is.

WALFORD, HR9 5QS
Tel.: 01989 562891
Website: www.millrace.info

3 mi south of Ross-on-Wye on B 4234. Parking.

PRICES
Meals: a la carte £ 23/35

MAP: 5

CLOSING TIMES
Open daily

BUTCHERS ARMS

Traditional cooking, with décor to match

The flags must surely have been flying at half-mast in this part of the world when Stephen Bull finally hung up his apron. He remains the owner of this cosy, timbered pub, but it now falls to Phil Vincent to feed the hungry hordes of Herefordshire. He's an experienced chef, and his cooking is unfussy and traditional, relying on quality local produce to deliver bold flavours. Expect game in season and plenty of offal; there's tasty home-baked bread and hearty, reasonably priced dishes like roast duck with orange sauce or wild rabbit, leek and cider pie. Like the cooking, the décor is traditional, with a welcoming log fire, wattle walls and beams slung so low you're forced to duck. Phil's daughters Leonie and Jemma run the show with aplomb.

WOOLHOPE, HR1 4RF
Tel.: 01432 860281
Website: www.butchersarmswoolhope.com

Midway between Hereford and Ledbury signposted off A 438. Parking.

PRICES
Meals: £ 9 (weekday lunch) and a la carte
£ 25/37

MAP: 6

CLOSING TIMES
Closed Sunday dinner in winter and
Monday except bank holidays

INN AT GRINSHILL

Cooking revolves around the seasons

Family-owned and very personally run, this inn stands in the middle of a pretty Shropshire village. Being a true country inn, the food offering revolves around the seasons, so expect catch of the day, shoot of the day or pie of the day, as well as a wide choice of dishes ranging from a simple sandwich or sharing board to pub classics like fish and chips – and more elaborate choices like rabbit loin with sage and juniper sauce or brill with wild mushrooms and fish cream. A cosy bar plays host to walkers and locals and there's a contemporary restaurant too, with purple chairs, clean white lines and a view to the kitchen. Six pretty bedrooms are individually decorated and comfortable. Can't find the television? Have a look behind the mirror.

The High St,
GRINSHILL, SY4 3BL
Tel.: 01939 220410
Website: www.theinnatgrinshill.co.uk

Between Shrewsbury and Whitchurch just off the A 49. Parking.

PRICES
Meals: a la carte £ 20/36

 6 rooms:
£ 70/120

MAP: 7

CLOSING TIMES
Closed first week January, Sunday dinner,
Monday and Tuesday

THE POUND INN

Run by an experienced couple

This large thatched pub sits on the busy A49 and is run by Sarah – who grew up in the village – and her husband Neil. There's been a hostelry on this site since 1457 and its name refers to the pens which once housed the animals of drovers staying overnight. It might have been modernised inside but there's still plenty of character to be found, courtesy of flagged floors, a large inglenook fireplace and a wooden bar. There are two different menus: the first offers a small selection of classics such as rib-eye steak or chicken Kiev; the second is slightly larger and lists more ambitious options like crab and cod ravioli, spring lamb with fondant potato or salted caramel parfait. They work closely with local suppliers, who are credited on the menu.

LEEBOTWOOD, SY6 6ND
Tel.: 01694 751477
Website: www.thepound.org.uk

3.75 mi north of Church Stretton on A 49. Parking.

PRICES
Meals: a la carte £ 23/30

MAP: 8

CLOSING TIMES
Closed first 2 weeks November, Sunday
dinner and Monday

CHARLTON ARMS

In a commanding position on the banks of the Teme

Claude Bosi is arguably the man who put Ludlow on the map, food-wise, with the original Hibiscus; the Charlton Arms is owned by his brother Cedric and his wife, Amy, who've given it a freshen up, bringing a modern touch to this traditional inn. It is situated in a commanding position next to the picturesque Ludford Bridge, on the banks of the River Teme, and remains all things to all people, with drinkers watching the sport in the snug and diners populating the airy lounge bar and the more comfortable restaurant with its superb river view. Menus also promise something for everyone and dishes are good value and full of flavour. Up-to-date bedrooms are named after famous plays and feature art from the Ludlow Festival; most have water outlooks.

Ludford Bridge,
LUDLOW, SY8 1PJ
Tel.: 01584 872813
Website: www.thecharltonarms.co.uk

On the south side of the town where B 4361 crosses the River Teme. Parking.

PRICES
Meals: a la carte £ 17/35

 9 rooms:
£ 90/160

MAP: 9

CLOSING TIMES
Closed 25-26 December

SUN INN

A real family affair

A traditional country pub on the English-Welsh border, the Sun Inn is a family affair, with experienced chef Peter in the kitchen and his wife Jean and daughter-in-law Sally delivering good old-fashioned hospitality to their customers – even the grandchildren help out on occasion. It's not a plush place but it's cosy enough, with a comfy bar on one side and a brightly painted dining room on the other. The concise, regularly changing menu offers comforting home-cooked dishes, so expect rich, creamy homemade soups followed by steak and ale pie or delicious homemade faggots with mash and peas – all finished off with a satisfying sticky toffee pudding. Keep an eye out for the glass board, where'll you find a list of tasty fish specials.

MARTON, SY21 8JP
Tel.: 01938 561211
Website: www.suninn.org.uk

5.5 mi northeast of Montgomery on B 4386. Parking.

PRICES
Meals: a la carte £ 24/38

MAP: 10

CLOSING TIMES
Closed Sunday dinner, Monday and lunch
Tuesday

THE HAUGHMOND

Stylish dining pub with a 'stag' theme

This stylish dining pub has a 'stag' theme, which can be seen everywhere from its logo and decorative features to the smart modern bedrooms and specially brewed Antler Ale. At lunchtime you'll find a good value selection of pub classics such as ham, egg and chips or steak and oxtail pie, while dinner moves things on a bit with the likes of haggis scotch egg with spiced raspberry purée or pistachio-crusted loin of lamb with goat's cheese and rosemary potato cakes. At the weekend they also open Basil's – an 18-seater restaurant which offers a sophisticated 5 course set menu – and as if that's not enough they also run a 'Village Shop', just across the way, which sells many ingredients from the menu, along with a ready-to-cook 'roast in a box'.

UPTON MAGNA, SY4 4TZ
Tel.: 01743 709918
Website: www.thehaughmond.co.uk

6 mi east of Shrewsbury by A 5064 and B 4380. Parking.

PRICES
Meals: a la carte £ 24/46

 5 rooms:
£ 72/120

MAP: 11

CLOSING TIMES
Closed 25 December and 1 January

THE GEORGE

In the same family for three generations

The moment you walk in the George, feel the warmth from the roaring fires and start to soak up the cosy, relaxed atmosphere, you just know that it's going to be good. A traditional pub set on the village green, it's simply furnished, with stone floors, scrubbed wooden tables and pictures of locals on the walls. The bubbly manager – the third generation of her family to have owned the pub – brings a woman's touch to the place, with the latest fashion mags for flicking through and candles and fresh flowers on every table. Like the décor, the food is simple but well done. The menus change daily according to the produce available; the team use local suppliers where possible and also grow some of their own vegetables in the garden.

ALSTONEFIELD, DE6 2FX
Tel.: 01335 310205
Website: www.thegeorgeatalstonefield.com

7.5 mi north of Ashbourne by A 515. Parking.

PRICES   MAP: **12**
Meals: a la carte £ 23/44

CLOSING TIMES
Closed 25 December

DUNCOMBE ARMS

A modernised country dining pub

Local residents must have been happy when this previously derelict pub reopened, as not only did they gain a stylish dining pub as their local, they also got the Hon. Johnny Greenall of the famous brewing family as its owner; add to this the fact that his wife is a descendant of the Duncombe family after which the pub is named and it's a sure-fire recipe for success. There are several cosy rooms to choose from, each with their own identity: 'Johnny's Bar' has a horse racing theme, 'The Augustus' is cosy and characterful and 'The Parlour and Oak Room' is airy and modern; there's also a lovely terrace with a wonderful view for sunnier days. Menus mix pub classics with more ambitious restaurant-style dishes and some have a playful element.

Main Road,
ELLASTONE, DE6 2GZ
Tel.: 01335 324275
Website: www.duncombearms.co.uk

Between Ashbourne and Uttoxeter on B 5032. Parking.

PRICES   MAP: **13**
Meals: a la carte £ 24/47

CLOSING TIMES
Open daily

THE TROOPER

Rare breed steaks and wood-fired pizzas

With the A5 starting life as the Roman military road to north Wales, and the hamlet of Wall host to what was once an important forces' staging post, it seems fitting that this pub should be named The Trooper. You can certainly feast like a Roman general at this self-styled 'Staffordshire steakhouse': choose from a wonderful selection of mature steaks, from local rump to fantastically marbled Kobe beef; rare breed steaks go up to 20oz for the truly ravenous and a fine array of sides includes the somewhat unusual parsley root fries. Not in a meaty mood? A wood-fired pizza oven, which takes three hours to reach the correct temperature, cooks tasty pizzas made to order from fresh dough. Grab a seat on the terrace when the weather allows.

Watling St,
WALL, WS14 0AN
Tel.: 01543 480413
Website: www.thetrooperwall.co.uk

Just south of Lichfield off A 5127, adjacent to the A 5. Parking.

PRICES

Meals: £ 12 (weekday lunch) and a la carte
£ 17/41

MAP: **14**

CLOSING TIMES

Open daily

FUZZY DUCK

Fashionably attired, with boutique bedrooms

The shower gel, shampoo and soap in the stylish boutique bedrooms of this delightful red brick country pub give a clue as to its owners: siblings Adrian and Tania also own Baylis & Harding, the toiletries company. Having made a success of the brand, and ready for a new challenge, they decided to take on their village local, transforming it from a boarded up boozer to a modern, fashionably attired dining pub. Seasonal British dishes might include roast duck with lentils and sprouting broccoli or braised ox cheek with French beans and celeriac mash; there's a 'pub classics' section with choices like the Aubrey Allen burger, and desserts like rice pudding are pleasingly old school, with the 'chocolate whatchamacallit' a must for chocoholics.

Ilmington Rd,
ARMSCOTE, CV37 8DD
Tel.: 01608 682635
Website: www.fuzzyduckarmscote.com

8.5 mi northeast of Moreton-in-Marsh off A 429 in village centre.
Parking

PRICES
Meals: £ 24 (weekday lunch) and a la carte
£ 21/44

 4 rooms:
£ 110/160

MAP: 15

CLOSING TIMES
Closed 26 December, Sunday dinner and Monday
booking advisable

KING'S HEAD

Hosted Shakespeare's parents' wedding breakfast!

Set close to the Cotswolds, in the picturesque village of Aston Cantlow, is the 13C Norman church where Shakespeare's parents were married... and they are thought to have had their wedding breakfast at this attractive inn. The timbered bar with its snug corners is hugely characterful and behind that, is a chic, country-style restaurant in pastel shades. The menu is guaranteed to please all, with its mix of generously sized classics, such as Lashford sausages and mash, and more modern dishes like beetroot terrine with creamed goat's cheese. Keep an eye out for the 'duck mix' of breast, leg, seared foie gras and orange chutney – a nod to the fact that during wartime rationing the landlord was unusually permitted to serve duck (he reared his own).

21 Bearley Rd,
ASTON CANTLOW, B95 6HY
Tel.: 01789 488242
Website: www.thekh.co.uk

6 mi northwest of Stratford-upon-Avon, signposted off A 46. Parking.

PRICES   MAP: **16**
Meals: a la carte £ 20/45

CLOSING TIMES
Open daily

CHEQUERS INN

Quirky pub with chandeliers and gilt mirrors

The signs outside scream country gastropub but to assume so would be off the mark; with its chandeliers, brushed velvet furniture and round-backed Regency chairs, this place is anything but formulaic. The open-fired bar is a popular spot with villagers, no doubt pleased with the large selection of beers as well as their local's transformation from run down boozer to smart, contemporary inn by experienced couple, James and Kirstin. When it comes to the cooking, menus display a broad international style so you'll find pub favourites and British classics alongside dishes of a more Mediterranean persuasion, like lobster risotto or sea bass with clam and mushroom tagliatelle. Tuesday is fish night, with fish and chips to eat in or take away.

91 Banbury Rd,
ETTINGTON, CV37 7SR
Tel.: 01789 740387
Website: www.the-chequers-ettington.co.uk

Southeast of Stratford-upon-Avon where the A 422 crosses the A 429. Parking.

PRICES   MAP: **17**
Meals: a la carte £ 22/38

CLOSING TIMES
Closed Sunday dinner and Monday

BLUEBELL

Daring to be different with plush furnishings

This part-timbered building on the high street is not your usual kind of pub. True, it comes with exposed beams, open fires and mix and match chairs – but some of those chairs have French-style gilding and one of the rooms has grey padded walls and sumptuous curtains fringed with peacock feathers. This mix of rustic character and formal elegance seems to be a hit with the customers, as does the wide-ranging selection of wines, beers and cocktails and the tasty British dishes. The chef uses the best local suppliers and cooking is honest and seasonal. The menu offers a mix of classics – like caesar salad or moules frites – and some more refined dishes such as duck with date purée and pickled shiitake or cod with Welsh rarebit and pea sauce.

93 High St,
HENLEY-IN-ARDEN, B95 5AT
Tel.: 01564 793049
Website: www.bluebellhenley.co.uk

8 mi northwest of Stratford-upon-Avon on A 3400. Parking.

PRICES   **MAP: 18**
Meals: a la carte £ 23/39

CLOSING TIMES
Closed Monday

CROSS AT KENILWORTH

Dishes not only look impressive but taste good too

When you first catch sight of this pub's smart exterior, you'll just know that they take things seriously here. When an eager member of staff greets you, settles you in and explains the menu, this first impression is confirmed. Further proof comes on your plate: skilfully executed, classical cooking uses prime seasonal ingredients, and dishes not only look impressive but taste good too. If you're seated in the back room, which opens onto the terrace, you get to watch the kitchen in action. The bright and airy room next door used to be a classroom – a fact alluded to by the eye-catching wall lamps shaped like hand bells. The front bar, with its adjoining snug and wood burning stove, makes a cosy place for a beer and a homemade sausage roll.

16 New St,
KENILWORTH, CV8 2EZ
Tel.: 01926 853840
Website: www.thecrosskenilworth.co.uk

On northwestern side of town on A 429, Coventry Rd. Parking.

PRICES   MAP: **19**
Meals: £ 30 (lunch) and a la carte £ 42/55

CLOSING TIMES
Closed Sunday dinner and bank holidays

BOOT INN

From picnic boards to sophisticated specials

Whether you're hastening down the M40 or pottering along on a narrow boat, it's worth stopping off at this large, buzzy pub. Set close to the junction of the Grand Union and Stratford-upon-Avon canals, it draws in a mixed crowd – from the young to the old; businesspeople to pleasure seekers – and you may well wonder where they all come from. With its traditional quarry-floored bar, modern restaurant and large terrace complete with a barbecue, it's deservedly popular, so booking is a must. Dishes vary greatly, from picnic boards and sharing plates to more sophisticated specials; the crispy oriental duck salad and the bubble and squeak are mainstays, and influences could come from Britain, Asia or the Med. In summer, eat outside in a tepee!

Old Warwick Rd,
LAPWORTH, B94 6JU
Tel.: 01564 782464
Website: www.bootinnlapworth.co.uk

2 mi southeast of Hockley Heath on B 4439. Parking.

PRICES
Meals: £ 15 (lunch and early dinner)
and a la carte £ 24/40

MAP: 20

CLOSING TIMES
Open daily
booking essential

RED LION

Tasty home-cooking and country-chic bedrooms

With its flag floors and log fires, this 18C former coaching inn has the character of a country pub, and its stylish interior boasts a warm, modern feel. The seasonal menu offers classic pub dishes like homemade steak and Hook Norton pie, pan-fried calves' liver or fish and chips, with old favourites like rhubarb crumble or warm chocolate fudge cake for dessert. These are tasty, home-cooked dishes from the tried-and-tested school of cooking – so if you're after something a little more adventurous, try the daily specials board instead. Staff are pleasant and smartly attired; Cocoa, the chocolate Labrador, also gives a warm welcome. Bedrooms may be slightly on the small side but they are stylish and contemporary, with a good level of facilities.

Main St,
LONG COMPTON, CV36 5JS
Tel.: 01608 684221
Website: www.redlion-longcompton.co.uk

Between Chipping Norton and Shipston-on-Stour on A 3400. Parking.

PRICES
Meals: £ 14 (lunch and early dinner)
and a la carte £ 27/36

 5 rooms:
£ 60/150

MAP: 21

CLOSING TIMES
Open daily

THE QUEENS

Reassuringly traditional, from looks to food

Having started life in the 16C, The Queens has been around nearly as long as the millstones in the wall which keep the neighbouring brook at bay. The pub might have been refurbished but its traditional look and feel remains – a conscious effort by the owners to respect the locals' preferences. There's a cosy bar-lounge with some nice leather benches for the drinkers and three small, traditional rooms neatly laid for dining. In true pub style you can get a hearty steak and ale pie or minted lamb sausages and mash but you'll also find the likes of pan-seared sea bass with glazed carrots and broccoli or tasting of Wiltshire pork with Bramley apple and caviar cream sauce. Come in September to check out the village's annual scarecrow festival.

Queens Hill,
BELBROUGHTON, DY9 ODU
Tel.: 01562 730276
Website: www.thequeensbelbroughton.co.uk

Between Stourbridge and Bromsgrove off A 491. Parking.

PRICES
Meals: £ 13 (weekdays) and a la carte
£ 23/39

MAP: 22

CLOSING TIMES
Closed 25 December and Sunday dinner

BUTCHERS ARMS

Refined British dishes and charming service

The Butchers Arms is a sweet, rural inn where wooden beams are fringed with hop bines and villagers meet for a pint at the end of the day. It's run by a young couple – he cooks, while she takes care of front of house – and both the pub and the food have an admirable lack of pretension. There may be only one chef in the kitchen but boy, what a chef! His mother is French and his culinary education began at an early age, with trips to the markets in the Loire. As such, he has a great appreciation for natural ingredients and knows how to use them to create simple yet wonderfully well-flavoured dishes, such as aged rib of Longhorn beef with crispy potato and butternut squash purée or Middle White pork faggots with black pudding and crispy polenta.

Lime Street,
ELDERSFIELD, GL19 4NX
Tel.: 01452 840381
Website: www.thebutchersarms.net

8.5 mi north of Gloucester by A 417 and signposted off B 4211. Parking.

PRICES
Meals: a la carte £ 39/53

MAP: 23

CLOSING TIMES
Closed 1 week early January, 1 week late August, Sunday dinner, Monday and bank holidays dinner only
and lunch Friday-Sunday booking essential

THE INN AT WELLAND

Designer touches and a lovely garden

With its minimalist modern sign, landscaped garden and decked terrace, it is clear that this country dining pub is a little bit different to the norm. Once inside, the designer touches continue – the designer in question being owner Gillian Pinchbeck, who together with her hands-on husband, David, turned this place from wreck to "by 'eck!" Inside, it's light, open and stylish with plenty of charming features like flagged floors, beams and a wood burning stove. You'd be forgiven for thinking that dishes might be elaborate and overambitious, but no – there are pub classics alongside dishes like spit-roasted poussin with sweet potato or pan-seared Cornish scallops with carrot and cumin mash; all tasty, generous of portion and sensibly priced.

Hook Bank,
WELLAND, WR13 6LN
Tel.: 01684 592317
Website: www.theinnatwelland.co.uk

Between Wynds Pont and Upton-upon-Severn on the A 4104. Parking.

PRICES   MAP: **24**
Meals: a la carte £ 25/43

CLOSING TIMES
Closed 25-26 December, Sunday dinner
and Monday

OLD RECTIFYING HOUSE

Great location, great atmosphere & great cooking!

With its shabby-chic décor, its young chefs hard at work in the open kitchen, and its soundtrack of jazz, blues and soul, this place is bringing a hipster vibe to Worcester, and so it comes as no surprise to see cocktail glasses hanging ready for action above the bar. Dating back to 1788, the striking mock-Tudor building stands in a great location overlooking Worcester Bridge and the River Severn and was originally where gin distilled across the river was brought for rectification, hence the name. There's a British slant to most of the dishes on the appealing menu, with the occasional international influence too, so expect potted gammon, dough balls, locally sourced steaks and battered haddock; all brought to you by friendly, easy-going staff.

North Par.,
WORCESTER, WR1 3NN
Tel.: 01905 619622
Website: www.theoldrec.co.uk

In city centre on north side of the River Severn overlooking Worcester Bridge. Pay and display car park adjacent.

PRICES
Meals: a la carte £ 24/43

MAP: 25

CLOSING TIMES
Closed Monday except bank holidays and
25 December

YORKSHIRE & THE HUMBER

—— England

© J. Arnold Images / hemis.fr

England's biggest county has a lot of room for the spectacular; it encapsulates the idea of desolate beauty. The bracing winds of the Dales whistle through glorious meadows and deep, winding valleys, while the vast moors are fringed with picturesque country towns like Thirsk, Helmsley and Pickering. Further south the charming Wolds roll towards the sea, enhanced by such Georgian gems as Beverley and Howden. Popular history sits easily here: York continues to enchant with its ancient walls and Gothic Minster, but, owing to its Brontë links, visitors descend on the cobbled street village of Haworth with as much enthusiasm. Steam railways criss-cross the region's bluff contours, while drivers get a more streamlined thrill on the Humber Bridge.

Yorkshire's food and drink emporiums range from quaintly traditional landmarks like the country tearoom and fish and chip shops proudly proclaiming to be the best in England, to warm and characterful pubs serving heart-warming local specialities.

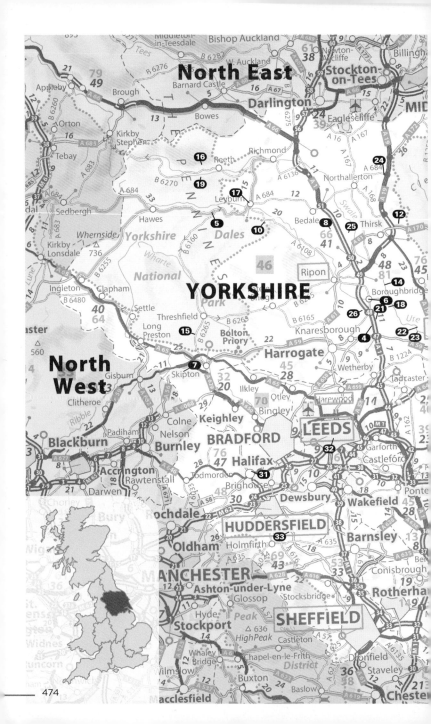

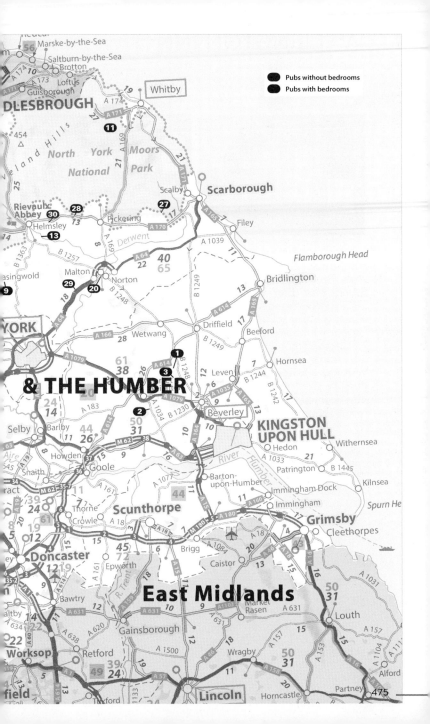

Pubs without bedrooms
Pubs with bedrooms

Marske-by-the-Sea
Saltburn-by-the-Sea
Brotton
Loftus
Guisborough
DLESBROUGH
Whitby

North York Moors
National Park

Scalby
Scarborough
Filey

Rievaulx Abbey
Helmsley
Pickering
Flamborough Head

asingwold
Malton
Norton
Bridlington

YORK
Wetwang
Driffield
Beeford
Hornsea

& THE HUMBER
Leven

Beverley
KINGSTON UPON HULL
Withernsea
Hedon
Patrington
Kilnsea
Spurn He

Selby
Barlby
Howden
Goole
Barton-upon-Humber
Immingham Dock
Immingham
Grimsby
Cleethorpes

Shaith
ract
Thorne
Crowle
Scunthorpe

Doncaster
Epworth
Brigg
Caistor

Bawtry
East Midlands
Market Rasen
Louth

altby
Gainsborough
Wragby
Worksop
Retford
Alford

field
Twxford
Lincoln
Horncastle
Partney

475

WELLINGTON INN

Well-run pub serving generous, flavoursome dishes

They may have called their company 'Warm Beer and Lousy Food' but that couldn't be further from the truth at the 'Welly', where they offer a good array of well-kept Yorkshire ales and an extensive range of dishes that capture the imagination. At lunch the blackboard 'Baaa...r Menu' lists appealing dishes such as warm crab and samphire tart or calves' liver and bacon, while in the evening there's a large à la carte offering the likes of loin of venison with parsnip boulangère or pork belly with scallops and hot and sour sauce. Dishes are generous, flavoursome and feature good quality ingredients. Eat next to an open fire in one of the beamed bars or in one of the numerous dining rooms, where you'll be served by a smart, efficient team.

19 The Green,
LUND, YO25 9TE
Tel.: 01377 217294
Website: www.thewellingtoninn.co.uk

10 mi northwest of Beverley just off B 1248. Parking.

PRICES   MAP: **1**
Meals: a la carte £ 30/39

CLOSING TIMES
Closed 25 December, 1 January, Sunday
dinner and Monday

STAR

The blackboard proudly lists local suppliers

Owners Ben and Lindsay bought this once down-at-heel pub in the small village of Sancton over ten years ago and have since set about establishing it and expanding it into the place you see today. There's a cosy, slightly rustic bar – its counter topped with homemade nibbles – where the locals like to come for a pint and maybe sausage and mash or a steak and ale pie. There are also two rooms with upholstered banquettes, smart wood-topped tables and plush carpets, which make up the restaurant; here you'll find a good value 'Yorkshire Lunch' menu and an à la carte offering hearty, boldly flavoured dishes which display a little more imagination. Regional suppliers are proudly listed on a blackboard; staff are young, local and full of smiles.

King St,
SANCTON, YO43 4QP
Tel.: 01430 827269
Website: www.thestaratsancton.co.uk

2 miles south of Market Weighton in centre of village on A 1034.
Parking.

PRICES   MAP: **2**
Meals: £ 17 (weekday lunch) and a la carte
£ 26/42

CLOSING TIMES
Closed Monday

PIPE AND GLASS INN

Superb cooking uses top quality regional produce

Very personally run by its experienced owners – he cooks, while she looks after front of house – the Pipe and Glass Inn is a deservedly popular place. Grab a drink and a seat beside the log burner or head straight for a table in the contemporary dining room to enjoy food that's carefully executed, big on flavour and generously proportioned. Dishes are made with local, seasonal and traceable produce, and might include venison and juniper suet pudding or roast loin of red deer; desserts like the Pipe and Glass chocolate plate (subtitled 'Five reasons to love chocolate') continue the decadent theme. Luxurious bedrooms are equipped with the latest mod cons and have their own patios overlooking the estate woodland; breakfast is served in your room.

West End,
SOUTH DALTON, HU17 7PN
Tel.: 01430 810246
Website: www.pipeandglass.co.uk

5 mi northwest of Beverley by A 164, B 1248 and side road west. Parking.

PRICES
Meals: a la carte £ 24/57

 5 rooms:
£ 155/225

MAP: 3

CLOSING TIMES
Closed 2 weeks January, Sunday dinner and Monday except bank holidays

BLUE BELL

In summer, sit on the smart front terrace

The Blue Bell might be a modern dining pub but it still has plenty of traditional character courtesy of hops hanging over the bar, sofas set in front of a wood burning stove and locals hanging out with their dogs. Venture round the bar and you'll find plenty of space for dining, with a mix of wood and fabric chairs set below wooden beams. When it comes to the food, everything is homemade, with starters like ham hock and black pudding scotch egg and main courses such as beef and root vegetable pie or monkfish and prawn curry. Sunday is quiz night and they also host regular evenings themed around different world cuisines. Upstairs, are four smart bedrooms with super king sized beds; one has a double-ended bath and his 'n' hers sinks.

Moor Ln,
ARKENDALE, HG5 0QT
Tel.: 01423 369242
Website: www.thebluebellatarkendale.co.uk

Midway beteween Knaresborough and Boroughbridge off A 6065.
Parking.

PRICES
Meals: a la carte £ 21/36

4 rooms:
£ 85/150

MAP: 4

CLOSING TIMES
Closed 9 January

AYSGARTH FALLS

Homely atmosphere and charming service

Just up the road from the triple flight of waterfalls at Aysgarth, you'll find this foliage-covered roadside inn. Keeping with the 'trio' theme, you'll find three different terraces and also three different rooms: local drinkers gather in the flag-floored bar and those after a meal can choose between two homely dining rooms. Menus evolve constantly and offer a mix of pub classics, homemade pizzas and more ambitious dishes like roast duck with confit leg or venison with black pudding; the specials are often based around fish, which arrives 6 days a week from the east coast. Contemporary bedrooms have views of the surrounding Dales and for those who want to get back to nature, they also own the neighbouring adults-only campsite.

AYSGARTH, DL8 3SR
Tel.: 01969 663775
Website: www.aysgarthfallshotel.com

Midway between Leyburn and Hawes on A 684. Parking.

PRICES
Meals: a la carte £ 20/37

13 rooms:
£ 85/170

MAP: 5

CLOSING TIMES
Open daily

GRANTHAM ARMS

Hearty dishes and comforting puddings

The Grantham Arms is a proper roadside inn, where the locals gather at high-level tables in the bar or come to watch the latest sporting events. If gin's your thing then this is the place for you – there are over 30 varieties available, along with a 'Gin of the Week'; while for wine lovers, the 'Wine & Nibbles' deal (Mon-Sat 5-7pm) offers a bottle of the house wine accompanied by olives and crisps. If you're after a proper meal there's the choice of two rooms – both with heavy wood tables and old black and white pictures of Boroughbridge back in the day – and the all-encompassing menu ranges from pie and mash to pan-roasted duck with Lyonnaise potatoes. Smart bedrooms come with contemporary oak furnishings and Egyptian cotton linen.

Milby,
BOROUGHBRIDGE, YO51 9BW
Tel.: 01423 323980
Website: www.granthamarms.co.uk

North of town centre by B 6265. Parking.

PRICES
Meals: £ 16 (lunch and early dinner)
and a la carte £ 21/30

7 rooms:
£ 60/150

MAP: 6

CLOSING TIMES
Open daily

BULL

Try the local meats and cheeses

The Bull is a member of the Ribble Valley Inns group – but don't expect some sort of faceless corporate brand – this is the pub company set up by Nigel Haworth and Craig Bancroft, co-proprietors of Lancashire's celebrated Northcote. They have led the way in promoting the specialities of their region and the Bull is no different. Expect real ales and local meats and cheeses, as well as traditional British dishes, rediscovered classics and the sort of puddings that make you feel patriotic. The Bull is an appropriate moniker as this pub is big and solid looking. It's at the side of Broughton Hall and is made up of assorted snugs and spaces, with beams, stone floors and log fires. It's cosy in winter and charming on a summer's day.

BROUGHTON, BD23 3AE
Tel.: 01756 792065
Website: www.thebullatbroughton.com

3 mi west of Skipton on A 59. Parking.

PRICES
Meals: £ 14 (weekdays) and a la carte
£ 22/46

MAP: **7**

CLOSING TIMES
Open daily

FOX AND HOUNDS

Family-run for over 30 years

It may be just a few minutes from the A1 but this traditional stone pub is a true country local. It's owned by hands-on couple Vincent and Helen and has been in the family since 1983. It's a fairly small place: to one side is a stone-walled bar with an open fire and an array of memorabilia on display; to the other side is a bright, neatly laid dining room with an old blacksmith's forge as its focus point. Good-sized menus offer unfussy home-cooked dishes; choose something from the daily changing blackboards, maybe ham hock terrine with piccalilli, followed by a satisfying steak and kidney short crust pie. Fruit and vegetables are from Snape, meats are from Bedale and fish is from Hartlepool. Local organic and homemade products are for sale.

CARTHORPE, DL8 2LG
Tel.: 01845 567433
Website: www.foxandhoundscarthorpe.co.uk

9 mi north of Ripon by minor road via Wath and Kirklington. Parking.

PRICES   **MAP: 8**
Meals: £ 16 (weekdays) and a la carte
£ 23/44

CLOSING TIMES
Closed first 2 weeks January, 25 December
and Monday

DURHAM OX

At 300 years old it has bags of character

Located in a sleepy little hamlet next to Crayke Castle is the 300 year old Durham Ox, a bustling pub which boasts pleasant views up to a medieval church and over the Vale of York. You'll receive a warm welcome whether you sit in the ornately panelled bar with its vast inglenook fireplace or in the more formal beamed dining room – but when the weather's right, head straight for the rear courtyard, as that's definitely the place to be. The regularly changing menu features plenty of fresh seafood and Crayke game and their grass-fed 40 day dry-aged steaks are a speciality. The cosy bedrooms are set in converted farm cottages and display original brickwork and quarry tiling; the suite is set over two floors and comes with a jacuzzi bath.

Westway,
CRAYKE, YO61 4TE
Tel.: 01347 821506
Website: www.thedurhamox.com

2 mi east of Easingwold on Helmsley rd. Parking.

PRICES
Meals: £ 18 (weekday lunch) and a la carte
£ 21/46

 6 rooms:
£ 70/120

MAP: 9

CLOSING TIMES
Open daily
booking advisable

BLUE LION

Game takes centre stage in season

Set in a delightful village, this former coaching inn boasts a rustic interior, pleasingly untouched by the minimalist makeover brigade. Dine in the charming flag-floored bar or in the high-ceilinged, wood-floored dining room; either way you'll sit at a polished wooden table in the glow of candlelight and enjoy unfussy, hearty, full-flavoured cooking of local produce. Dishes might include homemade pork pie, slow-cooked pigs' cheeks or roast wild venison, with game taking centre stage in season. The wine list is of particular note and offers a range of prices and plenty of variety by the bottle, carafe and glass. Bedrooms in the main house are furnished with antiques, while the rooms in the converted stable are more contemporary in style.

EAST WITTON, DL8 4SN
Tel.: 01969 624273
Website: www.thebluelion.co.uk

3 mi southeast of Leyburn on A 6108. Parking.

PRICES
Meals: £ 16 (weekday lunch) and a la carte
£ 26/45

 15 rooms:
£ 79/145

MAP: 10

CLOSING TIMES
Open daily
booking essential

WHEATSHEAF INN

Country feel with no-nonsense cooking

This late 17C inn is located at the centre of a delightful stone-built hamlet on the edge of the picturesque North Yorkshire Moors. There's a small garden and several rooms filled with framed prints and lithographs of hunting scenes, along with a delightful snug that boasts a lovely range – which acts as an open fire – and chunky tables crafted by one of the locals from thick slices of oak cut at the Castle Howard Estate. Menus offer a real taste of Yorkshire, utilising fresh produce from just outside the door, so you'll find the likes of lambs' kidneys, local steak, Whitby scampi and game shot within two miles, all accompanied by triple-cooked chips. It really is a family affair here, with mum cooking and her husband and daughter out front.

EGTON, YO21 1TZ
Tel.: 01947 895271
Website: www.wheatsheafegton.com

6.5 mi southwest of Whitby by A 171. Parking.

PRICES   MAP: **11**
Meals: a la carte £ 24/36

CLOSING TIMES
Closed 25 December and Monday

CARPENTER'S ARMS

Stylish bedrooms overlook the Vale of Mowbray

Mentioned in the Domesday Book, Felixkirk's claim to fame is that it was once a local Commandery of the Knights Hospitallers of St John of Jerusalem. Dating back to the 18C, the Carpenter's Arms may not be quite as old, but it really is a good old village pub, so you'll often find local groups such as the bell ringers in. When it comes to dining, there's a choice of blackboard specials or dishes from the seasonal main menu, which offers everything from gammon or venison casserole to sea bass with ratatouille. Be sure to save room for pudding before the steep climb back up Sutton Bank; if you don't fancy the ascent, spend the night under a duck down duvet in a well-equipped, stylishly appointed bedroom, overlooking the Vale of Mowbray.

FELIXKIRK, YO7 2DP
Tel.: 01845 537369
Website: www.thecarpentersarmsfelixkirk.com

Signposted off A 170, 3 mi northeast of Thirsk. Parking.

PRICES
Meals: a la carte £ 26/53

 10 rooms:
£ 95/185

MAP: 12

CLOSING TIMES
Open daily

STAR INN

To fully appreciate the character of this thatched 14C pub, head for the main low-ceilinged bar with its open fire and photo-filled walls, then grab the kidney-shaped Mousey Thompson table for the best seat in the house; alternatively, try the rustic middle room or the brighter, more modern, brasserie-like restaurant with its chef's table. Carefully executed, boldly favoured dishes have a skilled, classical style with subtle touches of originality; they use the very best of local produce including fruit and veg from the kitchen garden and meats from their own pigs and chickens. Coffee is taken in the loft, with complimentary cheese and nuts. Stylish bedrooms come with unique features: one has a snooker table and another, a suspended bed.

High St,
HAROME, YO62 5JE
Tel.: 01439 770397
Website: www.thestaratharome.co.uk

2.75 mi southeast of Helmsley by A 170. Parking.

PRICES
Meals: £ 25 (weekdays) and a la carte
£ 33/56

 9 rooms:
£ 150/260

MAP: 13

CLOSING TIMES
Closed Monday lunch except bank holidays
booking essential

OAK TREE INN

Yorkshire meats from the Bertha oven

Don't let the Brafferton Helperby sign confuse you – this did, in fact, start life as two even smaller villages; the Oak Tree being in the latter of the two. Younger sister to the Durham Ox and the Carpenters Arms, this is a place of two halves: there's a large bar, a tap room and two snugs in the main building, while the old hay barn houses a smart dining room with large windows overlooking a terrace. The same menu is available throughout, with cooking based around the Bertha charcoal oven; ingredients come from small local suppliers, with steaks, chops, poultry and fish to the fore. Overnight guests can relax in a spa bath in one of the chic modern bedrooms, which are named after different trees and come complete with 'Yorkie' bars.

Raskelf Rd,
HELPERBY, YO61 2PH
Tel.: 01423 789189
Website: www.theoaktreehelperby.com

5 mi northeast of Boroughbridge on T-junction entering village.
Parking.

PRICES
Meals: a la carte £ 20/45

 6 rooms:
£ 75/150

MAP: 14

CLOSING TIMES
Open daily

ANGEL INN

Try some of their 'Yapas' (Yorkshire Tapas)

The Angel was opened in 1983 by the late Dennis Watkins – who has been credited as the creator of the rural gastropub – and his memory lives on in this 18C stone inn, now run by his wife and son. It's a place of two parts: the appealing open-fired bar rooms known as the 'Brasserie' and two adjoining linen-clad rooms named the 'Restaurant'. For a casual dinner, sit in the Brasserie and pick something from the daily specials board; for a special evening out, book the Restaurant and choose from more refined, imaginative dishes. The in-depth wine list has an impressive catalogue of French growths and they offer tutorials in the wine cave across the road. Classical bedrooms are found in the 'Barn Lodgings' and more modern rooms in 'Sycamore Bank'.

HETTON, BD23 6LT
Tel.: 01756 730263
Website: www.angelhetton.co.uk

5.75 mi north of Skipton by B 6265. Parking.

PRICES
Meals: a la carte £ 27/45

 9 rooms:
£ 135/200

MAP: 15

CLOSING TIMES
Closed 2 weeks January and 25 December
booking essential

490

CHARLES BATHURST INN

18C hostelry set high in the hills

This characterful 18C hostelry is named after a local land and lead mine owner, and former resident. Sitting on the edge of the Pennine Way, high in the hills of Arkengarthdale, it boasts commanding views over the surrounding countryside and is so remotely set, that the only sound you'll hear is the 'clink' of quoits being thrown in the garden. Inside you're greeted by open fires, various timbered snugs and a charming dining room hung with old monochrome photos and sepia lithographs. Pub favourites are on offer at lunch, while the dinner menu – unusually written on a mirror – offers more ambitious dishes such as scallops with chorizo or moules marinière, with plenty of fresh fish and game in season. Bedrooms are spacious and comfortable.

LANGTHWAITE, DL11 6EN
Tel.: 0333 700 0779
Website: www.cbinn.co.uk

3.25 mi northwest of Reeth on Langthwaite rd. Parking.

PRICES
Meals: a la carte £ 22/42

 19 rooms:
£ 81/130

MAP: 16

CLOSING TIMES
Closed 25 December

SANDPIPER INN

Takes pride in the provenance of its ingredients

A friendly Yorkshire welcome is extended to the Dale walkers who come to refuel at this stone-built, part-16C pub, situated just off the main square. Visitors can rest their blistered feet by the fire in the split-level beamed bar or plump for a seat in the more characterful dining room. A small enclosed terrace out the back provides a third alternative for when it's sunny but you'll have to come inside to read the blackboard menus, found hanging on the walls amidst the general clutter of decorative pictures, books and ornaments. Subtle, refined cooking offers a modern take on the classics, so expect dishes like ham hock terrine and piccalilli, pressed Dales lamb or slow-cooked Wensleydale beef. Two homely bedrooms are on the first floor.

Market Pl,
LEYBURN, DL8 5AT
Tel.: 01969 622206
Website: www.sandpiperinn.co.uk

In town centre. Limited parking available in the Market Place.

PRICES
Meals: a la carte £ 25/44

 2 rooms:
£ 80/100

MAP: 17

CLOSING TIMES
Closed 2 weeks January, Tuesday in winter and Monday

THE DUNSFORTH

Menus offer admirable choice and value for money

There can be no sight more reassuring than a pile of Michelin Guides when you're about to order a meal! If you've spotted them, then you'll be enjoying the lively atmosphere in one of the fire-lit front rooms of this contemporary pub. If it's a quieter, more intimate meal you're after, head instead to the smart restaurant with its hunting print wallpaper and stag's head. Menus offer admirable choice and value for money and, when it comes to the ingredients, seasonality and freshness are key, with meat from Boroughbridge, fish from Hartlepool and as much homemade as possible, from the freshly baked bread to the ice creams and petit fours. Dishes tend to have a modern twist but they do traditional bar snacks too, if that's what you fancy.

Mary Ln,
LOWER DUNSFORTH, YO26 9SA
Tel.: 01423 320700
Website: www.thedunsforth.co.uk

4.25 mi southeast of Boroughbridge by B 6265. Parking.

PRICES
Meals: £ 20/45 and a la carte £ 24/54

MAP: 18

CLOSING TIMES
Closed Sunday dinner and Monday-Tuesday

PUNCH BOWL INN

A traditional inn deep in the heart of Swaledale

Deep in the heart of Swaledale is this traditional 17C stone inn, which is a popular stop-off point for walkers looking to refuel on hearty, classic dishes. At lunchtime there's filled panini along with a good choice of dishes like smoked loin of bacon or steak and Blacksheep casserole, while at dinner, the 'mirror' menu offers some more refined, interesting choices. Satisfying puddings could include homemade fruitcake or chocolate brownie; on Tuesdays they alternate between 'pie' and 'steak' nights, which prove popular with the villagers; and staff always go about their business with a smile. Supremely comfortable bedrooms are decorated in a fresh, modern style and all have dramatic views over Swaledale; those in the annexe are the best.

LOW ROW, DL11 6PF
Tel.: 01748 886233
Website: www.pbinn.co.uk

4 mi west of Reeth on B 6270. Parking.

PRICES
Meals: a la carte £ 20/39

 11 rooms:
£ 81/125

MAP: 19

CLOSING TIMES
Closed 25 December

NEW MALTON

Simple, honest and unpretentious

This 18C stone building has been serving the market town of Malton for many years, first as a pub, then a tea room and later, as a tapas restaurant – and now it's back as a pub again. There are three different rooms, all with open fires, reclaimed furniture and black and white photos of old town scenes; a style which is clearly a hit with the locals. The good-sized menu offers hearty pub classics with the occasional adventurous dish thrown in, and cooking is unfussy and flavoursome with an appealing Northern bias; the toad in the hole is particularly popular. Beers change regularly and food is served all day, every day; you're meant to order at the bar but if you catch one of the friendly team walking by, they'll happily save you the trip.

2-4 Market Pl,
MALTON, YO17 7LX
Tel.: 01653 693998
Website: www.thenewmalton.co.uk

In centre of town, ample on-street parking.

PRICES
Meals: a la carte £ 18/32

MAP: 20

CLOSING TIMES
Closed 25-26 December and 1 January

PUNCH BOWL INN

Ask for table 504 in the snug

You won't find Marton cum Grafton on your map but that's because it's two villages which have slowly joined together over the years. What you will find is this delightful whitewashed inn, which part-dates from the 14C and is part of an eclectic North Yorkshire group run by experienced owners. It has a strange, almost crescent shape, with a small seating area in front, a lovely terrace behind and various little rooms with open fires and old beams; not forgetting a private room with wine glass chandeliers. The all-encompassing seasonal menu features local produce and includes a seafood platter and a Yorkshire Board, along with excellent fish and chips and rib-eye steak; from 5.30-7pm they offer the 'Magnificent Seven' – 7 dishes at £7 each.

MARTON CUM GRAFTON, YO51 9QY
Tel.: 01423 322519
Website: www.thepunchbowlmartoncumgrafton.com

3.5 mi southeast of Boroughbridge by B 6265.
In the centre of the village. Parking.

PRICES   MAP: **21**
Meals: a la carte £ 23/50

CLOSING TIMES
Open daily

DAWNAY ARMS

It's not unknown for diners to arrive by boat!

In the shadows of the impressive 18C Beningbrough Hall and Gardens, you'll find this handsome pub. Step inside and you'll discover low beams, open fires and all manner of bric-a-brac, from old kitchen implements and horseshoes to a mincing machine and buffalo horns – head for the rear and find a spot in the delightfully airy dining room, with its view over the garden and down to the river. The experienced chef, a native Yorkshireman, lets the seasons guide him and offers gutsy, well-executed British dishes such as crispy pig's head with homemade black pudding or slow-cooked daube of beef. Game plays a big part in season and is locally shot – sometimes even by the chef himself. If you're a cheese lover, be sure to try their regional selection.

NEWTON-ON-OUSE, YO30 2BR
Tel.: 01347 848345
Website: www.thedawnayatnewton.co.uk

8 mi northwest of York sign posted off A 19. Parking.

PRICES
Meals: £ 14 (weekday lunch) and à la carte
£ 18/49

MAP: 22

CLOSING TIMES
Closed Sunday dinner and Monday except bank holidays

ALICE HAWTHORN INN

Owned by a local businessman

The Alice Hawthorn started life in 1787 as The Bluebell and was later renamed after a successful 1800s racehorse, itself named after the daughter of the local blacksmith. It's smart and stylish and sits on a picturesque village green which comes complete with a duck pond, grazing cattle and the country's tallest maypole. At lunch, choose from pub classics and sharing boards; at dinner you'll find more luxurious ingredients making an appearance in refined modern dishes like salmon ballotine with basil gravadlax and citrus potato salad, or wild garlic tortellini with goat's curd and tomato consommé. Service is friendly and helps to add to the 'village pub' atmosphere, which draws diners from York on one side and Harrogate on the other.

The Green,
NUN MONKTON, YO26 8EW
Tel.: 01423 330303
Website: www.thealicehawthorn.com

Signposted off the A 59 between Knaresborough and York. Parking.

PRICES
Meals: £ 20 (lunch and early dinner)
and a la carte £ 28/39

MAP: **23**

CLOSING TIMES
Closed Sunday dinner, Monday and
Tuesday lunch

GOLDEN LION

Atmospheric bar with over 80 different whiskies

This 18C stone inn sits overlooking the market cross of a historic village in the North York Moors National Park. With its low beamed ceiling, dark wood bar, church pew seating and welcoming wood-burning stove, it's the kind of place that the locals know and love; make for the atmospheric bar, which offers over 80 different whiskies and 15 gins. The cooking is traditional and satisfying, featuring filling dishes such as steak and kidney pie with a suet crust or homemade chicken Kiev. The main selection stays largely the same but there's also a more ambitious weekly changing specials board to consider – and be sure to save room for one of the tasty puddings with homemade ice cream. Modern bedrooms have heavy oak furnishings and good facilities.

6 West End,
OSMOTHERLEY, DL6 3AA
Tel.: 01609 883526
Website: www.goldenlionosmotherley.co.uk

6 mi northeast of Northallerton by A 684. Parking in the village.

PRICES
Meals: a la carte £ 23/33

 7 rooms:
£ 75/100

MAP: 24

CLOSING TIMES
Closed 25 December, lunch Monday and
Tuesday except bank holidays

NAGS HEAD COUNTRY INN

Try something from their rum collection

This rustic pub has been run by the same family for over 40 years. It has a small front terrace and a quirky interior, where over 700 framed ties hang on the walls of the open-fired Tap Room. Stop here for a beer with the locals, before heading through to the dining room with its comfy booths and hunting prints on the walls. At lunchtime choose from bar snacks and light meals; at dinner look for the blackboard menu, which features plenty of classics accompanied by seasonal vegetables and a jug of gravy (the owner is an avid shooter, so game season is always a good time to visit). If Rum's your thing, there's a great collection, including some from South America and the Caribbean, and if you fancy staying the night, cosy bedrooms await.

PICKHILL, YO7 4JG
Tel.: 01845 567391
Website: www.nagsheadpickhill.co.uk

7.5 mi northwest of Thirsk by A 61 and B 6267. Parking.

PRICES
Meals: a la carte £ 16/35

7 rooms:
£ 60/120

MAP: 25

CLOSING TIMES
Closed 25 December

CROWN INN

Taste every dessert with the 'assiette'

The tables out the front of this 14C inn make the most of its delightful position by the village green; don't be surprised to see a couple having a drink out here in the dark – although very lifelike, they are merely mannequins! All manner of bric-a-brac carries on the whimsical theme: look out for the grandfather clock, the stuffed stag's head and the fishing rods hanging from the ceiling. Menus offer pub classics like steak and ale pie alongside more ambitious dishes like 'Little Yorkshire Pig', comprising crisp belly pork, fillet medallions and black pudding; if you can't decide on a dessert, try them all with the 'assiette' of puddings. Well-appointed bedrooms come with feature beds, free-standing roll-top baths and plenty of extra touches.

ROECLIFFE, YO51 9LY
Tel.: 01423 322300
Website: www.crowninnroecliffe.co.uk

1.5 mi west of Boroughbridge by minor road. Parking.

PRICES
Meals: a la carte £ 25/43

4 rooms:
£ 80/120

MAP: 26

CLOSING TIMES
Open daily

ANVIL INN

Intimate dining room in a former smithy

As its name suggests, this charming inn was formerly a smithy and its old bellows, tools, forge and anvil still remain; in marked contrast, yet blending in seamlessly, is a boldly coloured contemporary sitting room. Cooking is classical in essence, with the odd international influence, so expect crispy duck pancakes alongside Shetland mussels or slow-roasted daube of beef. Local chef, Mark, prides himself on the use of regionally sourced produce; eggs come from the pub's own hens and the Stillington pork is a firm favourite. There are only seven tables in the intimate restaurant, so be sure to book ahead, particularly for Sunday lunch, which has become something of an institution. They also have two self-catering apartments behind the pub.

Main St,
SAWDON, YO13 9DY
Tel.: 01723 859896
Website: www.theanvilinnsawdon.co.uk

10 mi southwest of Scarborough by A 170, turning right at Brompton onto Sawdon Ln. Parking.

PRICES   **MAP: 27**
Meals: a la carte £ 25/39

CLOSING TIMES
Closed 25-26 December, 1 January,
Monday and Tuesday
dinner only and lunch Saturday-Sunday

FOX AND HOUNDS

Hearty Yorkshire cooking and homely bedrooms

It's always a good sign if a pub has regulars: diners so au fait with what's on offer that they don't even need to look at the menu – and this pretty, traditional 18C inn has plenty. What keeps them coming back is the generously proportioned, hearty Yorkshire cooking: pub classics like beer-battered haddock or calves' liver; maybe some classic slow braises or some brisket; and plenty of game in season. Customers not only return to eat but also to stay in one of the homely, individually decorated bedrooms, with second generations of families now returning to experience the pub's excellent hospitality. Keeping all the balls in the air is Helen – who worked her way up from chambermaid to manager – supported by a charming team.

Main St,
SINNINGTON, YO62 6SQ
Tel.: 01751 431577
Website: www.thefoxandhoundsinn.co.uk

Just off A 170 between Pickering and Kirkbymoorside. Parking.

PRICES
Meals: a la carte £ 24/48

10 rooms:
£ 59/140

MAP: 28

CLOSING TIMES
Closed 25-27 December

CROWN AND CUSHION

Local meat cooked on the charcoal-fired rotisserie

Two miles from Castle Howard, on the edge of the Howardian Hills, is this well-run 18C pub which makes a great start or stop-off point for the many walkers and birdwatchers that flock to the area. You can sip a beer by the fire alongside the locals in the Tap Room but the best place to eat is the lower rear dining area, which overlooks the semi-open kitchen – unless the sun's out, in which case head to the terrace with its country vista. The menu champions local meats and the kitchen's pride and joy is the charcoal-fired rotisserie known as 'Big Bertha'. This cooks meats and fish at 450 degrees, producing mouth-watering results and comes into its own with Sunday roast. Dishes are hearty, sandwiches are doorstops, and puddings are nursery style.

WELBURN, YO60 7DZ
Tel.: 01653 618777
Website: www.thecrownandcushionwelburn.com

6 mi southwest of Malton, village signposted off A 64. Parking.

PRICES
Meals: a la carte £ 25/43

MAP: 29

CLOSING TIMES
Open daily

PLOUGH INN

Choose a seat in the cosy, characterful restaurant

Retirement is an opportunity to take some time for yourself, to relax, maybe get a pet or potter round in the garden... alternatively, you could buy your local pub, like the owners of this 16C inn. Having installed an equally local chef behind the stove, they are making village residents very happy; you might even spot them having a swift pint themselves at the end of the bar. Sit in the restaurant if you can – it's in the older part of the building, is hugely characterful, and is kept cosy by wood burners. Traditional dishes are the order of the day, so expect classics like fishcakes or chargrilled rib-eye steak, with game in season and desserts such as sticky toffee pudding. Prices are laudably low and service, friendly and relaxed.

Main St,
WOMBLETON, YO62 7RW
Tel.: 01751 431356
Website: www.theploughinnatwombleton.co.uk

Signposted off A 170, 4 mi east of Helmsley. Parking.

PRICES   MAP: **30**
Meals: a la carte £ 22/37

CLOSING TIMES
Closed 25 December and Monday lunch

SHIBDEN MILL INN

A cosy, welcoming pub in a tranquil valley

This pub is situated in the middle of a deep-sided valley in the quiet, unspoilt countryside, yet is only a few minutes' drive from the centre of Halifax. In a previous life it was a corn mill and the stream which used to turn the wheel runs alongside, adding to the tranquil feel if you're dining alfresco. Character is not in short supply either, with beamed ceilings, welcoming fires and lots of cosy corners. Upstairs, a grill restaurant serves top notch steaks, ribs and fish on Thursday-Saturday evenings; downstairs the menu offers pub favourites like sausage and mash as well as more ambitious dishes like poached and sautéed wood pigeon. Staff are well-drilled and bedrooms, individually furnished; choose No.14 if it's luxury you're after.

Shibden Mill Fold,
HALIFAX, HX3 7UL
Tel.: 01422 365840
Website: www.shibdenmillinn.com

Signposted off A 58, 2.25 mi northeast of Halifax. Parking.

PRICES
Meals: £ 14 (lunch and early dinner)
and a la carte £ 22/40

11 rooms:
£ 90/195

MAP: 31

CLOSING TIMES
Closed 25-26 December and 1 January

CROSS KEYS

A traditional inn serving hearty British fare

This traditional brick-built pub stands in a regenerated area of the city and was once the watering hole for workers of the 19C Round Foundry, who would probably have appreciated the superb selection of bottled beers they serve today. The pub has a cosy, friendly feel and features flagged floors, old beams and wood-burning fires; the first floor dining room is named after James Watt, the inventor of the steam engine (although it's been said he stole many ideas from his inebriated workers!) Cooking is hearty, tasty and British through-and-through: the menu offers a mix of pub classics and more ambitious dishes, so expect cottage pie or fish and chips alongside haunch of venison or lamb shank. They are unsurprisingly busy, so be sure to book.

107 Water Ln,
THE ROUND FOUNDRY, LEEDS, LS11 5WD
Tel.: 0113 243 3711
Website: www.the-crosskeys.com

Just south of the River Aire in the Holbeck area.
Metered parking adjacent.

PRICES
Meals: a la carte £ 21/36

MAP: **32**

CLOSING TIMES
Closed 25-26 December and 1 January
booking essential

WOODMAN INN

Modern country pub with smart bedrooms

This dark stone pub is found in a lovely wooded South Pennine valley and is run by local father and son Graham and Craig Leslie. One side of the low beamed bar is kept for drinkers and the other is laid for dining, while upstairs there's a restaurant and a private dining room; or if you prefer to dine alfresco, there's a terrace just over the road. Menus strike a great balance between pub and restaurant style dishes, listing everything from corned beef hash to 28 day Bolster Moor farm rib-eye steak and from fish and chips to stone bass with crab risotto. The Yorkshire tapas sharing plate offers something a little different and comforting desserts could include crumbles and sponge puddings. Smart, modern country bedrooms include a 3 level suite.

THUNDER BRIDGE, HD8 0PX
Tel.: 01484 605778
Website: www.woodman-inn.com

5.75 mi southeast of Huddersfield, village signposted off A 629.
Parking.

PRICES
Meals: £ 28 (weekday dinner) and a la carte
£ 27/48

 19 rooms:
£ 50/100

MAP: 33

CLOSING TIMES
Open daily

SCOTLAND

Scotland may be small, but its variety is immense. The vivacity of Glasgow can seem a thousand miles from the vast peatland wilderness of Caithness and Sutherland's Flow Country; the arty vibe of Georgian Edinburgh a world away from the remote and tranquil Ardnamurchan peninsula. And how many people link Scotland to its beaches? But wide golden sands trim the Atlantic at South Harris, and the coastline of the Highlands boasts empty islands and turquoise waters. Meantime, Fife's coast draws golf fans to St Andrews and the more secretive delights of the East Neuk, an area of fishing villages and stone harbours. Wherever you travel, the scent of a dramatic history prevails in the shape of castles, cathedrals and rugged lochside monuments to the heroes of old.

🍽 Food and drink embraces the traditional, too, typified by Aberdeen's famous Malt Whisky Trail. And what better than Highland game, fresh fish from the Tweed or haggis, neeps and tatties to complement a grand Scottish hike...

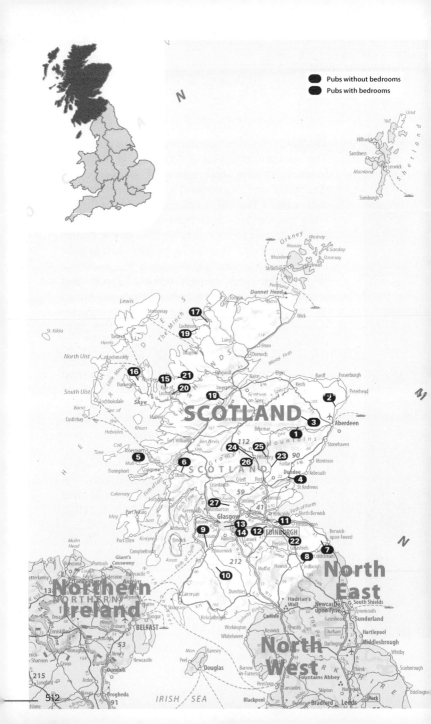

Pubs without bedrooms
Pubs with bedrooms

BOAT INN

Carefully prepared, traditional dishes

Pubs the length and breadth of Britain serve traditional bar meals like fish and chips and steak pie – what makes the Boat Inn stand out is the care put into preparing these dishes. The menu is kept short and simple while portions are generous; the occasional international dish makes an appearance – perhaps a Thai beef salad – and there are freshly baked cakes on the counter. A train runs around a shelf in the bright front room, there's a cosy bar at the back, a smart private dining room called the Pine Loft and spacious bedrooms which come with their own kitchenettes. The pub's name comes from the ferry which used to cross the River Dee here and the inn is reputed to be haunted by the ghost of a passenger who perished on the crossing.

Charleston Rd,
ABOYNE, AB34 5EL
Tel.: 01339 886137
Website: www.theboatinnaboyne.co.uk

On B 968 just along from the village green. Parking.

PRICES
Meals: a la carte £ 18/36

 8 rooms:
£ 65/110

MAP: 1

CLOSING TIMES
Closed 25-26 December and 1 January

COCK AND BULL

A fun place that doesn't take itself too seriously

The Cock and Bull is a quirky, atmospheric pub with a sense of fun befitting its name; check out the mural on the men's toilet door and the profusion of knick-knacks throughout. There's a choice of three rooms in which to dine: a cosy lounge with an open fire and low leather sofas, a more formal dining room and an airy conservatory. Wherever you sit, the menu's the same, and there's plenty of choice. You'll find classics like Arbroath smokie kedgeree or Cullen skink, alongside some more restaurant-style dishes such as confit pork belly or mushroom, watercress and ricotta tart; dishes are satisfying and everything arrives neatly presented. Some of the contemporary bedrooms are in a nearby annexe – a complimentary shuttle service is provided.

Ellon Rd,
BLAIRTON, BALMEDIE, AB23 8XY
Tel.: 01358 743249
Website: www.thecockandbull.co.uk

On A 90 6 mi north of Aberdeen. Parking.

PRICES
Meals: £ 18 and a la carte £ 21/34

6 rooms:
£ 75/110

MAP: 2

CLOSING TIMES
Closed 26-27 December and 1-2 January

KILDRUMMY INN

The perfect place to learn to fly fish

This 19C building has always served the local community in one way or another: over the years it has provided accommodation for farm workers, spent time as the local post office and been used as a garage – and now David and Neil (who met when they married two sisters) are taking it back to its original coaching inn roots. There's a plush dining room, a conservatory and a lovely open-fired bar where you can cosy up in an armchair and sample the local whiskies. The set menu offers the likes of home-cured salmon with capers, followed by roasted chicken with gnocchi and purple sprouting broccoli – finished off with more classical desserts. Cosy, contemporary bedrooms offer all you could want and they also have 4 miles of rights on the River Don.

KILDRUMMY, AB33 8QS
Tel.: 01975 571227
Website: www.kildrummyinn.co.uk

West 7 mi of Aldford by A 944 on A 97. Parking.

PRICES
Meals: £ 35

 4 rooms:
£ 89/99

MAP: 3

CLOSING TIMES
Closed January and Tuesday
dinner only and Sunday lunch

DROVERS INN

Freshly baked breads and local estate produce

Good cooking relies on good ingredients, so if the owner of a pub also has estates nearby that supply much of the produce, it's little wonder that the chef seems so content. This remote Highland inn with its immaculate lawns was once a crofter's cottage – and more recently spent time as the village post office. The bar with its open fires is a cosy spot but there's also a more formal dining room – to which the freshly baked breads add their wonderful aroma – and to the side, a lovely beamed room with a map of the area covering one entire wall. The well-priced menu makes particularly good use of the abundant local produce, including plenty of game and venison from the shoots in season. Tuesday is the ever-popular steak night.

MEMUS, DD8 3TY
Tel.: 01307 860322
Website: www.the-drovers.com

4 mi north of Kirriemuir by B 955 and minor road east. Parking.

PRICES
Meals: a la carte £ 26/39

MAP: 4

CLOSING TIMES
Closed 25-26 December

THE BELLACHROY

A well-priced selection of top-notch clarets

The Bellachroy sits in a pretty village at the head of Loch Cuin and, having been established in 1608, is the oldest inn on the island. Experienced owners Antony and Christine took over the running of it in 2013 and, although it might look a little shabby from the outside, it's characterful inside. The cosy bar and dining area have a rustic feel courtesy of wooden timbers, old sepia pictures and a selection of peat cutting tools on display (stick to this side, as it can get noisy in the locals bar, especially on a Friday and Saturday night). The concise lunch menu is followed by greater choice at dinner; go for the ultra-fresh local seafood – maybe mussels from Craignure, scallops from Tobermory or lobster from Croig. Bedrooms are simple.

DERVAIG,
ISLE OF MULL, PA75 6QW
Tel.: 01688 400314
Website: www.thebellachroy.co.uk

8.5 mi southwest of Tobermory by B 8073. Parking.

PRICES
Meals: a la carte £ 20/49

7 rooms:
£ 40/120

MAP: 5

CLOSING TIMES
Closed Sunday dinner and Monday
November-Easter

TAYNUILT

Its origins can be traced back to the 1400s

For centuries, this inn has been a staging post on the main road to Oban. Coleridge and Wordsworth enjoyed its hospitality back in 1803 and today it's run with pride and enthusiasm by the McNulty family. Food is their passion and the beautifully presented, assured modern cooking displays many intricate components. The Scottish larder is used to full effect: pancetta is made on-site and they smoke their own salmon over Springbank whisky staves, but they also aren't afraid to source ingredients from further afield. The pub sits between Loch Etive and Loch Awe and its well-kept bedrooms are named after these and other Scottish lochs. It may be simply furnished but what it lacks in character, it more than makes up for in the warmth of its welcome.

TAYNUILT, PA35 1JN
Tel.: 01866 822437
Website: www.taynuilthotel.co.uk

On main A 85 road through village, 12 mi east of Oban. Parking.

PRICES
Meals: a la carte £ 25/55

 9 rooms:
£ 95/195

MAP: 6

CLOSING TIMES
Closed Sunday, Monday and restricted
opening in January

ALLANTON INN

The regional cheese selection is a hit

This striking stone inn has stood in the Borders conservation village of Allanton since the 18C, when it formed part of the Blackadder Estate. A few years back it was bought by a young couple, William and Katrina, who wanted to move back to the area where Katrina's family had farmed for over 60 years. They immediately set about creating a welcoming inn and today you'll find a rustic bar, a cosy restaurant and, above it, six bright, simply furnished bedrooms. The cooking demonstrates a similar level of care, with a selection of thoughtfully prepared modern dishes crafted from local farm meats and Eyemouth fish. The regional cheese selection is a hit – as is the pretty garden with country views, where they hold the occasional hog roast.

ALLANTON, TD11 3JZ
Tel.: 01890 818260
Website: www.allantoninn.co.uk

1 mi south of Chirnside in centre of village. On-street parking.

PRICES
Meals: a la carte £ 17/38

6 rooms:
£ 65/95

MAP: 7

CLOSING TIMES
Open daily

ANCRUM CROSS KEYS

Watch the chef at work

You just know that a pub's going to serve a good pint when the river at the bottom of the garden is called the River Ale! The fact that the man in charge also owns the nearby Scottish Borders Brewery has got to help – and judging by the number of locals in the rustic front bar of this 200 year old pub, they certainly seem to agree. But what about the food? Well, what really sets this place apart is the cooking – and we're not talking everyday pub grub. In the style of a modern city restaurant, menus list only the ingredients of a dish – 'local pigeon, variations of beetroot, golden raisins, buckwheat' – and dishes are carefully crafted and tasty with a refined edge. Sit in the larger of the dining rooms to watch the chef at work.

The Green,
ANCRUM, TD8 6XH
Tel.: 01835 830242
Website: www.ancrumcrosskeys.com

Between St Boswells and Jedburgh signposted off A 68. Parking around The Green.

PRICES
Meals: a la carte £ 21/32

MAP: **8**

CLOSING TIMES
Closed Monday, Tuesday and lunch Wednesday

COCHRANE INN

Bright and modern with fresh, tasty dishes

If breakfast's your thing, come on a Saturday or Sunday morning – and if fresh, tasty, generously priced dishes are for you, come any day of the week. This is a pub that offers plenty of choice, from liver and bacon to salmon in puff pastry. Lunch includes a good range of sandwiches and steaks, the Express Menu is a steal and to finish you'll find proper puddings and their renowned sundaes. Service is friendly and copes well under pressure, but then that's what you'd expect of a pub that's part of an established group. The ivy-covered stone walls might have stood here for years but inside it's bright and modern, with copper lampshades hanging above the bar, coal-effect gas fires flickering in the grates and striking art adorning the walls.

45 Main Rd,
GATEHEAD, KA2 0AP
Tel.: 01563 570122
Website: www.costley-hotels.co.uk

2.75 mi southwest of Kilmarnock on A 759. Parking

PRICES
Meals: £ 15 (lunch and early dinner)
and a la carte £ 20/38

MAP: 9

CLOSING TIMES
Open daily

SORN INN

Family-run pub serving international dishes

It's a real family affair here, with the father checking you in to your bedroom and his son behind the stoves in the kitchen. The first clues as to the quality of food are the framed menus and the copy of the chefs' bible, 'Larousse' – and the cooking doesn't disappoint. The chef adopts an international approach – a result of his time spent on the QE2 – so along with prime Scottish beef and game from the Sorn estate come dishes like bacon carbonara, cod and chips or loin of pork with Morteau sausage. Dishes are well-priced, and there's plenty of flexibility here too: some dishes come in a choice of sizes and you can have them either sitting in a high-backed leather chair in the restaurant or with your dog beside your feet in the pub.

35 Main St,
SORN, KA5 6HU
Tel.: 01290 551305
Website: www.sorninn.com

In centre of village. Parking.

PRICES
Meals: £ 14 (weekday lunch)/17
and a la carte £ 19/35

 4 rooms:
£ 50/90

MAP: 10

CLOSING TIMES
Closed 10 days January and Monday

THE SCRAN & SCALLIE

A place to share good food with the whole family

Found in the smart, village-like suburb of Stockbridge, this pub is the more casual venture of well-known chef Tom Kitchin. It might seem an unusual name but 'Scran' means food and 'Scallie' means children, which reflects his desire for good food to be shared with the whole family. Pass through the heavy wood furnished bar to the dining room with its mix of rustic and contemporary décor; some walls are brick, others are stone, and some are boldly wallpapered and hung with old framed recipes. Extensive menus follow a 'Nature to Plate' philosophy, focusing on the classical and the local – and a map in the bar locates his suppliers. Where else can you start with sheep's heid broth and finish with jelly and ice cream?

1 Comely Bank Rd,
STOCKBRIDGE, EDINBURGH, EH4 1DT
Tel.: 0131 332 6281
Website: www.scranandscallie.com

On the northwestern side of the city. On-street meter parking.

PRICES
Meals: £ 15 (weekday lunch) and a la carte
£ 23/46

MAP: **11**

CLOSING TIMES
Closed 25 December
booking advisable

BRIDGE INN

Modernised local on the tow path

This friendly pub sits on the tow path between Edinburgh and the Falkirk Wheel and offers pleasant views over the canal. In summer, head out to the terrace or book a cruise on their restaurant barge; in winter, find a seat beside the fire. It might have a modern feel but this is a place that knows its role in the community and sets aside plenty of room in the bar for the locals and their dogs. The large menu offers everything from a pie of the day in a puff pastry case to seared scallops with pea and mint velouté or sea bass with sweet potato purée and smoked dulse seaweed. Fruit and veg come from their walled garden, pork comes from their saddleback pigs and the eggs, from their chickens and ducks. All of the cosy bedrooms have water views.

27 Baird Rd,
RATHO, EH28 8RU
Tel.: 0131 333 1320
Website: www.bridgeinn.com

10 mi southwest of Edinburgh signposted off A 71. Parking.

PRICES
Meals: a la carte £ 21/39

 4 rooms:
£ 70/120

MAP: 12

CLOSING TIMES
Closed 25 December

THE FINNIESTON

Small and cosy, with seafood from local waters

This was once a conventional old boozer but an enthusiastic young team with a real passion for food and drink have resurrected it, and it now specialises in seafood dishes and gin-based cocktails. It's small and cosy, with an intriguing ceiling, a welcoming fire and lots of booths. The anchor motif on the glass reminds you where their strengths lie and the Popeye and Olive Oyl pictures on the toilet doors continue the theme. All of the seafood is from Scottish waters, with mackerel from Peterhead, langoustines from Troon and oysters from Cumbrae. Dishes are light, tasty and neatly presented, relying on just a handful of ingredients so that flavours are clear; if you have the fish and chips, 50p will be donated to the local Fishermen's Mission.

1125 Argyle St,
GLASGOW, G3 8ND
Tel.: 0141 222 2884
Website: www.thefinniestonbar.com

On the west side close to Kelvingrove. On-street parking.

PRICES   **MAP: 13**
Meals: a la carte £ 23/37

CLOSING TIMES
Closed 25-26 December and 1 January

SALISBURY

Bijou pub with an eclectic menu

This bijou pub on the south side of the city proves that there are pubs which can successfully cater for both drinkers and diners. It's a small place with a relaxed feel and when it's full, it has a satisfyingly jovial air. Monthly menus are an eclectic mix of Scottish and international flavours with original twists, so you might find grilled sardines with chilli marinade, tomato concasse and homemade sourdough toast, or a scotch egg that comprises haggis wrapped around an egg, coated in breadcrumbs and accompanied by baked bean purée. Desserts are playful and worth saving room for — try the Snickers parfait with nougat, peanut brittle and rhubarb compote; for brunch, the Salisbury stack and the 11 ingredient Bloody Mary get top billing.

72 Nithsdale Rd,
GLASGOW, G41 2AN
Tel.: 0141 423 0084
Website: www.thesalisbury.co.uk

2.5 mi southwest of the city centre by A 8 and A 77. On-street parking.

PRICES   **MAP: 14**
Meals: £ 10 (lunch) and a la carte £ 23/34

CLOSING TIMES
Closed 25 December and 1 January

APPLECROSS INN

The freshest of seafood and a stunning seascape

Arrival at Applecross can involve a drive over the hair-raising, single-track Bealach na Ba, with its stunning views and hairpin bends; learner drivers and vertigo sufferers should travel the less scenic route along the coast road instead. This is an unpretentious sort of place, with a wood burning stove and an abundance of pine panelling. Service is friendly and the atmosphere, bustling; on sunny days, the terrace is unsurprisingly the most popular spot. Food-wise, the highlight is the freshest of seafood, often straight out of the sea and sometimes from within sight of the door; expect prawns, crabs and lobster from Applecross and oysters and mussels from Skye. Simple bedrooms in the next-door fishermen's cottages have marvellous sea views.

Shore St,
APPLECROSS, IV54 8LR
Tel.: 01520 744262
Website: www.applecross.uk.com/inn

From Kishorn via Bealach na Bo or round by Shieldaig and along the coast road. Parking.

PRICES
Meals: a la carte £ 16/40

 7 rooms:
£ 80/140

MAP: 15

CLOSING TIMES
Closed 25 December and 1 January
booking essential

EDINBANE INN

Bedrooms are comfy and cosy

This traditional-looking former farmhouse is the perfect place to cosy up by the fire on a misty night – Skye is the 'island of mist' after all – while the front porch is the place to be on sunnier days. The menu lists Scottish pub favourites like Cullen skink or local cheese and oatcakes but some more interesting dishes also make an appearance, such as Uist scallops with chorizo and chickpea stew or garlic and rosemary studded shoulder of lamb with red wine sauce; the daily specials chalked up on the blackboard are also a good bet. This is fast becoming the place to be on the north of the island and the traditional music sessions are a great draw too, with local musicians playing on Wednesday and Friday evenings, as well as Sunday afternoons.

Edinbane,
ISLE OF SKYE, IV51 9PW
Tel.: 01470 582414
Website: www.edinbaneinn.co.uk

Between Portree and Dunvegan on A 850. Parking.

PRICES
Meals: a la carte £ 25/38

 6 rooms:
£ 90/130

MAP: 16

CLOSING TIMES
Closed 2 January-2 February

KYLESKU

Fresh local seafood and breathtaking views

Breathtaking views of Loch Glendhu and the surrounding mountains make this 17C coaching inn an essential stop-off point if you're in the area. The open-plan bar and dining room are swathed in light thanks to a striking glass extension but, come summer, the waterside terrace is the place to be. Keep an eye out for 'Stumpy', the rather tame local stag, and also for Willie, who's been a customer for over 80 years. Fresh seafood is the order of the day, particularly the sweet langoustines and rope-grown mussels landed 200 yards away – push the boat out with the seafood platter or stick to the classics, which could include pie of the day or a hearty crumble. Bedrooms in the inn are cosy; two of the newer rooms have balconies with panoramic views.

KYLESKU, IV27 4HW
Tel.: 01971 502231
Website: www.kyleskuhotel.co.uk

32 mi north of Ullapool by A 835, A 837 and A 894. On street parking.

PRICES
Meals: a la carte £ 24/59

 11 rooms:
£ 73/170

MAP: 17

CLOSING TIMES
Closed late November-mid February

LOCH NESS INN

Considering its position, it would have been all too easy to make this inn a paean to all things 'Nessie' but thankfully, the only sign of the famous monster is in the pub's logo. The one place where the pub's location is justly celebrated is on the menu, so expect hearty, robust, flavoursome dishes which champion Scottish produce; perhaps Cullen skink, loin of venison or whisky-flambéed haggis. There are two main parts to the pub: the small Brewery Bar, home to locals and walkers fresh from the Great Glen Way; and the open-plan Lewiston restaurant with its wood burning stove and bright timbered beams. Service is sweet and well-meaning – and if you're after somewhere to lay your head, you'll find the bedrooms spacious and comfortable.

LEWISTON, IV63 6UW
Tel.: 01456 450991
Website: www.staylochness.co.uk

Between Inverness and Fort Augustus on A 82. Parking.

PRICES
Meals: a la carte £ 20/36

 12 rooms:
£ 55/112

MAP: 18

CLOSING TIMES
Open daily

CABERFEIDH

Enjoy generously sized 'small plates'

The informal lochside sister of the Albannach restaurant was designed with the Lochinver residents in mind, and it follows the same ethos of championing fresh local produce. Caberfeidh (Gaelic for a stag's antlers), sits on the main street, in a building that was once Mrs McKenzie's House and Shop – look out for the plans dating from the 1930s. The blackboard menu evolves throughout the day and has a seafood slant, with produce arriving from the nearby harbour. The majority of dishes are sharing 'small plates' but the portions are generous; you might find scallops with black pudding or cod goujons with homemade tartare sauce. Puddings are sticky and satisfying, service is cheerful, and the terrace has great views over the loch and river mouth.

Main St,
LOCHINVER, IV27 4JY
Tel.: 01571 844321
Website: www.caberfeidhlochinver.co.uk

In centre of village. Free public car park adjacent.

PRICES
Meals: a la carte £ 25/35

MAP: 19

CLOSING TIMES
Closed 25 December, 1 January and
in winter Monday and lunch Tuesday-
Wednesday

PLOCKTON HOTEL

Menus keep things pleasingly local

With its distinctive black exterior, this one-time ships' chandlery is easy to spot. Owned and run by the Pearson family for over 20 years, it offers a warm welcome as well as stunning views over Loch Carron to the mountains beyond. Most of the action takes place in the wood-panelled bar, with its red leather banquettes, tartan carpets and wood burning stove; though if the weather's good, the front terrace fills up the fastest. Cooking is honest, fresh and hearty, with a strong Scottish influence, so expect Talisker whisky pâté, Plockton smokies, haggis and whisky or herring in oatmeal – and don't miss the Plockton prawns. Simple, comfortable bedrooms are split between the pub and an annexe; those to the front have wonderful views.

41 Harbour St,
PLOCKTON, IV52 8TN
Tel.: 01599 544274
Website: www.plocktonhotel.co.uk

5 mi north of Kyle of Lochalsh.
Parking 50 yards away in village car park.

PRICES
Meals: a la carte £ 18/40

 15 rooms:
£ 45/140

MAP: 20

CLOSING TIMES
Open daily

TORRIDON INN

Perfect for those who enjoy outdoor pursuits

This is an easy place to miss, as from the outside it looks more like a Tourist Information Office than a pub, but it's well worth a visit, whether for a drink, a bite to eat or to take part in one of their many activities, from glen walks and kayaking to rock climbing and gorge scrambling. If these sound more like spectator sports to you, then simply sit back and enjoy the tranquil surroundings and glorious loch views from either the restaurant or the spacious, part-panelled bar decorated with stags' antlers and Ordnance Survey maps. The interesting menu and daily specials feature satisfying walkers' favourites and a few more elaborate dishes such as cheese soufflé or seared scallops. Simple, modern bedrooms are in the old stables.

TORRIDON, IV22 2EY
Tel.: 01445 791242
Website: www.thetorridon.com

1.5 mi south of Torridon on A 896. Parking.

PRICES
Meals: a la carte £ 18/36

 12 rooms:
£ 120

MAP: 21

CLOSING TIMES
Closed mid-December-January and
Monday-Thursday November, February
and March

SUN INN

Plans are afoot for an extension!

This smartly refurbished pub is set on the main road from Edinburgh to Galashiels and started life in the 17C as a blacksmith's, only later becoming a coaching inn. It's a large place, consisting of two open-fired rooms with a mix of wood and stone walls, which are hung with contemporary black and white photos of the area. Extensive menus feature good quality local produce and the suppliers are listed on a blackboard. Lunch keeps things simple but appealing – you might find ham hock potato cakes, kipper pâté or liver and bacon – while dinner is more ambitious, with the likes of pig's cheek and black pudding or sea bass with saffron risotto. Completing the picture are smart, modern bedrooms boasting handmade furniture and Egyptian cotton linen.

Lothian Bridge,
DALKEITH, EH22 4TR
Tel.: 0131 663 2456
Website: www.thesuninnedinburgh.co.uk

2 mi southwest of Dalkeith on A 7. Parking.

PRICES
Meals: £ 11 (lunch and early dinner) and a la carte £ 20/49

 5 rooms:
£ 75/150

MAP: 22

CLOSING TIMES
Closed 26 December and 1 January

DALMORE INN

A surprisingly stylish room hides within

With its whisky kegs out the front, it may look like a traditional pub, but cross the threshold and the Dalmore Inn reveals a surprisingly stylish modern interior. Brightly coloured walls hung with photos of Scottish scenes are juxtaposed with original stonework; giant potted plants occupy the centre of the room; and a life-sized picture of a Highland cow greets you at the door. The cooking is good value, unfussy and full of flavour – everything is freshly prepared to order and they like to use Scottish produce wherever possible; you might find ham hock terrine or Arbroath smokie risotto, followed by venison and black pudding meatballs or a homemade burger topped with haggis. Service is warm, welcoming and well-executed.

Perth Rd,
BLAIRGOWRIE, PH10 6QB
Tel.: 01250 871088
Website: www.dalmoreinn.com

1.5 mi southwest of Blairgowrie on A 93. Parking.

PRICES   MAP: **23**
Meals: £ 10 (weekday lunch) and a la carte
£ 20/44

CLOSING TIMES
Closed 25 December and 1-2 January

INN ON THE TAY

Superbly located on the banks of the Tay

As its name suggests, this smart modern inn is located on the banks of the River Tay. Head to either the terrace or the large dining room for superb views over the water – where you'll often see people rafting or canoeing – or on colder days bag one of the squashy sofas beside the log burning stove. At lunchtime expect gourmet sandwiches, burgers and hearty classics like Scotch broth; in the evening things become a little more structured, with tried-and-tested combinations like scallops and black pudding or beetroot-cured salmon gravadlax. The owners are cheery and welcoming, the atmosphere is laid back and if you're staying the night you'll find the bedrooms comfy and cosy. For a souvenir, visit their artisan chocolate shop opposite.

GRANDTULLY, PH9 0PL
Tel.: 01887 840760
Website: www.theinnonthetay.co.uk

5 mi northeast of Aberfeldy on A 827. Parking.

PRICES
Meals: a la carte £ 20/38

 6 rooms:
£ 70/110

MAP: 24

CLOSING TIMES
Open daily

STRATHARDLE INN

Be sure to try one of the classic Scottish dishes

This 18C drovers' inn sits opposite the River Ardle as you head south out of Kirkmichael towards Blairgowrie and its modern, wood-furnished bedrooms make a great base for exploring the area. Having organised plenty of corporate events, owner Abi knows a thing or two about hospitality – so whether you've popped in for a pint or have travelled from further afield, you'll always be greeted with a warm welcome. Regulars and their dogs gather in the cosy bar and those after a hearty meal head for the dining room. Lunch focuses on pub favourites so you might find fish and chips or pie of the day, while dinner offers tasty grills and roasts – you'll often see 'Arbroath smokies', 'stovies and oatcakes' or 'haggis, neeps & tatties' on the menu too.

KIRKMICHAEL, PH10 7NS
Tel.: 01250 881224
Website: www.strathardleinn.co.uk

Between Pitlochry and Blairgowrie on A 924. Parking.

PRICES
Meals: a la carte £ 20/34

8 rooms:
£ 50/95

MAP: 25

CLOSING TIMES
Open daily

AULD SMIDDY INN

Satisfyingly hearty dishes follow the seasons

As you might have guessed, this building started life as a blacksmith's, before spending a short spell as a tea room and later finding its calling as a pub. A small but colourful garden stands out against smartly whitewashed walls and there's a large terrace and courtyard round the back. Inside it has a likeable simplicity, with polished slate floors and wood burning stoves; sit at the front beside the counter or in the rear room where the blacksmith would once have worked. In the summer, salads and fish dishes fill the menu; in colder months, the choice may be smaller but the portions certainly aren't, with hearty classics such as haggis, neeps and tatties or local steak, sausage and ale pie. They also hold a seafood festival twice a year.

154 Atholl Rd,
PITLOCHRY, PH16 5AG
Tel.: 01796 472356
Website: www.auldsmiddyinn.co.uk

At northern end of the main street. Pay and display parking nearby.

PRICES
Meals: a la carte £ 20/43

MAP: 26

CLOSING TIMES
Closed last week January-first week February,
last week November and 25-26 December

THE INN AT KIPPEN

Attractive dishes from the bounteous local larder

Bigger than it looks from the outside; bright and subtly modernised on the inside; The Inn at Kippen is personally run by Alice and Mark Silverwood. The couple are keen to respect Scottish traditions and take full advantage of the bounteous local larder, so expect to see dishes like Cullen skink on the menu alongside Ayrshire beef and lamb, Scottish scallops and tasty sharing platters of Scottish fish and cheeses; all attractively presented in an elaborate, modern style. With Loch Lomond and the Trossachs National Park on the doorstep, it's well worth taking time to explore the local area; sample a couple of the local bottled ales on offer in the bar before retiring to one of the simply furnished, contemporary bedrooms upstairs.

Fore Rd,
KIPPEN, FK8 3DT
Tel.: 01786 870500
Website: www.theinnatkippen.co.uk

8 miles west of Stirling off A 811. Parking.

PRICES
Meals: a la carte £ 20/49

 4 rooms:
£ 65/135

MAP: 27

CLOSING TIMES
Closed 3-4 January

WALES

© R. Harding / hemis.fr

It's nearly six hundred years since Owen Glyndawr escaped the clutches of the English to become a national hero, and in all that time the Welsh passion for unity has bound the country together like a scarlet-shirted scrum. It may be only 170 miles from north to south, but Wales contains great swathes of beauty, such as the dark and craggy heights of Snowdonia's ninety mountain peaks, the rolling sandstone bluffs of the Brecon Beacons, and Pembrokeshire's tantalising golden beaches. Bottle-nosed dolphins love it here too, arriving each summer at New Quay in Cardigan Bay. Highlights abound: formidable Harlech Castle dominates its coast, and Bala Lake has a railway that steams along its gentle shores.

Hay-on-Wye's four pubs and eighteen bookshops turn perceptions on their head, and Welsh cuisine is causing a surprise or two as well: the country teems with great raw ingredients now employed to their utmost potential, from the humblest cockle to the slenderest slice of succulent lamb.

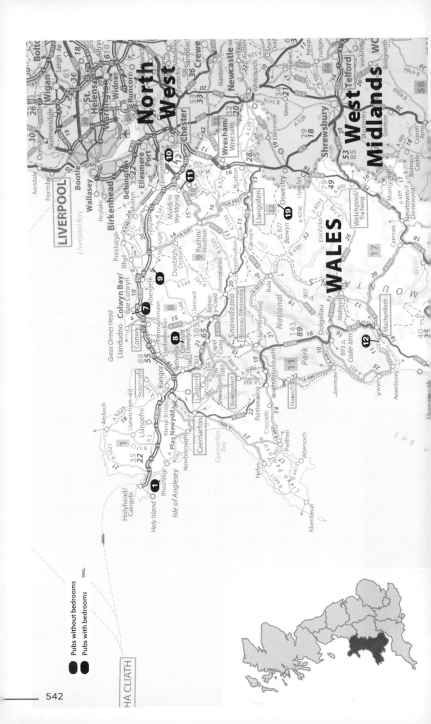

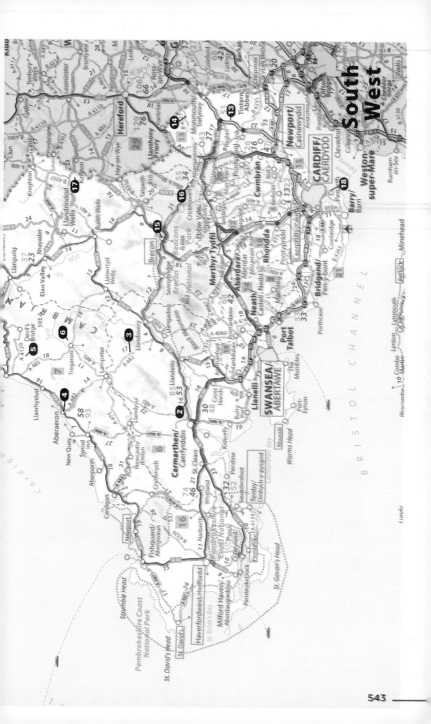

South West

CARDIFF/CAERDYDD

Newport/Casnewydd

SWANSEA/ABERTAWE

Carmarthen/Caerfyrddin

Merthyr Tydfil

Neath/Castell-Nedd

Bridgend/Pen-y-bont

Port Talbot

Llanelli

Hereford

Brecon

Aberdâr

Rhondda

Pontypridd

Cwmbrân

Barry/Barri

Weston-super-Mare

BRISTOL CHANNEL

Pembrokeshire Coast National Park

St. David's

Haverfordwest/Hwlffordd

Milford Haven/Aberdaugleddau

Pembroke/Penfro

Tenby/Dinbych-y-pysgod

Fishguard/Abergwaun

Newport/Trefdraeth

Aberaeron

New Quay

Cardigan/Aberteifi

Llandovery

Lampeter

Llandeilo

Devil's Bridge

Llanidloes

Knighton

Llandrindod Wells

Builth Wells

Hay-on-Wye

Llanthony Priory

Tintern Abbey

Monmouth/Trefynwy

543

WHITE EAGLE

Take in stunning sea views from the terrace

Set in a small coastal hamlet on the peninsula, this pub is a beacon for walkers and boasts stunning sea views from its dining room and spacious decked terrace. From the outside it may look more like a restaurant but swing a right through the door and you'll find the regulars nursing their pints in the cosy bar. It's rightly popular, so you might have to wait for a table; fill your time by looking over the menu, which offers something for one and all, including several different sharing boards, starters like pan-seared scallops or sweet potato fritters and main courses such as Best End of lamb or sautéed sea trout. If you've only got time for a flying visit, order some home-pickled cockles and clams to accompany a local Wrexham Ale.

RHOSCOLYN, LL65 2NJ
Tel.: 01407 860267
Website: www.white-eagle.co.uk

5 mi south of Holyhead by B 4545 and minor road south. Parking.

PRICES
Meals: a la carte £ 21/37

MAP: 1

CLOSING TIMES
Closed 25 December

Y POLYN

Welcoming to locals and visitors alike

The food is the focus at this small, rustic and pleasantly unfussy pub, which sits on a busy country road close to a stream and affords pleasant views. Mark, the owner, was previously an inspector with the AA, hence all the restaurant menus on display, which make quite a talking point. Pleasingly, he's just as welcoming to those on their first visit as to his trusty band of regulars. His wife Sue looks after the kitchen and her cooking is stout, filling and British at heart; the slow-cooked meats, fresh salads, satisfying soups and classic puds all hit the spot, both with the lunchtime couples and the more youthful crowd that gathers in the evening. Prices are kept realistic and the complimentary filtered mineral water is a nice touch.

NANTGAREDIG, SA32 7LH
Tel.: 01267 290000
Website: www.ypolyn.co.uk

6 mi east of Carmarthen by A 4300 on B 4310. Parking.

PRICES
Meals: £ 17 (weekday lunch)/35

MAP: **2**

CLOSING TIMES
Closed Sunday dinner and Monday
booking advisable

DOLAUCOTHI ARMS

Come on one of the homemade pie nights

This 300 year old drovers' inn sits in the picturesque Cothi Valley – close to the Roman gold mines – and its garden looks out over the river, where the pub has 4 miles of fishing rights. It's owned by the National Trust and leased by a friendly young couple, who moved here from the West Country with the aim of opening the 'ultimate' pub. It's a cosy, rustic kind of a place, where old stone slabs sit alongside red and black check tiled floors – and you can always guarantee a warm welcome from Lily the cat and the friendly team. There are two menus: one lists pub classics, while the second is more adventurous and offers the likes of fennel and lentil salad or lime chocolate brownie. Bedrooms are comfy and cosy – ask if you want a TV.

PUMSAINT, SA19 8UW
Tel.: 01558 650237
Website: www.thedolaucothiarms.co.uk

Between Llandeilo and Llandovery by A 40 on A 482. Parking.

PRICES
Meals: a la carte £ 17/29

 3 rooms:
£ 60/85

MAP: 3

CLOSING TIMES
Closed 16-29 January, 25-26 December,
Tuesday lunch, Monday except bank
holidays and midweek lunch November-
February

HARBOURMASTER

Nautical, New England styling and harbour views

With its vibrant blue exterior, you'll spot this place a mile off; not that the owners need worry about being noticed, as their reputation for good food and hospitality goes before them. As the name suggests, it once belonged to the harbourmaster and it offers lovely views out across the water. There's a bar-lounge with slate walls, a nautical New England style and an oval pewter-topped counter, as well as a modern dining room – make a play for 'cwtch', a table offering excellent harbour views. Choose between the bar menu or a more substantial evening à la carte supplemented by daily specials. Smart bedrooms, split between the house and a nearby cottage, are brightly decorated and well-equipped; some boast oversized windows or terraces.

Quay Par,
ABERAERON, SA46 0BA
Tel.: 01545 570755
Website: www.harbour-master.com

In town centre overlooking the harbour.
Parking on street and around the harbour wall.

PRICES
Meals: £ 28 (dinner) and a la carte £ 22/38

 13 rooms:
£ 75/250

MAP: 4

CLOSING TIMES
Closed dinner 24 December-26 December

Y FFARMERS

This really is the centre of the village

More than just the village pub, the passionately run Y Ffarmers is also the village hub and hosts everything from yoga classes and quiz nights to meetings of the local choir and bee keeping group. The characterful, whitewashed pub is situated in a remote, picturesque valley. It was originally a farm and subsequently a tax collector's office; turn right for the locals bar or left for the homely, open-fired restaurant which opens out onto the garden. The concise, monthly menu offers a good range of satisfying, original dishes that are big on flavour; the homemade lamb burger with redcurrant jelly is divine! Most produce comes from the valley, including locally grown organic veg, game from nearby shoots, and lobster and crab from Cardigan Bay.

LLANFIHANGEL-Y-CREUDDYN, SY23 4LA
Tel.: 01974 261275
Website: www.yffarmers.co.uk

7.75 mi southeast of Aberystwyth by A 487 and A 4120, turning right after Pant-y-crug. Parking in the village square.

PRICES   **MAP: 5**
Meals: a la carte £ 21/33

CLOSING TIMES
Closed first week January and Sunday
dinner-Tuesday lunch

Y TALBOT

Sit in the bar rooms, where the action is

Y Talbot was originally a drover's inn and its oldest part dates back to the 17C; a hotel extension was added with the arrival of the railways in the 1860s and you can clearly see the join. While there's a modern restaurant in the Victorian part of the building, the bar rooms in the older part are where the action is, and the best place to sit. The chef has a classical culinary background, so expect well-executed, full-flavoured traditional dishes made with Welsh produce. The daily changing pie is a hit with the locals, as is the burger with Snowdonia cheddar, while the daily fish special reminds you you're not too far from the coast. Bedrooms are bright and modern: ask for one of the newest. Oh, and there's an elephant buried in the garden!

TREGARON, SY25 6JL
Tel.: 01974 298208
Website: www.ytalbot.com

In the centre of town. Unrestricted parking in The Square.

PRICES
Meals: a la carte £ 22/38

 13 rooms:
£ 65/140

MAP: 6

CLOSING TIMES
Closed 25 December

PEN-Y-BRYN

Impressive bay views from the garden and terrace

You might need your sat nav, as even when you've located the right residential street, you could easily pass Pen-y-Bryn by. Looking more like a medical centre than a place to dine, it boasts impressive panoramic views over Colwyn Bay, especially from the garden and terrace. The spacious, open-plan interior is crammed full of pictures, bookcases and pottery, yet despite these and the oak floors, old furniture and open fires, it has a modern, laid-back feel. The extensive all-day menu offers plenty of choice, ranging from a classical ploughman's to more adventurous pheasant-based dishes; while during 'Beer and Bangers' weeks 12 varieties of sausage and over 20 beers are also offered. Large tables make it ideal for families or groups of friends.

Pen-y-Bryn Rd,
UPPER COLWYN BAY, COLWYN BAY, LL29 6DD
Tel.: 01492 533360
Website: www.penybryn-colwynbay.co.uk

1 mi southwest of Colwyn Bay by B 5113. Parking.

PRICES   MAP: 7
Meals: a la carte £ 20/37

CLOSING TIMES
Open daily

GROES INN

The first licensed house in Wales

A great location in the foothills of Snowdonia, tasty food, comfy bedrooms and friendly, cheerful staff: this pub has got the whole package. It dates from 1573 and was, as the sign on the front proclaims, 'the first licensed house in Wales', so it's got bags of character and is a great place to take shelter in winter or slake your thirst after a hike in the summer months. The appealing menu offers a good range of traditional dishes with the occasional international flavour; expect Welsh rarebit pepped up with Groes Ale, steak and kidney pudding, Welsh lamb or chicken curry. Bedrooms in the adjoining annexe are spacious and the best have a terrace or a balcony; ask for one at the rear with far-reaching rural views.

CONWY, LL32 8TN
Tel.: 01492 650545
Website: www.groesinn.com

3 mi south of Conwy on B 5106. Parking.

PRICES
Meals: a la carte £ 21/41

 14 rooms:
£ 100/200

MAP: 8

CLOSING TIMES
Closed Sunday dinner and Monday
November-mid March

KINMEL ARMS

They keep their own cows just over the road

This early 17C stone inn is hidden away in a hamlet by the entrance to Kinmel Hall. It's the type of pub that's not entirely sure if it wants to be a pub or a restaurant: true, there's a delightful open-fired bar with a slate-topped counter and low-level seating which hosts regular events for the locals; but there are also two spacious dining areas – one with chunky wood furniture and the other with a more conservatory-like feel. Lunch sees classic pub dishes and is followed by a traditional afternoon tea, while dinner steps things up a gear (some of the meat comes from their cows in the field over the road). Stylish, contemporary bedrooms boast smart bathrooms and large kitchenettes, so you can enjoy your continental breakfast in your PJs.

The Village,
ST GEORGE, LL22 9BP
Tel.: 01745 832207
Website: www.thekinmelarms.co.uk

In the centre of village. Parking.

PRICES
Meals: £ 15 (weekday dinner) and a la carte £ 27/45

 4 rooms:
£ 115/175

MAP: 9

CLOSING TIMES
Closed 25 December, 1 January, Sunday and Monday

GLYNNE ARMS

Classic dishes are given modern twists

This 200 year old coaching inn sits just across from the gates of Hawarden Castle and was once home to the Glynne family, hence its name. They're not the only family involved here though, as the descendants of PM William Gladstone, who own most of the village – including several farms and an interior design company – also have the Glynne Arms under their wing. Their experience with interiors means that the pub's been smartly refurbished and has a slightly funky feel. Cooking follows in a similarly modern vein by presenting classically based dishes with contemporary twists but traditionalists aren't forgotten, as there's also a range of bar snacks, along with steaks from the estate farm. Be sure to save room for one of the tasty desserts!

3 Glynne Way,
HAWARDEN, CH3 3NS
Tel.: 01244 569988
Website: www.theglynnearms.co.uk

In centre of the village. Parking

PRICES
Meals: a la carte £ 22/34

MAP: 10

CLOSING TIMES
Closed 25 December

TAVERN

A pub close to the chef-owner's heart

Having worked in various locations around the country, chef Peter Wright was thrilled when he got the chance to buy a pub close to his heart, near the place where he grew up and where his parents used to drink. He has given it a modern makeover and although the heavy tables and black and cream leather chairs may make it appear fairly formal, the menu is very much in a hearty, comforting pub vein – offering the likes of half a pint of prawns and Welsh Black beef and ale pie. The daily blackboard specials – particularly the grilled market fish dishes – prove popular and desserts are homemade and include all the favourites, from bread and butter pudding to Bakewell tart. The regular themed gourmet dinners best display Peter's talent.

Mold Rd,
ALLTAMI, MOLD, CH7 6LG
Tel.: 01244 550485
Website: www.tavernrestaurant.co.uk

2.5 mi northeast of Mold, on A 494. Parking.

PRICES
Meals: a la carte £ 20/39

MAP: 11

CLOSING TIMES
Closed 26 December and Monday

RIVERSIDE

Proudly Welsh, with a fresh, modern feel

If you fancy brushing up on your Welsh, head for this part-16C former coaching inn with the name 'Glan Yr Afron' (Riverside) above the door, then make for the 'Cwtch' (cosy corner) with its welcoming wood-burning stove. The pub stands on the main road in the small village of Pennal, backing on to a tributary of the River Dovey, and despite various additions and its Grade II listing, has a bright, modern feel inside. The friendly local team bring over tasty bread to nibble while you study the menu, which features all the usual pub favourites along with some sharing boards. Cooking is no-nonsense, full of flavour and keenly priced, and the portions are suitably hearty. Finish on a high with traditional puds like Eton mess, crumble or cheesecake.

PENNAL, SY20 9DW
Tel.: 01654 791285
Website: www.riversidehotel-pennal.co.uk

On A 493 between Aberdovey and Machynlleth. Parking.

PRICES
Meals: a la carte £ 19/37

MAP: 12

CLOSING TIMES
Closed 2 weeks January and Monday
October-May

RAGLAN ARMS

The hub of this small hamlet

The Raglan Arms' owners relocated here from the Isle of Skye and the chef moved up from Cornwall; both have kept in contact with many of their trusted suppliers, so alongside native Welsh ingredients you'll find Scottish black pudding and fish from the Cornish day boats. Menus feature a few pub favourites but cooking is very much in the modern vein, with dishes taking on an extra degree of refinement in the evening when you can choose from the likes of skate wing with king prawn risotto and cockle popcorn or duo of suckling pig with dauphinoise potatoes and caramelised apple. The set lunch is good value, as is the winter supper club menu. Dine by the open fire in the bar or in the bright conservatory which overlooks the spacious rear terrace.

LLANDENNY, NP15 1DL
Tel.: 01291 690800
Website: www.raglanarms.co.uk

In centre of village. Parking.

PRICES
Meals: £ 18 (weekday lunch) and a la carte
£ 25/43

MAP: 13

CLOSING TIMES
Closed 24-25 December, Sunday dinner
and Monday

BELL AT SKENFRITH

An impressive choice of champagnes and cognacs

The Bell offers uncomplicated warmth: a seat in a comfy sofa by the inglenook, candles and meadow flowers on the tables and friendly, unobtrusive service. The weekly changing menu features hearty, classical dishes with the occasional ambitious twist; these might include rolled fishcakes or sirloin of Brecon beef with a mini steak and kidney pudding. Ingredients are allowed to speak for themselves, with local suppliers credited on the menu and much of the produce coming from their organic kitchen garden. Fruits of the vine are also taken seriously, with a large selection of half bottles and an impressive choice of champagnes and cognacs. Bedrooms are understated in their elegance, with super-comfy beds, fluffy towels and personalised toiletries.

SKENFRITH, NP7 8UH
Tel.: 01600 750235
Website: www.skenfrith.co.uk

12.5 mi east of Abergavenny on B 4521. Parking.

PRICES
Meals: a la carte £ 28/38

 11 rooms:
£ 90/230

MAP: 14

CLOSING TIMES
Open daily
booking essential

FELIN FACH GRIFFIN

Attracts a great mix of customers

This terracotta-coloured former farmhouse in picturesque countryside is rather unique in that you'll find visitors aged from 1-100 and from all walks of life – which creates an almost bohemian atmosphere. Bright paintwork, colourful art and a scattering of magazines about the place provide a very 'lived in' feel and the atmosphere is extremely laid-back. The young staff interact well but just as importantly, have a good knowledge of what they're serving. Starters like local goat's curd with black olive purée or brawn with apricot chutney are followed by braised shin of Welsh beef or red mullet with salt cod brandade – and they're a cut above your usual pub grub. If you've eaten yourself to a standstill, pleasant bedrooms with comfy beds await.

Felin Fach,
BRECON, LD3 0UB
Tel.: 01874 620111
Website: www.felinfachgriffin.co.uk

4.75 mi northeast of Brecon by B 4602 off A 470. Parking.

PRICES
Meals: £ 22/29 and a la carte £ 30/37

 7 rooms:
£ 110/170

MAP: 15

CLOSING TIMES
Closed 25 December and early January

BEAR

It has stood proudly on this site since 1432

The well-maintained Bear stands proudly on the main street of this small town, its hanging baskets creating a riot of colour. Step through the front door into the hugely characterful lounge-bar with its shiny brass and open fireplaces and you can well believe it has been here since 1432. Diners can sit here or in the more formal restaurant; the latter may be more romantic but the former is undoubtedly the more appealing. The menu offers honest pub dishes like prawn cocktail, homemade faggots or braised Welsh lamb shank. The 'specials' add interest and a cheery young team provide swift, assured service, even when it's busy. Bedrooms are available in the main hotel: the most characterful feature exposed beams, four-posters and fireplaces.

High St,
CRICKHOWELL, NP8 1BW
Tel.: 01873 810408
Website: www.bearhotel.co.uk

In the town centre. Parking.

PRICES
Meals: a la carte £ 23/47

 36 rooms:
£ 84/177

MAP: 16

CLOSING TIMES
Closed 25 December
bookings not accepted

HARP INN

Panoramic views of the Radnor Valley

Built to house workers constructing the medieval church, this 15C stone inn welcomes drinkers and diners alike. On a warm summer's day take a seat outside and make the most of the glorious view; in colder weather, head through to the charming flag-floored room with its warming open fire and beams hung with hop bines. 'Seasonality' and 'sustainability' are keywords here; breads, ice creams and crackers are homemade and everything else is locally sourced. Menus may be concise but dishes are original; you might find leek and ale rarebit, scrambled egg and home-spiced chorizo, or mackerel fillet with fennel spelt risotto – while the Welsh Black beef with triple-cooked chips has become a mainstay. Simple bedrooms come with wonderful views.

OLD RADNOR, LD8 2RH
Tel.: 01544 350655
Website: www.harpinnradnor.co.uk

Signposted south off A 44 east of Llandrindod Wells just before crossing the border into England. Parking.

PRICES
Meals: a la carte £ 20/40

 5 rooms:
£ 65/110

MAP: 17

CLOSING TIMES
Closed Monday except bank holidays,
Tuesday and lunch Wednesday-Thursday

THE PILOT

Hearty cooking and the heart of the community

You might assume that it has something to do with planes but 'The Pilot' is actually a reference to the mariners who guide ships safely into the Cardiff docks. This once rundown neighbourhood boozer has been transformed into a neat dining pub and it really has become part of the local community: regulars gather in the front room to watch the latest sporting events, while diners head to the rear, with its wood-burning stove and partial bay views. Ingredients are laudably local, with produce from the kitchen garden, nearby suppliers and even some of the locals' allotments. A good-sized blackboard menu mixes classic pub dishes with more adventurous offerings; fish and chips, steak and chips and sausage and mash are perennial favourites.

67 Queens Rd,
PENARTH, CF64 1DJ
Tel.: 029 2071 0615
Website: www.knifeandforkfood.co.uk/pilot

5 mi south of Cardiff in residential area of the town.
Unrestricted on-street parking.

PRICES

Meals: a la carte £ 21/33

MAP: 18

CLOSING TIMES
Open daily

HAND AT LLANARMON

Cosy and welcoming with plenty of rustic charm

Set at the crossroads of two old drovers' roads, the Hand has been providing hospitality for several centuries and its current owners are continuing the tradition with flair, providing a warm welcome and hearty meals to travellers through this lush valley. There's a cosy bar, a spacious dining room and a pool room; and rustic charm abounds in the form of stone walls, open fires, ancient beams and quite a collection of taxidermy. The daily changing menu offers lots of choice, with plenty of wholesome pub classics like sausage and mash, steak and kidney pie or slow-braised lamb shank. Portions are generous, produce is local and the cooking, fresh and flavoursome. Cosy bedrooms have hill views and modern bathrooms; most feature a roll-top bath.

LLANARMON DYFFRYN CEIRIOG, LL20 7LD
Tel.: 01691 600666
Website: www.thehandhotel.co.uk

At the head of Ceiriog Valley northwest of Oswestry. Parking.

PRICES
Meals: a la carte £ 16/37

 13 rooms:
£ 55/150

MAP: 19

CLOSING TIMES
Open daily

NORTHERN IRELAND

© R. Spila / Sime / Photononstop

The presiding image of Northern Ireland for outsiders is buzzing Belfast, lying defiantly between mountain and coast. Its City Hall and Queen's University retain the power to impress, and it was within its mighty shipyards that the Titanic first saw the light of day. But the rest of the Six Counties demands attention, too. The forty thousand stone columns of the Giant's Causeway step out into the Irish Sea, part of a grand coastline, though Antrim can also boast nine scenic inland glens. County Down's rolling hills culminate in the alluring slopes of Slieve Donard in the magical Mourne Mountains, while Armagh's Orchard County is a riot of pink in springtime. Fermanagh's glassy, silent lakelands are a tranquil attraction, rivalled for their serenity by the heather-clad Sperrin Mountains, towering over Tyrone and Derry.

On top of all this is the cultural lure of boisterous oyster festivals and authentic horse fairs, while farmers' markets are now prominent all across the province.

Pubs without bedrooms
Pubs with bedrooms

BILLY ANDY'S

Rustic cooking and generous portions

It used to be the village store as well as a pub, and although the groceries are long gone, Billy Andy's still seems to be all things to all people, with drinkers, diners, overnight guests and music lovers all flocking here. There are two snug drinking areas, their walls filled with vintage posters; a wood burning stove and several open fires; and a pool table, a rustic dining room and a fine selection of whiskies – as well as four modern bedrooms, chatty staff and welcoming locals. Cooking is filling, with a strong Irish accent; expect Glenarm salmon, Finnebrogue venison, mature braised beef and rare breed pork. Desserts come in miniature so you can enjoy more than one; Friday is steak night and Saturday music sessions pack the place out.

66 Browndod Rd,
MOUNTHILL, BT40 3DX
Tel.: 028 2827 0648
Website: www.billyandys.com

5 mi southwest of Larne by A 8 on Browndod Rd. Parking.

PRICES
Meals: £ 17/20 and a la carte £ 23/38

 4 rooms:
£ 40/85

MAP: 1

CLOSING TIMES
Closed 25-26 December

PHEASANT

Children are well catered for

Set in the heart of County Lisburn, this sizeable creamwashed inn has a typically Irish feel, from the Guinness-themed artwork to the warm welcome and laid-back atmosphere. With its stained glass and dark wood, it has a somewhat Gothic style; the traditional open-fired bar is the place to sit when it's cold and the patio provides the ideal spot in warmer months. Internationally influenced menus showcase seasonal produce, with local seafood the speciality in summer and game from the nearby estate in winter. Children are well catered for too, with a dedicated selection of freshly prepared dishes, as well as toys and climbing frames. It's a popular place, so if you're in a group it could be worth booking the snug or the 'Game Keepers Loft'.

410 Upper Ballynahinch Rd,
ANNAHILT, BT26 6NR
Tel.: 028 9263 8056
Website: www.thepheasantrestaurant.co.uk

1 mi north of Annahilt on Lisburn rd. Parking.

PRICES   **MAP: 2**
Meals: £ 13 (lunch and early dinner)
and a la carte £ 20/38

CLOSING TIMES
Closed 12 July and 25 December

PIER 36

Welcoming, family-run pub overlooking the harbour

You couldn't pick a better spot for this family-run pub: it sits on the quayside overlooking the picturesque harbour and the lighthouse. But it's not just its location that marks it out; the hospitality here is pretty good too and the owners continually work to give their customers what they want – which explains why so many keep coming back. When it comes to the food, the menus are traditionally based and offer something for everyone. They purchase only the freshest seafood – so you can't go wrong with the local sole or mussels – and they also sell an impressive number of steaks, which is due, no doubt, to the fact that they hang and mature the meat themselves. Bedrooms are bright and modern, and some have great harbour and sea views.

36 The Parade,
DONAGHADEE, BT21 0HE
Tel.: 028 9188 4466
Website: www.pier36.co.uk

On the harbourfront. Parking in the street and at the rear.

PRICES
Meals: a la carte £ 20/48

 6 rooms:
£ 50/120

MAP: 3

CLOSING TIMES
Closed 25 December

PARSON'S NOSE

Proudly classical cooking – go for a fish special

The second venture for Danny Millar and Ronan Sweeney is this characterful Georgian inn, which started life as a private house built by the first Marquis of Downshire and dates back to the 18C. The rustic, open-fired bar displays a collection of brewing and distilling paraphernalia, while the dining room above overlooks the Queen's Lake in the grounds of the castle. Food is important here and those in the know will immediately get the culinary reference in the pub's name. Menus are unashamedly traditional and portions are generous; Dundrum oysters and mussels play a big part and the daily fish specials are always a hit – as is the slow-cooked Dexter beef. Puddings are classical and comforting, and the service, quick and efficient.

48 Lisburn St,
HILLSBOROUGH, BT26 6AB
Tel.: 028 9268 3009
Website: www.theparsonsnose.co.uk

In centre of the town. On-street parking.

PRICES
Meals: £ 17 (weekdays) and a la carte
£ 21/39

MAP: 4

CLOSING TIMES
Closed 25 December
booking advisable

PLOUGH INN

There's plenty of choice in where and what to eat

From its lush forest and glistening 40 acre lake to its impressive 17C castle and steep streets lined with antiques shops, picturesque Hillsborough has plenty to offer, including the locally acclaimed Plough Inn. Having been trading since 1752, it's extremely well-established in the community – but it's not your usual kind of pub and offers three eateries in one. Regulars can be found enjoying pub classics in the traditional bar or, on Thursday, Friday and Saturday evenings, in the adjoining seafood restaurant, where the daily blackboard specials are a hit. The younger crowds tend to gather in the ground floor café-cum-cocktail-bar or in the trendy bistro above which offers an international menu. There are numerous multi-level terraces too.

3 The Square,
HILLSBOROUGH, BT26 6AG
Tel.: 028 9268 2985
Website: www.theploughhillsbrough.co.uk

At the top of the hill in the square. Parking.

PRICES   MAP: **5**
Meals: £ 15 and a la carte £ 21/39

CLOSING TIMES
Closed 25-26 December

BALLOO HOUSE

Smart dining pub dating from 1867

This characterful stone building is named after the Balloo Crossroads that it sits upon, and is run by Danny Millar, a well-known local chef and an ambassador for Northern Irish produce. It started life as a farmhouse, before becoming a pub in 1867 – not that it had the smart dining pub feel then that it does today. Locals come together in the snug bar, the original range is still on display, and the far wood-panelled room is named 'McConnell' in honour of the family who once lived here. Lengthy menus offer a mix of pub classics and dishes with more international leanings. Pies are popular, as is High Tea, which is served every day except Saturday. Cooking is honest and hearty; to start, everyone is brought tasty Guinness wheaten bread.

1 Comber Rd,
KILLINCHY, BT23 6PA
Tel.: 028 9754 1210
Website: www.balloohouse.com

On A 22 between Comber and Killyleagh at Balloo crossroads. Parking.

PRICES   MAP: **6**
Meals: £ 15 (weekday lunch)/35
and a la carte £ 30/43

CLOSING TIMES
Closed 25 December
bookings advisable at dinner

POACHER'S POCKET

The Dexter beef is a hit

This neat, modern-looking pub might be rurally located but it's clear that plenty of people know about it. It's owned by Danny Millar – one of Northern Ireland's leading chefs – and, wisely, he's kept the cooking rustic and satisfying. Start with a tempting selection of homemade breads and tapenade, then move on to a tasty Dexter beef burger or grill. Two courses should fill you up, so if you can't quite make it to dessert, visit their deli, the Poacher's Pantry, to pick up some homemade cakes and artisan chocolates. To the front it retains a traditional pubby feel, while at the back you'll find the best seats in the house, in a rather smart two-tiered extension overlooking a small internal courtyard. Come at the weekend for a laid-back brunch.

181 Killinchy Rd,
LISBANE, BT23 5NE
Tel.: 028 9754 1589
Website: www.poacherspocketlisbane.com

3.5 mi southeast of Comber on the main road to Killinchy. Parking.

PRICES   **MAP: 7**
Meals: £ 15 (weekdays) and a la carte
£ 20/39

CLOSING TIMES
Closed 25 December

REPUBLIC OF IRELAND

© R. Mattes / hemis.fr

It's reckoned that Ireland offers forty luminous shades of green, and of course an even more famous shade of black liquid refreshment. But it's not all wondrous hills and down-home pubs. The country does other visitor-friendly phenomena just as idyllically: witness the limestone-layered Burren, cut-through by meandering streams, lakes and labyrinthine caves; or the fabulous Cliffs of Moher, unchanged for millennia, looming for mile after mile over the wild Atlantic waves. The cities burst with life: Dublin is now one of Europe's coolest capitals, and free-spirited Cork enjoys a rich cultural heritage.

Kilkenny mixes a renowned medieval flavour with a taste for excellent pubs; Galway, one of Ireland's prettiest cities, is enhanced by an easy, boho vibe. Best of all, perhaps, is to sit along the quayside of a fishing village in the esteemed company of a bowl of steaming fresh mussels or gleaming oysters and the taste of a distinctive micro-brewery beer (well, it makes a change from stout...).

Pubs without bedrooms
Pubs with bedrooms

MORRISSEY'S

Careful cooking shows respect for ingredients

As a boy Hugh McNally helped out at his mother's fish and chip shop; when he was older he worked at his grandparents' pub just across the road; and today that pub in the small coastal village of Doonbeg is his. It's been smartly refurbished, with banquettes along the walls, scrubbed wooden tables and walls filled with local artwork and books. There's also a decked terrace which overlooks the river and the castle ruins and is great for sunny days. The menu may be a simple affair but cooking is carefully done and shows respect for ingredients. Locally caught fish and shellfish feature heavily and the crabs in particular are worth a try. Bedrooms are smart and modern – two overlook the river – and they have bikes and even a kayak for hire.

DOONBEG
Tel.: (065) 905 5304
Website: www.morrisseysdoonbeg.com

In centre of village by the bridge. On-street parking.

PRICES
Meals: a la carte € 26/45

 5 rooms:
€ 50/100

MAP: 1

CLOSING TIMES
Closed January, February and Monday
dinner only

VAUGHAN'S ANCHOR INN

Self-taught chef offering ambitious cooking

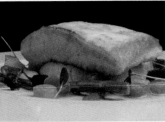

If you need to pick up some groceries in the picturesque fishing village of Liscannor, why not stop off at this family-run pub? Its cosy, pleasantly cluttered bar comes complete with a small shop selling everything from sea salt to birthday candles. The self-taught chef has travelled widely and has visited some of the world's best restaurants, so although lunch might feature traditional scampi and chips, the scampi will be made from langoustines and come in panko breadcrumbs and the chips will be homemade. Seafood plays an important role and will be on your plate just a few hours after it's landed; the seafood platter is a real hit – and how many pubs do you know that serve caviar? Smart bedrooms feature bright local art and colourful throws.

Main St,
LISCANNOR
Tel.: (065) 708 1548
Website: www.vaughans.ie

2 km from Lahinch by coast road, on main route to Cliffs of Moher. Parking.

PRICES
Meals: a la carte € 24/50

 7 rooms:
€ 60/100

MAP: 2

CLOSING TIMES
Closed 25 December

WILD HONEY INN

Classic dishes presented in a modern manner

With the Cliffs of Moher and the limestone landscape of The Burren on the doorstep, this roadside inn makes a great base for exploring County Clare; but it's also a great place to discover good cuisine. From the outside, the three-storey building looks nothing like a pub – in fact, it started life as a hotel, and the garden was once the dance hall. It's a welcoming place, with a turf fire in the cosy bar and a peaceful guest lounge for those staying in the simple bedrooms. When it comes to the food, they offer well-priced classics presented in a modern way; they also champion local produce, particularly seafood, with the kitchen showing respect for natural ingredients and allowing their flavours to shine through. Bookings are not accepted.

LISDOONVARNA
Tel.: (065) 707 4300
Website: www.wildhoneyinn.com

Just south of the village, on the Ennistimon rd. On-street parking.

PRICES
Meals: € 35 (weekday dinner)
and a la carte € 33/48

 14 rooms:
€ 65/100

MAP: 3

CLOSING TIMES
Closed November-February and weekdays
March-April
bookings not accepted

LINNANE'S LOBSTER BAR

Started life as a cottage, over 300 years ago

If you've not been before, leave plenty of time, as this tiny hamlet can be something of a challenge to find. Linnane's started life over 300 years ago as a traditional thatched cottage and is a simple but likeable place; roaring peat fires welcome you in the winter and the full-length windows are opened onto the terrace in summer. From the front it overlooks The Burren and to the rear you can watch the local boats unloading their catch on the small pier – some of which is brought straight into the kitchen. Unsurprisingly, they specialise in fresh fish and shellfish, with the lobster being a particular favourite. Some dishes are cooked simply, others, with a little more imagination, but all are tasty, well-prepared and sensibly priced.

New Quay Pier,
NEW QUAY
Tel.: (065) 707 8120
Website: www.linnanesbar.com

11 km northeast of Ballyvaughan following signs for Finavarra from N 67.

PRICES
Meals: a la carte € 23/57

MAP: 4

CLOSING TIMES
Closed 25 December, Good Friday and
Monday-Thursday October-Easter

POACHERS

Neighbourhood pub that's a hit with the locals

It's not big, brash or colourful, but that doesn't mean the Poachers Inn is lacking in a good old Irish pub atmosphere; in fact, if you're looking for the locals, this is probably where you'll find them. There's a whole array of menus to choose from. Lunch offers light snacks (the steak sandwich on homemade bread is particularly popular), supplemented by a good range of gutsy blackboard specials – the seafood dishes are the ones to choose; while dinner steps things up a gear and proudly showcases West Cork produce – maybe crab from Kinsale or fish from Skibbereen. Sit among framed maps and local prints in the wood-panelled front room or cosy-up in the snug. If you're feeling creative, book yourself in for one of the popular cookery courses.

Clonakilty Rd,
BANDON
Tel.: (023) 884 1159
Website: www.poachers.ie

1.5 km southwest on N 71. Parking.

PRICES
Meals: € 22 (weekday dinner)/32
and a la carte € 24/42

MAP: 5

CLOSING TIMES
Closed 25 December

MARY ANN'S

Complete with a gallery of modern Irish art

You've little chance of missing this boldly painted pub or, for that matter, its larger than life owner. It's set in the heart of a sleepy village, up a steep, narrow street and the walk is sure to help you work up an appetite; if not, then while away some time in The Warren, the pub's art gallery, where the owner proudly displays his collection of modern Irish art. After this, head for the rustic bar, the linen-laid restaurant or, if the weather's right, the garden, where an enclosed dining area with gingham tablecloths and a mature fruiting vine provides the perfect suntrap. Menus are all-encompassing and offer plenty of choice; seafood is often a feature and there's usually several authentic Asian dishes courtesy of the Malaysian chefs.

Main St,
CASTLETOWNSHEND
Tel.: (028) 36146
Website: www.maryannesbarandrestaurantcork.com

Between Rosscarbery and Skibbereen south of N 71. On-street parking.

PRICES
Meals: a la carte € 26/51

MAP: **6**

CLOSING TIMES
Closed 10 January-3 February, 24-26 December and Monday-Tuesday November-March dinner only

DEASY'S

Gloriously dated interior with a nautical feel

Hidden away in a picturesque hamlet, this appealing pub and its small decked terrace offer lovely views out across the bay. It's well run by a confident team but they aren't open regularly all year, so be sure to check the opening times before you go. The open-fired, stone-floored interior is gloriously dated, with mismatched wood furniture and a maritime feel, courtesy of framed fish prints and old boat propellers hung on the walls. Dishes change from day to day and are dictated by the seasons and the latest catch brought in by the local boats; you might find roast monkfish or surf clams with braised pork belly, and the Thai coconut fish soup is well worth a try. Puddings are, in the main, traditional, but they do a tasty panna cotta too.

Ring,
CLONAKILTY
Tel.: (023) 883 5741

3 km southeast, signposted off N 71 following signs for Ring. Limited parking.

PRICES
Meals: € 32 (early dinner) and a la carte
€ 30/48

MAP: 7

CLOSING TIMES
Closed 24-26 December, Good Friday,
Sunday dinner, Monday, Tuesday and
restricted opening in winter

CRONIN'S

Run by the third generation of the Cronin family

Having been in the family since 1970, this good old Irish pub is now being run by the third generation of Cronins; you're still likely to find Mr Cronin Snr about the place, only this time on the other side of the bar. The keen team welcome one and all and, being just a stone's throw from the harbour, that usually includes a yachtsman or two. The long bar is adorned with interesting artefacts, while the back room is filled with boxing memorabilia. During the week, they serve straightforward seafood dishes, while at weekends and midweek in summer, the restaurant is open for dinner, offering maybe scallops with leeks, fresh salmon tartare or their renowned shellfish platter. Produce is from nearby Oysterhaven and Ballycotton.

CROSSHAVEN
Tel.: (021) 483 1829
Website: www.croninspub.com

In the centre of town with free parking adjacent.

PRICES
Meals: a la carte € 25/38

MAP: 8

CLOSING TIMES
Closed 25 December and Good Friday

TODDIES AT THE BULMAN

Maritime-themed pub with excellent bay views

The Bulman is set in a great location, looking out over the bay towards Kinsale, and its décor is fittingly maritime themed; look out for the interesting mural of Moby Dick and the carving of the famed Bulman Buoy. Scrubbed tables and open fires give it a rustic feel and pictures from yesteryear fill the walls. The cosy bar is the venue for live music nights – when locals and visitors alike can be found enjoying the craic; while upstairs, the well-travelled owner – formerly of Toddies restaurant – can be seen cooking in the more formal dining room. Simple pub classics and interesting specials feature at lunch and carefully prepared, globally influenced dishes follow in the evening. Unsurprisingly, fresh local seafood is the star of the show.

Summercove,
KINSALE
Tel.: (021) 477 2131
Website: www.thebulman.ie

East 2 km towards Summercove signposted to Charles Fort. Small free car park opposite.

PRICES
Meals: a la carte € 32/50

MAP: 9

CLOSING TIMES
Closed 25 December and Good Friday

CHOP HOUSE

Some dishes can be surprisingly elaborate

In a prominent position on the main interchange, just a drop goal from the Aviva Stadium, you'll find this imposing pub. Once a rather spit 'n' sawdust affair, it's been given a new lease of life by a local restaurateur – so much so, that dinner bookings are now advisable. For warmer days there's a small terrace; in colder weather head up the steps, through the bar and into the bright conservatory area. Lunchtimes see a relaxed menu of maybe beer-battered cod, wild mushroom tagliatelli or Landes chicken but to truly experience the kitchen's full talent come for dinner, where you'll discover the likes of North African spiced lamb breast with orange confit, raw tuna with teriyaki glaze or their speciality, 35 day dry-aged prime Irish steaks.

2 Shelbourne Rd,
BALLSBRIDGE
Tel.: (01) 660 2390
Website: www.thechophouse.ie

5min walk from Lansdowne Rd DART station.
On-street pay and display parking.

PRICES   MAP: **10**
Meals: € 32 and a la carte € 30/55

CLOSING TIMES
Closed Saturday lunch

OLD SPOT

Come on Sunday for a roast for two

You'll find this grey pub with striped canopies just a stone's throw from the stadium. The appealing bar has a stencilled maple-wood floor and offers a selection of bottled craft beers that's second to none, alongside a regularly changing English ale on draught. It also serves all manner of bar snacks – try the pork croquettes or perhaps some Carlingford oysters. The adjoining downstairs restaurant is relaxed and characterful with its mix of seating and wide variety of vintage posters and signs. Here, pub classics are given a modern edge. Home-made black pudding vies with smoked ham and foie gras terrine; pressed lamb shoulder with chicken and tarragon pie – and on Sundays you can get roasts for two. Service is suitably relaxed and friendly.

14 Bath Ave,
BALLSBRIDGE
Tel.: (01) 660 5599
Website: www.theoldspot.ie

5min walk from Lansdowne Rd DART station.
On-street pay and display parking.

PRICES
Meals: a la carte € 31/51

MAP: 11

CLOSING TIMES
Closed 25-26 December and 1 January

MORAN'S OYSTER COTTAGE

Straightforward cooking and great hospitality

The name says it all: it's been run by seven generations of Morans; its speciality is oysters; and with whitewashed walls and a lovely thatched roof, it's every bit a country cottage. It's set in a tiny hamlet down winding country lanes and you'd never find it unless you knew it was there; on a summer's day, however, it soon becomes apparent that plenty of people do. Catherine is the latest Moran to take the helm and she continues the family's philosophy of straightforward cooking and good hospitality. The menu barely changes – but why change something that works so well? You'll find tasty prawns, mussels, crab, smoked salmon and lobster, along with daily baked brown bread; September – being native oyster season – is the best time to visit.

The Weir,
KILCOLGAN
Tel.: (091) 796 113
Website: www.moransoystercottage.com

5min from the village of Clarinbridge. Parking in road.

PRICES
Meals: a la carte € 26/50

MAP: 12

CLOSING TIMES
Closed 24-26 December and Good Friday

O'DOWDS

Run by the same family for over 100 years

The O'Dowd family have been dispensing gastronomic delights at this eye-catching blue-hued pub for over one hundred years. Sit in either the cosy fire-lit bar or the more spacious wood-panelled dining room to enjoy fresh, simply cooked seafood. Tender, sweet crab arrives straight from the shore, teamed with a glorious garlic butter to make the perfect meal; while the likes of brill, turbot and plaice are given the respect they deserve – simply lightly dusted with flour and then shallow fried. If you're coming for dinner, be sure to book ahead, and if lunch is your thing, then arrive early, otherwise you may find yourself watching enviously from the quayside as others tuck into home-baked soda rolls and steaming bowls of seafood chowder.

ROUNDSTONE
Tel.: (095) 35809
Website: www.odowdsseafoodbar.com

On R 341 13 km from Clifden. Parking outside and on the quayside.

PRICES
Meals: € 20 (dinner) and a la carte € 17/53

MAP: 13

CLOSING TIMES
Closed 25 December
booking advisable

O'NEILL'S (THE POINT) SEAFOOD BAR

Generous portions of locally landed seafood

This smart pub has been run by the O'Neill family for over 150 years and, amazingly, several different generations are still involved. It sits in a great spot beside the Valentia Island car ferry slipway (sit on the terrace for views over the sea and island), and has a pleasantly traditional feel, courtesy of family photographs, all manner of bric-a-brac and plenty of seafaring memorabilia. The menu offers generous portions of simply prepared, deliciously fresh, locally landed seafood. Lobster and crab are perennial favourites, salmon comes from the adjacent smokehouse and local fishermen bring their day's catch – which might include squid, monkfish or lobster – to the door. Unusually, they don't serve chips or puddings.

Renard Point,
CAHERSIVEEN
Tel.: (066) 947 2165

4.5 km west of Cahersiveen: follow the signs for the Valentia Island ferry. Parking.

PRICES
Meals: a la carte € 27/35

MAP: 14

CLOSING TIMES
Closed November-March and lunch March-May,October-November and Sunday
bookings not accepted

BALLYMORE INN

Proud to use small artisan producers

Set in a small village close to the Aga Khan's stud, this pub's claim to fame is that Clint Eastwood, Bono and the late Larry Hagman have all popped in on their way to the races. To the rear, a large bar screens sporting events; to the front there's a spacious dining area with red leather banquettes, mosaic flooring and a Parisian brasserie feel. Lunch sees salads, homemade pizzas and risottos, with more substantial dishes appearing at dinner. The owner is keen to promote small artisan producers, so you'll find organic veg, meat from quality assured farms and farmhouse cheeses – as well as produce from their own kitchen garden. A small deli sells homemade breads, pickles, oils, cakes and jams; if you see fudge then be sure to grab a packet.

BALLYMORE EUSTACE
Tel.: (045) 864 585
Website: www.ballymoreinn.com

South of Naas on R 411. Parking.

PRICES
Meals: € 24 (weekday lunch)/38
and a la carte € 26/51

MAP: 15

CLOSING TIMES
Open daily

FALLON'S

Save room for the tasty homemade puddings

Once half of the successful Fallon & Byrne food emporium in Dublin, Tom Fallon has taken his knowledge to the heart of Kildare, to share with the appreciative locals of Kilcullen. Satisfyingly, this is a proper bar, with a long wooden counter and a flagged floor – albeit one that's undergone a slight modernisation, courtesy of a boutique colour scheme and purple sofas – and at lunch the place is crammed with local office staff and ladies who lunch. Explore further, and you'll find a conservatory-style room at the back, while a linen-clad dining room provides a bit more formality in the evening. The menu offers plenty of choice, from a 'pie of the day' to grilled salmon with local black pudding, followed by tasty homemade desserts.

Main St,
KILCULLEN
Tel.: (045) 481 260
Website: www.fallonb.ie

At the Naas end of the main street. Parking.

PRICES
Meals: a la carte € 31/55

MAP: 16

CLOSING TIMES
Closed 25 December, Good Friday and Monday

HARTE'S

Spirit-lovers should try the 3-gin tasting board

This welcoming pub, built in 1838, sits right in the centre of a busy market town in the heart of horse racing country. To the right is a snug bar with an open fire, where they serve a selection of local artisan beers; opposite is a small but popular restaurant where large mirrors hang on exposed brick walls. Kick things off with a gin tasting board, comprising three different gin and tonics, then move on to the tasty, well-prepared dishes with modern twists. You might find Ardsallagh goat's cheese and beetroot or thyme roasted chicken on the good value set menu, while the more ambitious à la carte steps things up a level with the likes of crab with chilli, cucumber and apple gazpacho or mature Irish rib-eye with Crozier Blue béarnaise sauce.

Market Sq,
KILDARE
Tel.: (045) 533 557
Website: www.harteskildare.ie

Between Naas and Portlaoise off E 20.
On-street parking in main village square.

PRICES
Meals: € 26 (weekdays)/35 and a la carte
€ 29/40

MAP: 17

CLOSING TIMES
Closed Monday except bank holidays

OARSMAN

A local guitarist plays 4 nights a week

With the River Shannon just 50m away and always a boatman or two inside, this pub's name is perfectly apt. Its double-fronted windows are filled with pottery, county flags and old artefacts, while a plethora of objects adorn the walls and an array of fishing tackle sits above the bar. This is a traditional pub through and through: family-owned, with rough wooden floors, old beams and stone-faced walls; and, unsurprisingly, is frequented by the locals – especially at lunch. Snacks are available in the afternoon and there's a fairly substantial bar menu in the evening, while later in the week the comfy upstairs room offers dishes such as confit of Thornhill Farm duck or trio of Kettyle lamb. Cooking is flavoursome and produce, laudably local.

Bridge St,
CARRICK-ON-SHANNON
Tel.: (071) 962 1733
Website: www.theoarsman.com

In the town centre. On-street parking meters.

PRICES
Meals: € 22 (weekdays)/35 and a la carte
€ 23/46

MAP: 18

CLOSING TIMES
Closed 25-27 December, Good Friday and
Sunday-Monday October-April

FITZPATRICKS

Memorabilia and antiques feature inside and out

On the coast road to the peninsula, at the foot of the Cooley Mountains, you'll find this classical whitewashed pub overlooking Dundalk Bay. To call it characterful would be an understatement: this is a place where you can take in the whole of the Irish experience in one go. The car park and gardens are filled with colourful flowers planted in old bicycles, boots and even a bed; while inside there's a beautiful bar chock-full of antiques and memorabilia, including a fascinating collection of chamber pots and Victorian toiletries. The extensive menu features hearty, flavoursome portions of traditional dishes, with local steaks and seafood something of a speciality; come on a Tuesday evening for specials which are centred around lobster.

Rockmarshall,
JENKINSTOWN
Tel.: (042) 937 6193
Website: www.fitzpatricks-restaurant.com

9 km northeast of Dundalk following N 52 on R 173. Parking.

PRICES
Meals: € 11 (weekday lunch)/35
and a la carte € 30/52

MAP: 19

CLOSING TIMES
Closed 24-26 December and Good Friday

TAVERN

Classical dishes include a great chowder

Most people come to the area to visit Croagh Patrick, the famous rock with a chapel perched on top, but this vibrantly painted pub has also put itself firmly on the map in recent years. With its designer colours, leather banquettes and quirky basket lampshades, it's the type of place that would fit right into a 'Country Living' magazine. In keeping with this style, staff are smart and attentive, and the kitchen produces an array of dishes with wide-ranging influences and a touch of refinement. Local seafood and meat arrive in classical combinations and the specials board lists the fruits of the latest catch. The chowder is award-winning, the chicken with chargrilled bacon is a perennial hit, and the daily cheesecake is an absolute must.

MURRISK
Tel.: (098) 64060
Website: www.tavernmurrisk.com

9 km west of Westport on R 335. Parking.

PRICES
Meals: a la carte € 23/49

MAP: 20

CLOSING TIMES
Closed 25 December and Good Friday

SHEEBEEN

Live music every Friday and Saturday night

This pretty whitewashed pub stands in a remote location in the shadow of the magnificent Croagh Patrick mountain and boasts lovely views out across the bay. On warmer days, grab a seat on one of the outside tables; when it's colder, head for the traditional snug, the rustic open-fired bar or the slightly more formal first floor dining room. The owner is passionate about keeping his pub honest and true, so along with the laid-back atmosphere and cheery groups of locals drinking Guinness, you'll find a selection of hearty, unfussy dishes on offer, including the likes of mussels, oysters and lobsters from the bay, and lamb and beef from the fields nearby. To top it all off, there are live music sessions every Friday and Saturday night.

Rosbeg,
WESTPORT
Tel.: (098) 26528
Website: www.croninssheebeen.com

West of the town beyond Westport Quay. Parking.

PRICES
Meals: a la carte € 24/43

MAP: 21

CLOSING TIMES
Closed 25 December, Good
Friday and lunch weekdays November-mid
March

HARGADONS

Stone walls, sloping floors and character aplenty

Built in 1864 by a local merchant-cum-MP, this building started life as a grocer's (the original comestible drawers are still on display), before being acquired by the Hargadon brothers in 1909. To say it's characterful would be an understatement. There's a narrow passageway with booths; anterooms with oak-topped tables; thick walls hung with Guinness and Jameson's memorabilia; and a sloping stone floor designed to prevent flooding – there's even a lovely little "Ladies' Room" complete with its own serving hatch. Cooking is warming and hearty, offering the likes of Irish stew or bacon and cabbage, followed by tasty nursery puddings. They also have a good wine list, which makes sense when you see the large wine shop that adjoins the pub.

4-5 O'Connell St,
SLIGO
Tel.: (071) 915 3709
Website: www.hargadons.com

In the centre of town. Public parking nearby.

PRICES   MAP: **22**
Meals: a la carte € 18/36

CLOSING TIMES
Closed Sunday
bookings not accepted

LARKINS

Thatched pub in a charming loughside location

This thatched, whitewashed pub dates back around 300 years. It is set in a charming location on the shores of Lough Derg and is popular with the sailing set, particularly in summer. As traditional inside as it is out, it boasts old flag and timber floors, a long wooden bar and original open fireplaces. This is very much a locals' pub and it plays host to regular Irish folk music sessions and traditional Irish dancing groups. Having come from farming backgrounds, the owners are passionate about sourcing local produce and the menu offers straightforward, unfussy dishes, with plenty of fresh seafood; maybe half a roast duck or fillet of pork with black pudding mash, with classic puddings such as sticky toffee pudding or a chocolate brownie.

GARRYKENNEDY
Tel.: (067) 23232
Website: www.larkins.ie

9 km west of Nenagh by R 494 and minor road north.
Free public car park opposite.

PRICES   MAP: **23**
Meals: € 20/38 and a la carte € 25/42

CLOSING TIMES
Closed 25 December, Good Friday,
Monday-Tuesday and Wednesday-Friday
lunch November-April

LOBSTER POT

Carne's not-so-well-kept secret

If you're on your way to the ferry crossing at Rosslare or returning from a stroll along the nearby beach, this bold green pub is definitely worth calling in at. The interior is spotless and as soon as you see the staff in their smart waistcoats, you know they take things seriously here. Make for a cosy, characterful nook amongst the huge array of memorabilia and study the extensive menu of tasty home-style cooking, which offers a simple selection of light bites at lunch and a dinner menu exclusively for adults – as children must leave by 7pm. There are a few grills, but, as the name suggests, it's mostly seafood, with oysters and lobster cooked to order the specialities. But be sure to arrive early, as this is Carne's not-so-well-kept secret.

Ballyfane,
CARNE
Tel.: (053) 913 1110
Website: www.lobsterpotwexford.ie

Off N 25 following signs for Our Lady's Island. Parking.

PRICES
Meals: a la carte € 27/58

MAP: 24

CLOSING TIMES
Closed 1 January-10 February, 24-
26 December, Good Friday and Monday
except bank holidays

BYRNE & WOODS

Arguably the second highest pub in Ireland

A smartly restored Morris Traveller stands outside what is arguably the second highest pub in Ireland, set up in the Wicklow Mountains. Built from stone, it looks older than it really is and, as its name may suggest, consists of two parts. 'Byrne' is a small, cosy bar with a stone fireplace and wood-burning stove – and is where you'll find the local drinkers and thrice-weekly live music sessions; while spacious, dimly lit 'Woods', is where the majority of diners head, characterised by dark wood furnishings, brown leather seating and a clubby feel. Cooking is fresh and straightforward, with lighter dishes on offer during the week, and the likes of pork belly with sage and apricot chutney or salmon with rocket pesto at the weekend.

Main St,
ROUNDWOOD
Tel.: (01) 281 7078
Website: www.byrneandwoods.com

On R 755 between Laragh and Killough. Parking.

PRICES
Meals: € 14/35 and a la carte € 24/42

MAP: 25

CLOSING TIMES
Closed 25-26 December

INDEX OF **TOWNS**

INDEX OF **PUBS & INNS**

Notes

Notes

CREDITS

P2: C.Joiner / age fotostock ▪ **P4-5:** Zoomar / Julin Garbare / Zoonar GmbHM age fotostock - Gloucester Old Spot, Piff's Elm - Lazy Toad, Brampford Speke - Swan Inn, Swinbrook ▪ **P8-9:** Ali Mobasser / Anabel Navarro Llorens / Jorge Monedero ▪ **P14:** FOTOSEARCH RM / age fotostock - Ron Bull / Alamy / hemis.fr ▪ **P181:** Alan Dawson / age fotostock ▪ **P217:** Robert Harding / hemis.fr ▪ **P473:** J. Osmond / Photolibrary / Getty Images ▪ **P511:** imageBROKER/ hemis.fr ▪ **P565:** R. Harding / hemis.fr ▪ **P604:** © Lluís Real / age fotostock

Thanks to:
Michelin would like to thank those pubs that provided us with their photographs.

Cover photographs:
Bunch of Grapes, Bradford-on-Avon (Front cover)

MICHELIN TRAVEL PARTNER ─────────────────────────

Société par actions simplifiées au capital de 11 288 880 €
27 Cours de L'Île Seguin - 92100 Boulogne Billancourt (France)
R.C.S. Nanterre 433 677 721

Hannay House, 39 Clarendon Rd
Watford WD17 1JA
Tol: (01023) 205217
www.ViaMichelin.com
eatingoutinpubs-gbirl@michelin.com

© Michelin et cie, Propriétaires-éditeurs
Dépôt légal octobre 2016
Printed in Italy 09-16
Typesetting: Nord Compo, Villeneuve-d'Ascq (France)
Printing and binding: Geers offset - GENT

YOUR OPINION MATTERS!

To help us constantly improve this guide, please fill in this questionnaire and return to:

Eating out in Pubs 2017
Michelin Travel Partner,
Hannay House, 39 Clarendon Road,
Watford, WD17 1JA, UK

First name: ....

Surname: ....

Address: ....

Profession: ....

< 25 years old	☐	25-34 years old	☐
35-50 years old	☐	> 50 years	☐

1. How often do you use the Internet to look for information on pubs?

Never ☐

Occasionally (once a month) ☐

Regularly (once a week) ☐

Very frequently (more than once a week) ☐

2. Have you ever bought Michelin guides before?

☐ Yes   ☐ No

3. If yes, which one(s)?

Eating out in Pubs ☐

The Michelin Guide Great Britain & Ireland ☐

The Green Guide (please specify titles) ☐

....

Other (please specify titles) ☐

....

4. If you have previously bought Eating out in Pubs, what made you purchase this new one?

....

....

5. If you buy the Michelin Guide Great Britain & Ireland, how often do you buy it?

Every year ☐

Every 2 years ☐

Every 3 years ☐

Every 4 years or more ☐

ABOUT EATING OUT IN PUBS :

6. Did you buy this guide:

For holidays? ☐

For a weekend/short break? ☐

For business purposes? ☐

As a gift? ☐

For everyday use? ☐

7. How do you rate the different elements of this guide?

NB: **1. Very Poor**   **2. Poor**   **3. Average**   **4. Good**   **5. Very Good**

	1	2	3	4	5
Selection of pubs	☐	☐	☐	☐	☐
Number of pubs in London	☐	☐	☐	☐	☐
Geographical spread of pubs	☐	☐	☐	☐	☐
Menu Prices	☐	☐	☐	☐	☐
Practical information (services, menus)	☐	☐	☐	☐	☐
Photos	☐	☐	☐	☐	☐
Description of the pubs	☐	☐	☐	☐	☐
Cover	☐	☐	☐	☐	☐
The format & size of the guide	☐	☐	☐	☐	☐
Guide Price	☐	☐	☐	☐	☐

8. How easily could you find the information you were looking for ?

....
....

9. Please rate the guide out of 20 ..../20

10. Which aspects could we improve?

....
....
....
....
....
....

11. Was there a pub you particularly liked or a choice you didn't agree with? Perhaps you have a favourite place of your own that you would like to tell us about? Please send us your remarks and suggestions.

....
....
....
....
....
....
....
....
....
....